Marketing, Management and Motivation

Marketing, Management and Motivation

Successful Business Development for
Professional Services Firms

Dianne Bown-Wilson and Gail Courtney

The Law Society

ISBN 1–85328–810–1

Published in 2002 by the Law Society
113 Chancery Lane, London WC2A 1PL

Typeset by J&L Composition Ltd, Filey, North Yorkshire
Printed by TJ International Ltd, Padstow, Cornwall

Contents

Preface and acknowledgements

A journey of 10,000 miles starts with a single step.

No saying, we feel, more perfectly summarises the process of establishing and developing a business, whatever its focus. Taking the first, faltering steps towards realising your goals and those of the organisation you work with, having the tenacity to stick with it and the ability to encourage and inspire your colleagues to do the same, is what differentiates those who become successful from the also-rans.

Our aim in writing this book was two-fold: to provide some with the impetus needed to begin proactively developing their business (whatever their particular priorities) and to give others, who are part way along the journey, practical advice and encouragement.

Unfortunately for the pessimists, business development is a never-ending journey. However, the good news is that constant change, evolution and innovation are key drivers in all those businesses who don't merely flourish, but stand head and shoulders above the rest. They are the enviable minority who manage to realise not just their own desires and ambitions but, equally importantly, those of their clients and staff.

The exercise of writing this book has been our own 'journey of 10,000 steps' and along the way we have been grateful for the help of numerous generous people who have either given freely of their support and encouragement, or have contributed to our knowledge of how things happen by simply being there and allowing us to get to know them and their challenges and experiences. Rather than risking alienation through omission, we do not list individual names, but instead take this opportunity to thank everyone – clients, friends, family and others – who have unstintingly given of their time, interest and enthusiasm.

To anyone reading this with a view to engendering improved business development within their own organisation we have one overriding message: none of this is easy, but it is a lot less difficult if you can always look at the positive side of what improved marketing, management and motivation can do for your organisation and, most of all, try to *enjoy* the process.

Dianne Bown-Wilson and Gail Courtney
The M³ Consultancy
Lower Farm Barn
Lower St
Islip
OX5 2SG
www.m3consultancy.co.uk

Introduction

Why another book on professional services marketing?

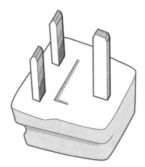

Figure 0.1 Marketing, Management and Motivation work together like the three prongs of an electrical plug – unless they're all correctly wired up and perfectly aligned, the whole thing won't work even though it appears to be fine

Is there a need for another book on professional services marketing? Obviously, we think there is and the very fact that you as a professional have picked it up and are, at least, scanning the first page, presumably means that you feel you don't have all the answers yet. If there's one thing we are sure of, it's that for 99 per cent of professionals business development is right at the bottom of the list when casting about for an interesting read.

So what brought you to this book? From our experience, it could have been any of a number of reasons, but behind them all there seems to be a common theme: you – as a managing or marketing partner or director, or practice manager – are looking for the key to *making it happen*.

Professional services firms have long held an exalted position. As recently as a generation ago, lawyers, accountants, surveyors and architects were held in awe – alongside doctors, teachers and bank managers. These days, however, the position has changed. Small to medium-sized professional firms – even those which are financially profitable – are facing a number of serious problems, including:

- inability to keep up with commercial and technological changes;
- uncertainty about how and in what direction to develop their business;
- poor public image;

- diminishing client loyalty;
- increasing stress levels of those who work within the firm;
- changing attitudes and legislation in respect of working practices;
- increasing competition.

Such firms are being squeezed on all sides, as Figure 0.2 illustrates, yet lack of information on how to tackle these issues doesn't seem to be the problem. There is a bewildering plethora of management and marketing advice on offer ranging from the academic approach – heavy on theory and short on implementation – to the quick fix, 'how to' guides, usually focusing on basic marketing communications activities, such as writing press releases and holding seminars. But, as they say, there is a big difference between reading about how to fly a plane and actually being able to do it, and the gap between knowing what should be done in respect of business development, and actually being able to do it, doesn't seem to be getting any smaller.

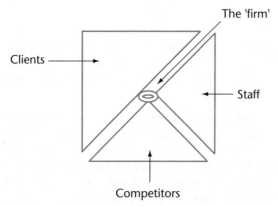

Figure 0.2   How the traditional professional services firm is being squeezed

Business development, in its broadest sense, basically comes down to effective marketing, and these days, most small to medium-sized firms are no longer complete novices. Most have undertaken at least one SWOT analysis (see Chapter 1), carried out some marketing activity (often with some success), and are familiar with a range of marketing communications tools. Despite this they usually demonstrate an erroneous understanding of what marketing actually is. Even when intellectually they know better, they still tend to approach marketing as a separate bolt-on item, regarding it as a tangible set of marketing communications activities rather than as a complete, all-embracing, externally focused ethos with implications for every aspect of running their firm. Consequently they are baffled by their inability to get it right – rather as if they had introduced a new accounts processing system and found it didn't work.

What they are seeking is assistance in answering the following questions:

- 'We spend quite a bit on marketing, but it doesn't seem to make much difference. Where are we going wrong?'
- 'We know we ought to be doing more marketing, but resources are limited – how can we make it happen?'
- 'We market ourselves adequately to our existing clients, but how can we crack new markets?'
- 'We start off well, but marketing projects repeatedly fall by the wayside. What can we do about it?'

There is plenty of advice about, but for leaders and staff of professional firms, understanding it and acting on it are two entirely different things and comments like these are still disturbingly commonplace:

- 'It's about time I set a few hours aside to do some marketing.'
- 'Planning is a waste of time and achieves nothing.'
- 'If we ask our clients for feedback, they'll just complain.'
- 'We don't have to market, we know we're the best.'
- 'Marketing doesn't work.'
- 'I'm a professional, not a salesman.'

As a starting point to helping them adopt a different approach, we look to the Chartered Institute of Marketing (CIM)'s definition of marketing: 'the management process responsible for identifying, anticipating and meeting customer needs, profitably' and also that of marketing strategist Kotler who summarised it as 'an approach to doing business'.

These two definitions, with their holistic, management- and client-focused implications, make it fairly clear that the problems most firms face are likely to lie in their lack of commitment to operating as a truly market-facing business dedicated to meeting the current and anticipated needs of their existing and potential clients.

Much traditional marketing theory is based around the four Ps of

Product
Price
Place
Promotion

These are the elements of your service (discussed further in Chapter 2) which can be manipulated in order to ensure that what your business is offering meets the needs of your market place. The four have been extended to cover other factors of importance to service-based industries (Physical evidence, Process, People, Profitability, Positioning, Planning systems, Period and Performance). However, we have found that in professional services firms there are more important factors which override these, which we refer to as the six Cs:

Communication
Culture
Common sense
Continuity
Charisma
Change

These are areas which, although not part of the service offering itself, control and influence the delivery of the whole package. They are factors to which firms frequently pay very little formal attention, but which insidiously act to prevent efficient and effective service delivery and consequently inhibit the development of the firm.

Over time, as we repeatedly battled with the six Cs and other issues and problems associated with the implementation of marketing in professional services firms, it occurred to us that all of these could essentially be distilled into three key areas: marketing, management and motivation, and behold – a new business development model was born!

The M³ model

The common focus of each chapter of this book is, therefore, the interplay of marketing, management and motivation in the dynamics of firms, and the associated issues and shortcomings which prevent them from achieving real progress. The M³ model (see Figure 0.3) is based on the premise that the success of any firm relies on its abilities in three areas:

- how the firm is managed;
- its approach to marketing;
- the willingness of its staff.

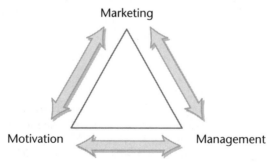

Figure 0.3 The M³ model

Our focus is on successful *marketing*, because that is what every firm must achieve in order to grow and prosper. Equally importantly, we look at the effects of this on how the firm and the process is *managed* and how staff (and clients) are *motivated*. Hence, the M^3 model overturns the premise that the three are separate, fundamentally unconnected disciplines and proposes that each should be considered in parallel with the other two, with progress depending entirely on the ability of each firm to achieve its own workable balance.

We believe that consistently high levels of client care, a market-focused ethos and the 'edge' that creates distinction can all be created through understanding the interrelationship of marketing, management and motivation and adopting and applying a policy of consistent, sustained application within the firm. As no two firms are the same in terms of their combination of strengths and weaknesses in these areas, off-the-shelf solutions which may be beneficial to one firm, may be completely unworkable in another. In general terms our approach seeks to enable each firm to identify:

- where it currently is;
- where it wants to be;
- problems, weaknesses and obstacles, unique to the firm, that prevent it from getting there.

Our approach helps firms to establish sensible plans and objectives, implement realistic programmes of activity and monitor progress. We also aim to provide management with the insight to be able to recognise growing imbalances between the three Ms, equipping them with the tools needed to put matters right and continue on course.

Feedback shows that the M^3 model is useful because it is a diagnostic rather than purely solutions-based approach, focusing on helping each firm identify its areas of strength and weakness, alongside a realistic understanding of the intrinsic factors which will help or hinder its success. For example:

- Marketing cannot operate in isolation from the on-going activity of the firm – it needs a framework of strategic business planning and clear objectives.
- Successful business development often involves a complete cultural (and possibly operational) re-alignment on the part of the firm (from an internally focused to an externally focused approach) in order to provide a climate in which it can flourish.
- Systems and operations must be brought into the twenty-first century in order to underpin what is on offer.

- Adopting a commercial ethos and operating as a business – benchmarking progress against other small and medium-sized enterprises (SMEs) – aids dynamism and innovation.
- Marketing throughout the firm must be directed, managed and supported from the top.
- Marketing is a specialist skill which requires the investment of a significant amount of both time and money.

Who are we writing for?

This book is aimed specifically at small to medium-sized firms, those where the leaders and managers of the firm are still doing the work and where there is probably little in-house professional support in terms of marketing, human resources (HR), training or information technology (IT) personnel. Large firms who have the resource to carry their own professionals tend to have, as a result, more in common with large, commercial organisations than with smaller professional services providers. For this reason, many professional firms come unstuck when looking for benchmarks for performance. They look at what larger firms are doing within their own industry instead of looking at what the same size organisations are doing within other sectors.

With professional services firms, we believe the differences between small and large organisations very much outweigh the similarities, for some of the following reasons:

- Small to medium-sized professional services firms find differentiation almost impossible to achieve because of the nature of the services being provided (services tend to be across the board rather than niche or specialist) and broad similarities in their client base (largely comprising SMEs and private clients).
- Unlike commercial enterprises, professional services firms have only had to compete in the commercial market place comparatively recently. Generally, smaller firms have a very long way to go to catch up with commercial operations and the large professional firms, and they continue to struggle with adopting a truly commercial (i.e. market-focused) approach.
- Professional services tend to be a 'distress' purchase. This means that they are used to solve problems, and function in a support role, rather than being proactively sought out by clients as a source of advice. Although larger firms will often actively collaborate with their clients in re-engineering their processes and service offering to better meet the client's needs, few small to medium-sized firms make the effort to do so. This is largely due to their ingrained reactive stance and inflexible charging arrangements.

Thus, the standards of SMEs in the commercial market place should be used as a yardstick wherever possible. By stepping outside the box and refusing to be constrained by industry norms for professional services, firms can set their sights much higher, take a more realistic view of what can actually be achieved, and start to realise that the sky's the limit when considering the future of their business.

No firm is looking at a blank sheet of paper when it considers its future. It has a history, some sort of management system (anarchy is rare) and a complement of personnel. What determines the position of the firm on the evolutionary business scale between embryonic and evolved sophistication, and moulds and shapes its future progress, are its approach to marketing and how the leaders of the firm interweave the two strands of management and motivation into it in order to develop a market-focused business. Some key factors are included in Figure 0.4.

This is not a 'how to' manual. We are not looking at either formal management or marketing theory: we start from the premise that as a managing/ marketing director or partner, or a practice manager, you will have – at the very least – a basic familiarity with both. Our approach is to look at business development in its entirety and we concentrate on how to make it work in practice. As you will have seen from the contents pages, the book is structured in a fairly straightforward format, considering each of the three areas of marketing, management and motivation in turn. However, rather than concentrating on the niceties of theory and practice, we look at the issues related to each which hamper achievement of excellence and growth and suggest practical approaches to overcoming them.

Lack of success in marketing, for example, is not usually due to lack of technical knowledge about marketing but rather to much deeper, ingrained problems such as inertia, suspicion, stagnation, resentment, insecurity and cynicism. Management tends to be 'administration' dressed up as something finer, while motivation provided by anything other than financial reward, is so rare as to be non-existent.

So, throughout the book, we give examples of worst practice and best. What we try to do is highlight some of the areas we believe you need to take into account, providing a little more information where we think either that you may find yourself overwhelmed if you start looking into the topic in depth, or where very little else seems to have been written about it.

Demons and disguises – identifying where your problems lie

Do you recognise any of these problems in your firm in respect of business development?

Embryonic	Primitive being	Evolved sophisticate
Poor understanding of 'marketing'	Understand marketing theory	Overall market orientation
No plans/objectives	Some limited planning	Hierarchy of plans
Consistently reactive	Largely reactive	Proactive
Fee-driven	Fee-driven but will consider other drivers	Client-, market- and staff-driven
Partner-driven internal structure	Team structure based on service delivery	Structure built around client needs
All clients treated equally	Limited recognition of importance of some clients	Key client management programmes
All knowledge held by individuals	Some shared knowledge	Firm-wide knowledge management systems
Consensual management style	Some delegation of responsibility	Commercial devolved structure
Motivation is linked to fees earned	Some motivation to meet 'soft' targets	Motivation to deliver in all business development areas
Quality is promoted but not practised	Some common internal standards	Quality accreditation and benchmarking

Figure 0.4   The evolution of marketing

- Identifying the dividing line between providing a professional service and running a business.
- Wading through the plethora of approaches/consultants.
- Lack of clarity about problems/issues you face.
- Characteristics of successful firms not fully understood.
- Quick bolt-on solutions sought.
- Concern about the expense of non-core activities, e.g. marketing, training, IT.
- The ethos of the firm is markedly different to that of a commercial SME.
- Poor communication and team-working – internal and external.
- Difficult to differentiate the firm from the competition.
- Overemphasis on technical skills.

There is a major difference between recognising problems and implementing solutions – this book will help you recognise where you are, identify where you should be aiming to be, and assist you to get there. As such, it's all about *change*. There again, plenty has been written about change management, but it is change in the context of marketing, management and motivation that we believe is important in the professional services market place.

Marketing and soft-skills training, client care programmes, communication channels, resource management, profitability and quality assurance are just some areas where concentrated effort can pay real dividends. But which to tackle first, why, and how much to invest? The problems are myriad, which is why – again – we refer to the three key areas:

1. Marketing

Telling many smaller firms that the way forward in marketing terms is to concentrate primarily on one-to-one client care, when they believe that is what they already do highly successfully, is to invite disdain. What they believe will have an effect are the comforting, tangible items such as a new brochure, a website, a folder of press releases. That allows them to say, 'we've done our bit but if the market doesn't respond, it proves our point that marketing doesn't work'. Regrettably, this is the stage that many firms have now reached and their bewilderment is palpable. They have invested significantly in marketing, IT, and all the other trappings of what on the surface should have been a ground-breaking strategy, yet have little to show for it in terms of results.

It all comes down to understanding the significance of, and channelling resource into, those areas that matter. But even at the top this doesn't necessarily happen, as a research report undertaken by Wheeler Associates demonstrated (*Marketing the Advisers II*, McCallum Layton and

Wheeler Associates, 1999). The study looked at marketing within the top 50 law firms and showed that a quarter of top firms still failed to measure client satisfaction even though they were spending a small fortune on promoting their service message. At a far more basic level, a research survey we undertook in 2000 into response to telephone enquiries at small to medium-sized firms showed that 10 per cent of firms nationally refused to reveal the names of key personnel (e.g. managing partner) to telephone enquirers, a simple but telling indicator of a lack of openness and a completely internally-focused ethos.

In addition to focusing on the wrong areas of activity, there is a common, usually unspoken, attitude among professionals that 'marketing's fine – as long as someone else does it'. This correlates with the fact that marketing skills are rarely regarded as being of any great importance to the individual or the firm. As a result, insufficient training takes place and most still approach marketing activities with a mixture of fear mingled with a conviction that a do-it-yourself approach will do.

2.   Management

Professional services firms across the board suffer inherent management difficulties, many of which are a direct result of the partnership structure – current or historical – even in those firms which appear to have taken a more commercially oriented approach. Managing a professional services firm is, as they say, akin to 'herding cats', with a range of potentially conflicting personalities each with ideas of how to do things, fostering a lack of accountability and consensus and coordinated activity. Lip-service is paid to the need to devolve sufficient management power and leadership to drive things forward, with a formal view of 'management is necessary and good' being undermined by individual, unspoken attitudes of '. . . for everyone but me'.

Even firms with apparently quite sophisticated management structures rarely have the supporting processes to underpin them. Many small to medium-sized firms are, in fact, near-anarchies where management is merely administration of some predefined group activities, rather than any significant means of organisation, supervision and control. Although this usually causes few problems in carrying out day-to-day technical work, planned and sustained marketing effort cannot succeed in such an environment, as the means uniformly to set and agree objectives and direct resource to their achievement simply do not exist.

3.   Motivation

Realistically, there is little or no motivation within most small to medium-sized firms for partners and fee-earners to devote time and effort to marketing. With few exceptions, all that is seriously measured, valued, or rewarded is fees earned on the basis of this simple equation:

Work on desk = Amount billed = Degree of success

What that work is, where it came from, how it was obtained, whether it will lead to more work, even whether it was truly profitable, is usually not measured or rewarded. This being the case, all efforts are ultimately focused on the bottom line, thereby reinforcing the image of marketing as a bolt-on activity. Even more damaging, this approach ignores key motivational issues such as cost-effectiveness and efficiency, incentive and reward, resource management, return on investment, future growth, and so on.

A further consequence of the lack of serious measurement of client satisfaction is also reflected in the lack of motivators driving improvements in client care. After all, if you can bury your head in the sand and pretend that if you don't get too many formal complaints, not much is wrong, there is very little motivation for change.

These are just a few examples of the problem areas in business development, and firms wanting to move forward have tackled the problems in a number of ways, including:

- appointing management consultants to help the firm decide its strategy, and structure and re-engineer its processes;
- appointing marketing consultants to, for example, produce print material, a website and undertake public relations;
- appointing HR consultants to look at issues such as training and appraisal;
- appointing someone internally to organise marketing events and set up a client database;
- sending fee-earners on training courses to address problems such as time management.

Unsurprisingly, as none of these approaches in themselves addresses the very heart of the culture, operating systems and people of the firm, they fail to produce any real long-term change. As those providing the service cannot be separated from the service they provide, what we believe really needs to happen is (to return to our original six Cs):

Common sense and cultural change, founded on communication, continuity and charisma

So that, in a nutshell, is what this book will help you bring about, at least in terms of recognising where your problems lie and assessing some practical solutions.

Today's professional, tomorrow's entrepreneur

'Why can't a woman be more like a man?' lamented Professor Higgins in *My Fair Lady*, and, echoing this, we ask 'why can't a professional be more like a businessman?'.

Ten to fifteen years ago in the early days of marketing within the professions, in-house marketing professionals had to be recruited from commercial or industrial backgrounds for the simple reason that there were insufficient people with professional services experience. Although this should have been beneficial in terms of the amount of commercial experience and acumen they could introduce, what tended to happen was simply that both sides went through a very painful learning curve – more painful for the marketer than the professional firm if statistics of how short a time most stayed in their positions are to be believed. The professions simply were not ready for it, and, typically, the marketers simply accepted that their lot in life was to produce brochures and organise seminars or they left and were replaced by someone who was happy to do so.

Times have now moved on – but things have come full circle. Because there is now a pool of people with experience in marketing within professional firms these are the people who now tend to be recruited to fill such positions because 'they understand how things work within professional firms'. We would argue, however, that 'the way we do things' is now one of the biggest factors which is holding many firms back, and we would recommend looking further afield and recruiting support staff from those with experience in other service industries. Not only will they have fresh ideas, they will also have proof and experience that, yes, it can be done.

Some firms are taking a realistically commercial orientation, but where they are slow to change is in breaking down the simple barriers that still divide them from the rest of the commercial market place. As you will see, throughout the book we use the language of professional firms in order to dispel any fears that what we are saying might have been written for any business in any market, and to reinforce the fact that 'yes, we do mean *you*'.

As ours is a business which has both professional services clients and service-focused commercial company clients, we are quite used to having to change our language entirely when talking to each group. Although this may seem a small point, we believe it's the tip of the iceberg in terms of where some of the problems of professional services firms lie.

Just look at the examples in Table 0.1. The list goes on and on yet we are talking to both groups about the same things, aiming to solve the same problems. So why do we have to speak to each with an entirely different forked tongue?

Table 0.1 The significance of language

Professional firm	Commercial company
Firm	Company
Partners	Managers
Clients	Customers
Managing partner	Managing director
Practice manager	General manager
Bills	Invoices
Fee-earning	Profit-making
Fee-earners	Staff
Terms of engagement	Terms of business
Senior partner	Chief executive
Management committee	Board of directors
Staff partner	Personnel manager
File review	Quality control
Timesheet	Work record/roster
Coffee and chat	Appraisal meeting
Client partner	Account manager

Most professional services firms say that they consider commercial acumen to be very important – by 'commercial acumen' they mean knowledge and understanding of the commercial market place, and how their clients' businesses operate. All well and good, but, by continuing to perpetuate the mystique of professionalism through their language, they are failing to underpin this by their behaviour. We believe that much of this continuing mystique is driven by insecurity, lack of confidence and fear emanating from the fact that professionals are trained technically to be lawyers, accountants, surveyors – and not much else.

Even more damaging is the unfortunate propensity of some professional services firms still to regard themselves as 'better' or 'more important' than commercial companies. The pomposity of this is exasperating, but the real frustration lies in the inherent false sense of security it creates that they will somehow, therefore, be absolved from treading the same long hard road of change and development as every other business. We trust that the mere fact that you are browsing through this book means you are not one of these, but, should you be harbouring any doubts, the fact is that change and development are unavoidable challenges for every business – and if you are bringing any baggage with you, you will have an even more arduous job ahead of you to catch up.

Equally detrimental is the fact that in many firms, the personal tools that professionals need to implement an efficient, effective and profitable service are considered not to really matter, even though a considerable amount of lip-service may be paid to them. Nothing could be further from the truth. Today's professionals need a whole armoury of skills to survive, including:

- marketing skills;
- relationship-building and motivational skills;
- research and knowledge management skills;
- IT skills;
- management and decision-making skills;
- team-working skills;
- leadership skills;
- coaching skills;
- communication skills;
- time-management skills.

But where do they learn these? From attending a few seminars if they are lucky – for the simple reason that these attributes are still regarded as being an incidental part of the job.

To return to our earlier point, the only way most firms can differentiate themselves is through superior performance in respect of these personal skills, not through the technical excellence that they still so greatly revere. When recruiting staff, most firms still base their selection primarily on technical excellence, yet this often results in staff with technical skills above and beyond what their clients require, which may impress you, but holds little sway with clients who just want to get the job done.

So, remember, next time you recruit: good enough can be enough, and, if your firm is short on charisma and rainmaking skills, a brilliant socialiser may be ten times more valuable to you than an intellectual. Ultimately, training a person in technical skills is comparatively easy, whereas instilling a winning personality into someone with all the kudos of a cod is virtually impossible.

The key factors for success – knowing what to aim for

Writing in *Professional Marketing* in 1998, editor Richard Chaplin said: 'Being distinctive is the future . . . once all firms are the same in service delivery and client care, then those with an edge will succeed' (winter 1998).

Unfortunately, some years on, gaining edge still isn't the problem for most smaller firms, although many believe it is. All firms are still far from being the same in service delivery and client care – unless in the light of a recently published *Which?* report on legal services, one takes the rather cynical view that most are still uniformly poor (*Which?*, 8 August 2001, p. 8). The good news is that, as a result, it is still possible for firms to differentiate themselves through service delivery and client care, with the possibilities being limitless for those who manage to create additional edge in whichever way they do it.

Over time, as we have developed our M³ model, we have also identified a list of what we believe are the defining characteristics of successful small to medium-sized professional services firms. Of course, they are open to debate but you could do worse than bear with us and use them as a focus for your efforts:

1. Acceptance by all that delivery of the technical service is only one part of the job.
2. Focusing on the client, not on the work being done for them.
3. Taking a commercially focused approach to doing business and looking outside the professions for business models.
4. Giving priority and *time* to consistent business development and management.
5. Strong, charismatic leadership and an energetic approach.
6. Modern flexible employment policies and a democratic culture.
7. Excellent proactive communication (internal and external).
8. Soft skills training programmes tailored to all staff levels.
9. Creation of a shared vision and sense of purpose throughout the firm.
10. Understanding and utilising the value of existing clients and contacts.

We are not suggesting that you should try to address them all at once – creating change in any of these areas will take a massive amount of time. In fact, as every firm will undoubtedly be better in some areas than others, we suggest you identify those most in need of improvement and consider how you are going to engineer significant change. We hope that by the time you have read this book, you will have a clearer idea of why you should do so and how to go about it.

CASE STUDY   **The builders merchants' showroom – a parable for professional firms**

When Jones & Co Builders' Merchants decided to develop their business, they wasted no time in analysing their requirements. As their existing premises were old and ramshackle, an impressive new showroom was obviously needed to attract new customers. So within minutes the directors sketched out a design and agreed to start work immediately. Budgets, timescales, architects' plans – they could circumvent them all. The important thing was simply to get on with it and create an imposing new edifice as fast as they could.

Then something strange happened – instead of using their own carefully chosen and stored building materials, they went in search of them elsewhere. Why? Because their mindset said 'Stock is stock, and materials for building are something else.'

In the event, they had difficulty obtaining what they needed. Immediately available supplies were hard to come by; they were pipped at the post by other purchasers; ended up paying more than they should; and in some instances found they couldn't get what they wanted at all. The months dragged by until eventually, in disgust, they threw in the towel. It had all turned into an enormous waste of time and effort and at the end of the day the old building would have to do – developing the business was simply too difficult.

In the meantime, customers had been leaving in droves due to difficulty accessing the old showroom and the fact that the staff obviously had their focus elsewhere. In reality, the customers hadn't minded the showroom at all, as long as it provided them with what they wanted. They went there for efficient and friendly service, and the firm's previous 'if we haven't got it, we'll get it for you' attitude – the physical surroundings of the builders' merchants had had little effect on their loyalty at all.

Many professional services firms tackle business development in this way too. They don't ask their clients what they want. They are over-ambitious and they don't work to written plans or within realistic budgets and timescales. Worst of all, when it comes to building the business, they completely fail to take into account the vast stocks of potential surrounding them in terms of their existing client base, network of contacts and pool of expertise. 'Clients are clients and new business is something else' . . . Instead, they choose to waste enormous amounts of time, money and energy trying to obtain new clients . . . and often fail.

Marketing

Basic planning techniques

Think about your firm – do you recognise any of these problems?

	YES	NO
In our firm planning is just something that happens on paper, no one's actual marketing activities ever seem particularly planned.		
We've had written plans in the past but no one ever refers to them subsequently.		
Our team plans are totally unrelated in format, style or content.		
We have difficulty translating group plans into personal objectives.		
We never seem able to get our plan finished till halfway through the year.		
Measuring achievement against the plan is always a nightmare.		
If we try to involve everyone in the planning process, we end up with a typical committee-designed camel.		

We keep being told that our marketing objectives should be SMART, but we're not really sure what this means.		
Following our bi-annual partners' meetings, all our partners know what they need to do, it's difficult to see the need for anything more formal.		
We've little enough spare time to devote to business development as it is – we don't have the luxury of being able to waste weeks on planning.		

Assuming you didn't answer 'no' to all the above, then you should read on.

Even if you think planning is not an area of concern for your firm, we suggest you still skim through this chapter and compare our advice with what you currently do. Our experience shows that in many firms, over time, the process of planning has become mechanical to the extent that those most directly involved almost seem to have lost sight of the point. Revisiting what your plans should be covering and aiming to achieve might well be worthwhile.

Planning is both a natural human activity and an essential business activity if you want some control over your environment and events. Yet despite this, business planning is often one of the areas where professional services firms experience some of their greatest difficulties. So, in this chapter, as we run through the essentials of the planning process and why you need to plan, we will also be providing some pointers on keeping your head above water long enough to reach the magical 'other side' where at last you will be able to start 'doing'.

Why plan?

We believe there are three main reasons why planning is important. First, the prime function of planning is to provide you with a set of instructions to get you to where you want to go. The most important implication of this is that it will set you off in a direction which you have consciously chosen to follow, which means that you are in a position to take control of the future, rather than drifting precariously, subject to the force of circumstance. Whichever area your planning process relates to – broadbrush business development, or functional activity plans – it involves a number of questions which remain constant:

- Where are we now?
- Where do we want to get to?
- How do we get there?

- What exactly are we going to do?
- Are we on the right track?

An equally important reason is that a plan records specifically, for the benefit of others, what you are intending to do, so that they can support you and know what is expected of them.

Finally, as a professional adviser – whatever your area of expertise – you should be in a position to offer your clients general commercial advice in respect of their own business and marketing plans, whether start-up or expansion. It's difficult to be credible if you're not familiar with the process yourself.

So unless you are prepared to let the firm drift out of control, planning is not an optional extra and yet, as mentioned above, it seems to be one of the biggest stumbling blocks for professional services firms embarking on taking a more formal approach to their business development. Repeatedly, one hears of firms who have become so bogged down in the planning process, that by the time they get to the end of it (if they ever do) they have lost all impetus.

There seem to be several reasons for this:

- In many ways, planning is the most essential process in running a business, and certainly the most crucial aspect of marketing, and therefore professionals – who are used to 'getting it right' – are unduly afraid of preparing a less than perfect plan.
- Unfortunately, planning has to be done first. You need to have a plan before you can do anything else, but the coordination, analysis and foresight required for the complex business of drafting a plan can be taxing for a team who may be unused to working together, or simply unfamiliar with the planning process.
- Professionals tend to have overly analytical minds. Through their very nature and training they have a tendency for 'paralysis through analysis' caused by over-analysing and trying to take into account every possible eventuality.

So it is important to be wary of the dangers of overly meticulous planning if you have suffered previous marathon planning ordeals or are embarking upon a formal planning process for the first time. It is better to view the initial plan simply as a way of getting started.

| CASE STUDY | **Mixing up a miracle** |

One of our favourite analogies is to compare a plan to a recipe. This idea originally came to us when dealing with the managing partner (we'll call him George) of a medium-sized accountancy firm. In discussing the firm's needs, he was personable and enthusiastic in respect of most of what we had to say, but was adamant, as were his staff, that formal planning was a complete waste of time. We persisted with our premise that it was impossible to introduce a meaningful business development programme throughout the firm without going through the planning process, but he continued to take the stance that it would be a total turn-off and would sabotage whatever enthusiasm existed.

For a while it seemed as if the stand-off would continue irreconcilably – until we remembered that George was an enthusiastic amateur chef, having made numerous references to his hobby in our discussions.

During our own brain-storming session on how best to solve the problem, it came to us that we might suggest to him that we develop the planning–cooking analogy as a way of getting across the message about the importance of planning to the firm and how practically they should go about it. Fortunately, George seized upon the idea with relish and in a highly entertaining presentation a few weeks later, supported by George hamming it up like Keith Floyd on location, we were able to get the following message across:

A plan should provide:

- a clear and appetising idea of what the end result will look like;
- a list of appropriate ingredients – including details of quantities;
- clear step-by-step guidance as to the techniques to use to combine them;
- information on how to tell at each stage whether things are right;
- timings and estimated costs.

At the end of the demonstration, the firm had not only wholeheartedly taken on board the message about planning and were prepared to give it a go but as an added benefit could sample their leader's impressive stir-fry as well!

Taking the pain out of planning

Whether you are undertaking formal planning for the first time, or implementing a change in approach, there are a number of things you should bear in mind in order to make the process easier and to ensure you achieve results:

- Start in plenty of time – several months before the anticipated start date of your plan. The planning cycle should ideally mirror your financial year so if you let things slip you'll have the problem of planning coinciding with all the other tasks to be undertaken at your year-end.

- Start small and don't try to change everything all at once. Most disillusioned marketers have been over-ambitious in what they set out to achieve and have fallen at the first hurdle, overwhelmed by what lay before them. Easier by far to break your plan up into discrete stepping stones and take them one at a time, spurred on to success by what you have already achieved.
- Communicate with others at the outset about what you are doing, what the stages will be and the anticipated timescale.
- Allow for slippage by setting deadlines for others before the time you actually need their input.
- Indicate that by its very nature the planning process will result in change.
- Don't agonise over the process. Plan to get a good draft written in as short a time as possible and then review it and seek acceptance. Even if there are still a couple of months to go until the start of your new business year, not much is actually going to change in that time, so any amendments you may have to make will only be minor. (Aiming to have the process finished well in advance usually means that you will have a realistic chance of completing the planning process on time.)
- Having written your plan(s) and gained commitment – leave it alone – don't tinker unnecessarily.
- Test the validity of your plan through backwards planning. Look at your final objectives – have you taken into account all the stages you need to achieve it?
- If formal planning is new to your firm's culture, aim to spend the first six months of implementation just concentrating on working to a plan – focusing on the process – rather than worrying too much about exactly what you are achieving at this stage.

Top-down or bottom-up planning?

Whether the firm's plans are devised by those at the top and filtered downwards for the rest to flesh out with team and individual plans, or whether the input and aspirations of the majority are what form the building blocks of the firm's corporate plan, is always a difficult issue. In fact it is one which can cause either total paralysis or a state of overwhelming confusion, unless a stance is quickly taken. Our belief is that there is no right way – but there is one way which is more effective than others.

Common sense dictates that even in a firm which has not previously had a formal plan, the managing or senior partner will have a clear idea (or has the historical evidence on which to form one) of the firm's achievements to date, its capabilities, and its position in the market place. This being the case, it should not be impossible to draft a formal business plan and marketing plan, taking into account this information and putting forward reasonable objectives for the firm's future growth and development. This plan can then be circulated for comment and, if necessary, adjustments made before it is finalised.

The reason for taking this approach is twofold:

1. If a firm is new to the formal planning process it certainly should not be considering any radical or contentious objectives or strategies in its first year of working with such a system, otherwise it is almost certainly destined to fail.
2. It is difficult enough for one person to get together a reasoned and sustainable plan without wasting tortuous weeks on the process. To throw the process open to committee is, again, to court disaster.

Of course, if you are familiar with working within the formal planning process and have previous business plans to refer to – ideally supported by subsidiary marketing, HR, IT and service team plans – then the whole process changes somewhat. The managing partner will undoubtedly be producing an overall business plan for the firm on a 'more of the same' basis – indeed as most business plans cover a three- to five-year period, annual adjustment is frequently all that is required. This can usually be done at the stage when those at the top have had an opportunity to consider and approve the above-mentioned subsidiary plans, and will use these as the basis for updating the overall business plan.

What tends to happen in a *meaningful* planning process is that this stage becomes something of a tennis match, with the managing partner or board on one side of the net and the subsidiary teams on the other. Each puts forward their proposals in their draft plans and has them volleyed back to them as often as it takes in order for their content in terms of objectives, strategies and performance targets to equate to their piece of the overall picture. Think of it as a jigsaw puzzle – the piece the team may think it wants to fashion may be all well and good in isolation, but ultimately it needs to come up with a plan that represents the size and shape of the piece in the overall corporate business puzzle. See Figure 1.1.

Business vs marketing planning

When you're talking planning – you're not just talking one plan. You need to have an overall business plan and a number of executive functional plans. Figure 1.2 illustrates this. As each plan flows from the one above it in the planning hierarchy (as demonstrated in Figure 1.3) you

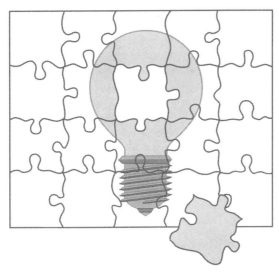

Figure 1.1   The corporate planning puzzle

need to start with the firm's business plan. However, the planning stages you need to go through for each are identical – only the areas on which you focus are different.

    Even the smallest firm will probably have a formal written business plan to outline the way forward for the entire firm. In essence, such plans are usually mainly concerned with money – which services will generate it, how it will be spent, how any shortfalls or surpluses will be dealt with – and often only exist simply because banks or other financial advisers require it.

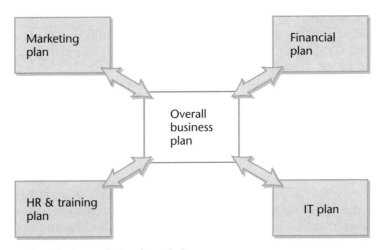

Figure 1.2   The interrelationship of plans

Figure 1.3   The hierarchy of plans

The marketing plan

Having looked at how the marketing plan fits into the overall planning picture and why you need one, we will take a look at what goes in it. The marketing plan will detail the specifics of the marketing programme you are about to undertake and ideally will sit alongside other detailed functional plans for the firm, e.g. IT, training, and so on. Most firms will need more than one marketing plan in as much as every service team or work group should have a subsidiary plan of how they are going to market their services to current and potential clients and other potentially useful third parties.

This being the case, the marketing plan is the summation of all those plans – much in the same way that the firm's business plan summarises all the service plans which hang off it. An obvious consequence of this hierarchy of plans is that the further down the pyramid you go, the more detailed the plans become and certainly the marketing plan should include details of which team, group or individual is responsible for certain activities.

Marketing plans can be structured in numerous different ways – there is no single 'right way'. Sometimes, it is easiest to write a central marketing plan by reference to the marketing mix (see Chapter 2), that is by listing various marketing communications tools, such as advertising, public relations (PR), seminars, website development, and so on – simply because the marketing budget may be broken down in this way.

However, your marketing plan should include:

- a brief marketing situational analysis – in short, setting the background to your marketing-related issues;
- reference to corporate objectives and strategies – in particular you need to make it clear how these are driving marketing objectives;
- marketing objectives – these must be SMART objectives (more about SMART later in the chapter) and must relate to purely marketing matters, e.g. sales, profile-raising, new-client generation, etc.;

- marketing strategies – the way in which you are going to achieve your marketing objectives;
- tactical plan – how you are going to use the promotional mix (see Chapter 2 for more details);
- timescales and budgets;
- monitoring and review processes.

Where you have several subsidiary team-based marketing plans supporting the central, overarching marketing plan, the tennis game referred to above is likely to be even more furiously played. There are two scenarios your firm is likely to face:

- A team has devised an over-ambitious plan and has to 'tone it down' in order to take into account the resource needs of other teams.
- A team has devised a most undemanding plan which it then has to 'beef up' in order to ensure that it has a hope of achieving the level of results needed to fill its slot in the overall jigsaw.

Either way, this can be a very sensitive process, which will need a great deal of time and careful management to ensure that everyone is happy with the plan they end up with.

What your plans should encompass

Fundamentally, a plan should cover the who, what, where, when, how and why of what the firm is going to do. As we have seen, there are different levels of planning, but that same simple formula can be applied to each. Cutting out all the niceties of management and marketing theory, the function of a plan is to:

- remind you of *why* you need to do things (achievement of objectives);
- act as an aide-memoire for *what* you are supposed to be doing and which stage comes next;
- ensure that all the team/firm is 'singing from the same hymn sheet';
- underpin the apportionment of human and financial resource (i.e. time and money);
- provide timescales for the achievement of objectives;
- encapsulate how and when you measure what you are (or aren't) achieving;
- stand as a frame of reference against which to measure opportunities (i.e. is this relevant?);
- enable you to be able to recognise achievements and 'tick things off'.

Or, to take a more formal view:

Planning is the dynamic force which helps to drive an organisation forward by coordinating resources and channelling them towards the achievement of predetermined goals.

The starting point for considering the issue of motivation in respect of planning is to ascertain whether or not the firm has a plan. If the answer is affirmative, the next question is 'do you refer to it?' Most will answer 'no'. So what's the point of having a plan? Reduce this to its most fundamental level and what you are actually asking is 'what's the point of your business and where is it going'? To answer this, consider your financial predictions for the coming year:

- What do you hope/need to earn?
- What are you likely to earn (based on past/current performance)?

The difference (business growth) between these two points is generated through business development, more specifically by marketing. People say, 'but we already market ourselves and have done so for some years and it doesn't seem to make much difference'. What they fail to realise is that most businesses have to undertake a certain amount of business development just to effectively stand still, whereas a programme of focused marketing effort is required to achieve financial results above and beyond that level.

However, as you will see later in this chapter, there is much more to be considered than simple financial objectives when making decisions about why to plan and what your plans should cover. But we have found – and we suggest this is the approach you should take with your firm if you are new to planning – that concentrating on the financial improvements planning can bring about generates immediate interest. Having gained that interest, you can move on to the other benefits later.

Stages of planning

Figure 1.4 illustrates the significance of each stage of planning, which we shall now look at in more detail.

1. Situational analysis

Situational analysis (SA) is jargon for research and investigation. It is also sometimes known as the audit process, and although part of planning, it must – by definition – precede the formulation of the plan. Unfortunately, it is usually a tedious process and may involve trawling back through dozens or even hundreds of client files and vast amounts of accounts data, and even spending hours on the Internet researching

Planning stage	Key issue
Situational analysis	Where are we now?
Vision	Why are we in business?
Objectives • corporate • service (e.g. IT, marketing)	What do we want to achieve?
Strategy • corporate • service (e.g. IT, marketing)	How are we going to achieve it?
Tactics	What tools are we going to use?
Review	How are we doing?

Figure 1.4   The significance of each planning stage

various aspects of your existing client base and the market in which you operate, or want to operate.

Most people, human nature being what it is, try and cut corners in this area – *don't!* There are two simple reasons for doing all this:

1. You need historical information. You need the best possible information you can glean about the relevant factors which have:

    (a) contributed to your current level of performance/turnover;
    (b) affected your current levels of profitability;
    (c) established the profile which you currently retain.

2. You need accurate information now. What you are doing is akin to laying the foundations of a building – if you don't get it right now, whatever you build on top is almost certainly destined for disaster.

People often tell us 'we know where our strengths lie' or 'we've got a good idea of what's what, we don't need figures'. However, looking at the need for specific, measurable objectives, and considering the large amount of resource – both time and money – that such people are about to risk on the whole process, we don't believe that such an informal approach is sufficient.

SA involves past, present and future analysis – and the only encouraging thing to say if you are embarking upon it for the first time, is that having done it once, you will be able in future to monitor as you go. You will thereby be cutting out the whole of the 'past' exercise, and much of the 'present', while making monitoring of the future an on-going and continuous task. In short, the pain will be a diminishing factor.

What exactly your firm needs to look at is governed by your size, geographical location, skills set, etc. – but, as a general rule, you should be looking at the following factors:

- External
  - environment: political, economic, social, technological and legal/regulatory factors;
  - competitors: who and how they operate and your respective position;
  - clients: existing and potential client groups;
- Internal
  - staff: quality, skills, motivation satisfaction levels;
  - client relationships: nature and strength, retention levels;
  - service quality: hard evidence of current status;
  - service portfolio: range and price.

What you are doing is trying to identify those factors which exert a significant positive or negative force on your business. We suggest you draw up a list of these opposing forces – both in respect of where you are now, and where you would like to be in, say, three or five years' time. When doing so, decide how important each area is and identify those where you need to exert effort to bring about change. No doubt you will have quite a long list of different factors at this stage, so how do you identify where to place your focus? Our general rule is: *Don't try to improve on what is already good and what you already do well (positive forces). Put your effort into reducing negative forces.*

For example, if your firm's use and application of IT is generally good, don't focus on making it better, rather focus on those areas – people, teams, functions perhaps – where poor performance is undermining the efforts of the majority. See Figure 1.5.

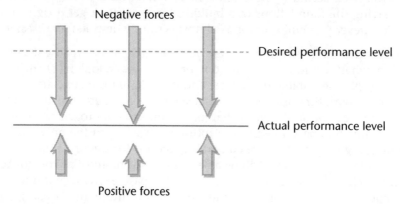

Figure 1.5 The force field

At the end of this exercise, you will find you have the basis of both a gap analysis (a comparison of where you want to be with where you are now, enabling you to consider how the gap between the two might best be bridged) and a SWOT analysis (an outline of your firm's Strengths, Weaknesses, Opportunities and Threats). As most firms are familiar with the latter, all we will say here is ensure that your SWOT is based on fact, and that the strengths and opportunities are not mere wish-lists, or representative of the way you like to see yourselves.

Some firms, when planning, are best advised to turn the SWOT analysis on its head to avoid everyone becoming so swamped in the mire of perceived marketing weaknesses that they are unable to focus on the opportunities and lose heart completely when considering threats. Try doing a SOWT – and you may find morale and analysis improves enormously. Having said this, other firms may need to focus rather more on weaknesses and threats to overcome a general air of complacency and unreal interpretation of market forces.

Having done your situational analysis, you will be in a position to measure reality against aspiration in terms of shared personal goals (e.g. ratio of salary to time input) and values (e.g. an ethical approach to doing business) and postulate a long-term *vision* for the firm.

2.   Vision and values

The foundation stone of the business plan, and indeed the firm's entire approach to doing business, is its Vision of where it wants to be and the values which it will seek to protect in conducting business. Distinctions can be made between vision statements, mission statements, value statements and goals – but there is little point in getting worn down by all of that here. What is important is that you should be able to write down, succinctly and meaningfully, what your firm stands for and where it is going in a way that both provides everyone in the firm with a shared sense of direction, and acts as a clear call to action.

Many organisations publicise such a summary about their firm as a mission statement, but we suggest you don't approach the exercise from the point of view of trying to devise something which will look good on your corporate literature or emblazoned across your website. In doing so, all too often people end up with something which is folksy, trite and completely indistinguishable from any other firm's. So just concentrate on getting your vision into words that will mean something for your own people, then run with it for a couple of years or so before you start proclaiming it to the outside world. After all, it can be highly dangerous to lay out your stall as a 'provider of high quality services' if your clients think 'not in my opinion'.

More about values and the way in which they underpin development of a brand can be found in Chapter 3. The key point to take on board here is that, as research has found, values cannot be created, they can only be discovered, so by definition the workforce as a whole must be involved in this discovery as it is within their ranks that your values lie.

3.   Objectives

Corporate objectives are the practical summary of what the business wants to achieve and should reflect the findings of your gap and SWOT analyses (remember, not every weakness, threat, or negative force needs to be addressed – there will always be a hierarchy of importance, or some things that you can, practically, do little to influence). Corporate objectives should relate to key financial factors for business success, e.g. growth, profitability (return on investment), cash flow and market share/competitive position. Objectives can be both long and short term.

Figure 1.6 demonstrates the way corporate objectives represent the firm's position at an overarching level, providing a framework for objectives in subsidiary plans – for example, human resources, IT and, of course, marketing.

Whenever you have an objective it must be a SMART objective:

Specific
Measurable
Achievable
Realistic
Time-bound

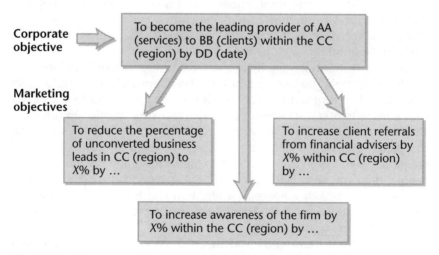

Corporate objective

To become the leading provider of AA (services) to BB (clients) within the CC (region) by DD (date)

Marketing objectives

To reduce the percentage of unconverted business leads in CC (region) to X% by ...

To increase client referrals from financial advisers by X% within CC (region) by ...

To increase awareness of the firm by X% within the CC (region) by ...

Figure 1.6   How corporate objectives influence functional objectives

Non-SMART objectives, for planning purposes, just aren't satisfactory. They will probably be unachievable because they are too ambiguous, or too ambitious or ill considered, success or failure can't be measured, and no one is clear about the timescale over which they should be achieved. As objectives are crucial to the whole planning process and occur in every level of plan from corporate down to personal, we suggest that you stop at this point and spend a few minutes thinking about SMART objectives. It really is that important.

Of course, it is not always easy turning what sounds a reasonable sort of objective into a SMART objective. Your aim may be 'to increase the amount of business we get from the XY market'. Yes, but by how much? By when? The usual answer is that such detail is impossible to predict, in which case you must make a reasonable guess along the lines of '. . . by 30 per cent over three years'.

Take another common objective: 'To raise our profile for doing such and such work'.

- To raise your profile with whom?
- How can you measure it; how will you know?
- By when?

At this stage it should be clear that corporate objectives must be underpinned by meaningful supporting objectives. For instance, in the last example, the marketing plan should include reference to undertaking research – albeit fairly rudimentary – to establish the current baseline of awareness about the firm within the specified market place.

The key benefit of setting SMART objectives is that it generates questions in the minds of those setting them, along the lines of:

- How will we know if we're achieving that?
- What happens if we exceed our targets almost immediately?
- Is measuring the result in that way realistic?
- What will be the ramifications of not keeping to time?

Systems need to be put in place to enable the firm to measure its results and to review progress periodically. As you go along, your objective can and should be changed, e.g. at the end of year one, if it becomes clear that either it has been exceeded already or is patently unattainable, but other than that it should stand as something the firm needs to achieve.

A word of warning – if you have been reading books on commercial business planning, you may be tempted to set objectives relating to market share. We have seen so many examples of objectives along the lines of 'to increase our market share in the area of XX' that we know this happens. In the field of professional services, market share is often very difficult to establish or to measure – so we suggest you steer well clear of it unless you know you are providing a service which, quite literally, only has a few competitors and little prospect of many more jumping on the bandwagon. Quite simply, it is meaningless and unmeasurable. If you think you are in such a strong position that you can achieve measurable results, try rephrasing your objective to 'to become the service provider of choice for AA service for clients in the BB market place within the next three years'. Of course, that means you will have to conduct research to show who is the supplier of choice at present, and periodic research to establish whether you are achieving your objective as time progresses.

4.   Strategy

A strategy, to quote the dictionary definition is: 'a large-scale plan or method for winning a war'. Strategy deals with the *how* of the planning process and basically, it is the *way* in which you're going to achieve your objectives and gain long-term competitive advantage.

   A number of approaches can be taken to devising strategies:

- the military approach
- the common sense approach
- the long-haul approach.

Marketing and business strategists often draw powerful parallels between various military strategies and the way they relate to business, but we think that is probably a little excessive. Suffice it to say that no great wars were ever won by the generals merely turning up at the battle ground with their troops and saying 'go for it guys – just do what you want . . .'

   Marketing guru, Michael Porter, has said of strategies, 'The best strategy for a given firm is ultimately a unique construction reflecting its particular circumstances'. So, effective strategies are formed through assessing the combination of your strengths, your clients' and potential clients' needs and wants, and your competitors' weaknesses. Because of the nature of professional services, a strategy which proposes simply going out and telling the world how good you are and expecting them to respond to that message is unlikely to work (see Chapter 2 and the section on advertising for more on this).

   Confusion often arises with strategy and objectives over the level to which they relate. Remember, corporate strategy should relate to the approach the entire firm is going to adopt, whereas marketing strategies, since they may be generated by teams who are directing their services at different market sectors, may vary. However, the basic message remains: corporate strategy must be underpinned by team or function strategies which in turn must combine to implement the corporate strategy.

   In respect of marketing strategies, there are in reality only four strategies open to you although they can be couched in many different ways depending on the detail of the markets and services involved. These are to provide:

1. (More) existing services to existing markets.
2. New services to existing markets.
3. Existing services to new markets.
4. New services to new markets.

These options are encapsulated in one of the most useful marketing models to be devised, the Ansoff matrix (see Figure 1.7). It is easy to remember, it makes crystal clear what your options are, and it succinctly indicates the level of risk associated with each.

For most firms, we would advise a very careful risk assessment of each strategy, aiming for a comfortable balance between those which you have an extremely high likelihood of achieving (low risk) and those which have potentially the highest positive or negative impact on your business (probably high risk). The achievability factor is key – if your whole business development is based around strategies which will be difficult to achieve, the likelihood of success is low and for you they become high-risk strategies in terms of moving the business forward.

	Services	
	Existing	New
Markets — Existing	**Market penetration strategy (lowest risk):** • sell more to current clients • win competitors' clients • cross-sell to existing clients	**Service development strategy:** • introduce 'new' service • significantly modify service delivery • develop different service packages
Markets — New	**Market development strategy:** • attack new market segments • infiltrate new geographic areas	**Diversification strategy (highest risk):** • mergers/takeovers • multi-disciplinary partnerships

Figure 1.7   Marketing strategies (the Ansoff matrix)

5. Tactics

As mentioned above, corporate plans will ideally have several supporting tactical plans covering various functions of the firm and these represent the real meat and potatoes of the process – in essence, who is going to do what, presented in as short and sharp a form as possible.

Struggling with the difference between strategic and tactical decisions is a common problem and Table 1.1 contains some pointers which may help you differentiate between the two. It is important that you get to grips with this, otherwise your hierarchy of plans won't add up to what is required.

Ideally, as it deals with very precise activities, your tactical plan should be presented as succinctly as possible. Although you may need to provide some supporting narrative, we have always found that there is nothing like a Gantt chart (see Figure 1.8) for making it all crystal clear. If necessary, get it blown up to A1 size and put it on the wall as an aid to help people remember and focus on what they should be doing.

6.   Timescales and budgets

We deal more with budgeting in Chapter 2, and of course, we have stressed above that objectives must be time-bound so, by implication, your tactical activities must be also. Timescales and budgets should be clearly indicated in every tactical plan, but should not necessarily be cast in stone (see below).

7.   Monitoring and review

It is essential that as part of the planning process you agree monitoring and review mechanisms and stick to them if only for the very simple reason that human nature dictates if no one is checking, nothing gets done.

Table 1.1   Differentiating between strategic and tactical decisions

Factor	Strategy vs tactics
Timespan	Strategy is long term; tactics are short term
Importance	Strategy has long-term gravitas; tactics can be easily changed
Detail	Strategy is broad; tactics are detailed and specific
Information needed	Strategic matters require extensive external analysis, past, present and future, much of which is speculative; tactics depend more on empirical, internally-generated information
Nature of problem	Strategic problems are usually unstructured and involve risk and uncertainty; tactical problems are more fact-based with less risk and more previous evidence to work with
Occurrence	Strategy evolves continuously; tactics are time-bound and often repetitive

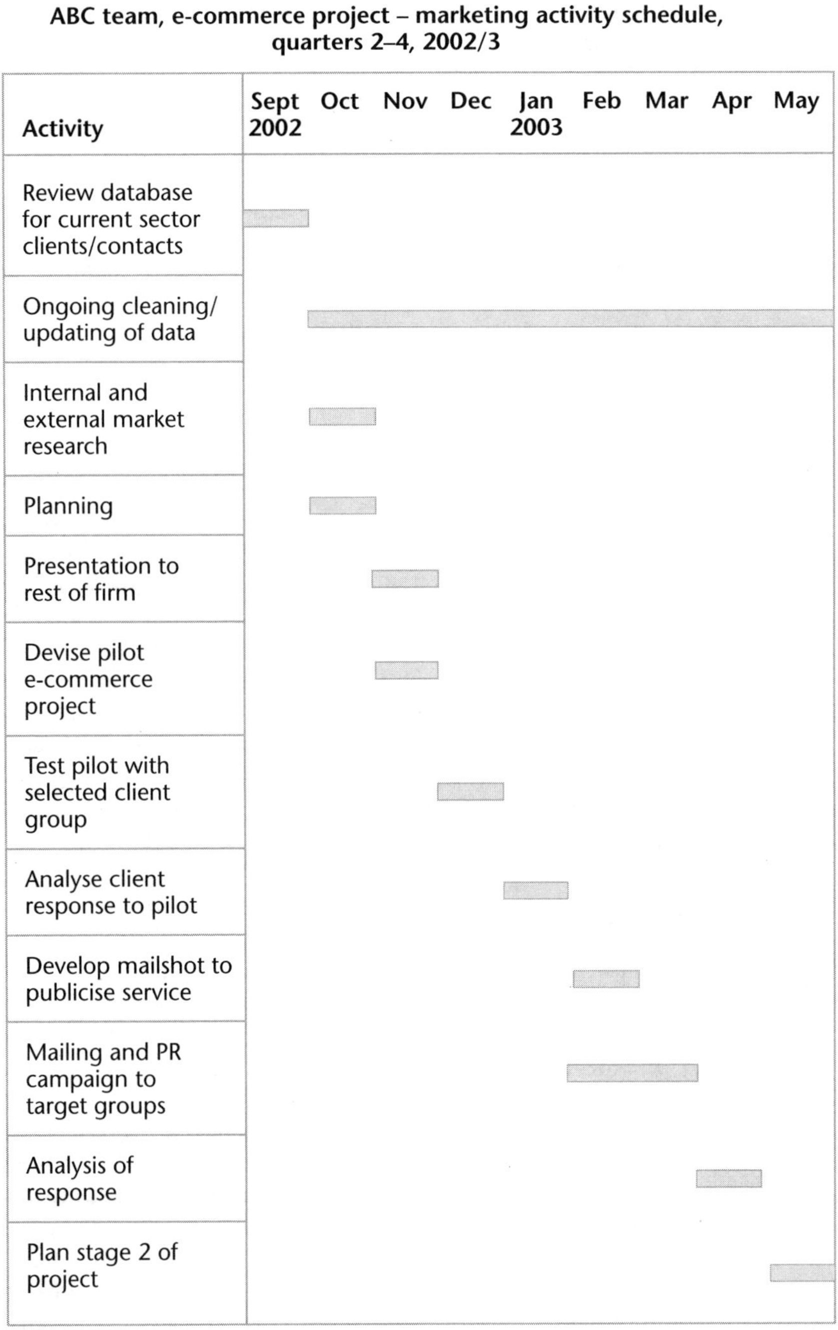

ABC team, e-commerce project – marketing activity schedule, quarters 2–4, 2002/3

Activity	Sept 2002	Oct	Nov	Dec	Jan 2003	Feb	Mar	Apr	May
Review database for current sector clients/contacts	▨								
Ongoing cleaning/ updating of data		▨▨▨▨▨▨▨▨▨▨▨▨▨▨▨▨							
Internal and external market research		▨							
Planning		▨							
Presentation to rest of firm			▨						
Devise pilot e-commerce project			▨						
Test pilot with selected client group				▨					
Analyse client response to pilot					▨				
Develop mailshot to publicise service						▨			
Mailing and PR campaign to target groups					▨▨▨▨				
Analysis of response								▨	
Plan stage 2 of project									▨

Figure 1.8   A typical Gantt chart

This is where management of the process is crucial in terms of keeping control of what is going on.

Such control should include the following:

- regularly comparing marketing costs against budget, and activity undertaken against timetables;
- analysing the profitability of various service types, teams, or whatever criteria you have decided;
- checking that strategy is being adhered to and that no one is pursuing a different route;
- reviewing results of activities against their initial objectives.

And it goes without saying, of course:

- checking actual fees earned against budget.

It may be useful to mention at this point the balanced scorecard technique as a useful means of on-going measurement and review (further information is given in Chapter 7). Using a balanced scorecard is a way of regularly reviewing comparative information from different teams or departments on a periodic basis to ensure that their activities are meeting the optimum balance of performance, as previously agreed by the firm's management. The practical advantage of this is that it enables the firm to establish which variables are important, what performance levels are acceptable, and to ensure that teams are not letting their performance in one or more areas slip through a misplaced concentration on some other area.

A word about contingencies

A common complaint by those trying to defend their indefensible position of why they shouldn't plan is that 'we can't predict what will happen in the future – if we have a plan, it will mean that we'll be unable to respond to unexpected opportunities'. This is nonsense. Every plan should address, as standard, the way in which the market will be scanned for these opportunities, how they will be flagged up, and who will decide whether or not to pursue them. The person deciding (most likely the team leader or managing partner) will use the existing strategies and objectives as a benchmark for helping him/her to reach a decision, but ultimately it is a risk. The point is, that because the risk has been reduced in all other areas through planning, the firm then has a greater ability to respond to contingencies and crises without being too damaged. And yes, a certain amount of the budget should always be reserved for contingencies (probably as a 'slush fund' held and controlled by the managing partner).

Common planning pitfalls

'If you were just starting up, would you obtain funding from a bank on the strength of this plan?' That is the test we ask clients to apply when looking at the quality of their business and marketing plans, and in many cases, the answer is 'no'.

There are numerous areas where it is easy to go wrong. Plans can:

- be too long;
- have unrealistic objectives;
- be poorly budgeted;
- have no involvement / no link to personal objectives;
- be over-ambitious;
- lack feedback mechanisms;
- overlook the role of management and motivation.

Too long

We helped one firm move from having a marketing plan for each department, which filled an entire ring-binder, to plans which were no more than two or three A4 sheets. It was a difficult process, but the benefits in terms of clarity of vision were enormous. Because their plans are now so accessible, everyone refers to them frequently, updates them regularly and can see how they form part of 'the bigger picture.'

Unrealistic objectives

The most essential part of the plan is to have realistic, SMART objectives. To hark back to an earlier point, checking to see that your objectives are SMART isn't something peculiar to the planning process – it is something which, if you haven't already, you should take on board, and try applying to every objective you set, in every area of your life.

Poor budgeting

We go into the budgeting process in more detail in Chapter 2. For now, it is important just to realise that everything has a cost, even a negative cost (e.g. choosing to do one thing means losing the profits to be gained by doing something else) and that all your efforts can be sabotaged if you run out of available budget at a key point.

No involvement / no link to personal objectives

A plan is only a way of directing what people should do. If people don't know what exactly they should do, and are not committed to the plan, it will achieve nothing. Everything within the plan needs doing by some-one – if it is a team plan, it won't be the 'team' who will do it, it has to be one or more individuals from within that team – so it must be made clear exactly who.

Over-ambitious

When planning, there is a fine line between being realistic and being challenging. Don't expect to be able to achieve miracles simply because you have written it all down.

Lacking feedback mechanisms

Finally, make sure the board or the managing partner or whoever is driving the planning process provides feedback – initial and ongoing – both on the formulation of the plan and its execution. There is nothing more frustrating for those who have been hounded to provide their plan by a certain date (usually a partners' away-day or weekend) and then to hear nothing more about it. Having worked themselves into a frenzy of focus and enthusiasm they – and their team – are left wondering 'was it agreed?', 'which bits did they like most', 'when should we start?'. So make initial, fast feedback stage one of the monitoring and review process referred to above.

Similarly, on an on-going basis, make sure that processes are in place for feeding back results – good or bad – to those involved in an initiative, whether those results are financial or relate to 'softer' issues. This is directly connected with the most overwhelming pitfall . . .

Overlooking the role of management and motivation

This we regard as probably the biggest reason for failure. Managing partners may have gone through the entire consultation process with their partners and staff in compiling the plan, but devised it essentially as an academic exercise. The issue of 'how is it going to happen?' has been largely ignored. Two key issues to consider, therefore, are *who* is going to lead, cajole, and coordinate (management) and *how* are you going to get buy-in and commitment from everyone involved (motivation). Table 1.2 shows an example taken from a marketing plan.

Planning is not a one-off, we've-done-it-now, set-in-stone, process. Without management and motivational support, the plan is unlikely to be implemented at all and the whole process will have been for nothing. Particularly in areas such as marketing where people may feel uncomfortable and unsure about what they need to do, individuals will need constant leading and pushing from step to step, rewarding and chastising as appropriate for their efforts or lack of them, and constant reminders of what they should be doing and why.

Table 1.2 Example of the management and motivational implications of a typical marketing objective

Marketing objective	Management implication	Motivational implication
To win XX% more business from market YY	Does the team involved have sufficient power, authority and support to be able to implement the plan?	What will ensure that every member of the team carries out his/her part of the plan?

What often happens is that team marketing plans are drafted and implemented by those 'at the sharp end' who are doing the work and thereafter no interest is taken in their implementation by anyone outside the team. Then what tends to happen is . . . nothing. There is always some reason why the team has not been able to deliver and by the time this is discovered, it is too late to encourage them back on course. So in any firm it is crucial that senior management is seen to take a regular, sustained interest in team progress and generates motivation through feeding back information to the team and the rest of the firm about the positive outcome of those efforts.

If you are reviewing the planning process in your firm as you read this, and feel that what you do currently is probably far from sufficient, or if you are embarking upon formal planning for the first time, this is one area where we would strongly advise you to seek external advice. Yes, you can do it yourself, but it is difficult, and your firm's plans are as important as an architect's plans are to a builder. If they are not right, everything that follows from them just won't work. So think very carefully – professional assistance, in this instance, can be very worthwhile.

POINTS TO REMEMBER

➤ The object of planning is to ensure that the business decides where it wants to go and how to get there, rather than drifting aimlessly.

➤ Planning provides a coordinating vision.

➤ Planning involves looking at past, present and future performance against a background of internal and external positive and negative forces in order to ensure that the firm, in future, minimises its weaknesses, tackles or avoids threats and plays to its strengths.

➤ Planning helps firms seek the most beneficial business strategies and maximise the best opportunities.

➤ There are only four main marketing strategies – existing services to existing clients, new services to existing clients, existing services to new clients, new services to new clients.

➤ Management and motivational elements are key to success.

2

The marketing and promotions mix

- Managing the marketing mix
- Aspects of promotion
- Motivation and the marketing mix
- The marketing communications tool-kit
- Marketing resource implications
- Choosing and using suppliers
- Budgeting
- Market research

Think about your firm – do you recognise any of these problems?

	YES	NO
We can't seem to overcome the contradiction in needing to strengthen our profile for some areas of work, while remaining a generalist full-service firm.		
It's a chicken and egg situation – do we recruit a specialist so we can offer a service, or wait till we have a client that needs the service and then see how we might deal with it?		
Our profile isn't as high as some other firms in this town.		
We've lost business to fixed-fee conveyancers and others offering fixed-price packages. How do we compete without entering into direct competition?		
We have a couple of branch offices that are an on-going problem – how important is a 'local' presence these days?		
We've spent the last three years discussing what should go on our website with the result that we still haven't got one.		

We should make more use of PR but very little of note ever happens here.		
We hold seminars and we send newsletters – but the problem is, so does every one of our competitors!		
Ninety per cent of our marketing budget goes on advertising, but it's difficult to see what we get out of it.		
We know we should communicate more regularly with our clients, but doing these things takes time.		
We should do more mailshots but our database is a disaster zone.		

Assuming you didn't answer 'no' to all the above, then you should read on.

Managing the marketing mix

In essence, marketing is all to do with matching your services to client needs. According to marketing strategist Kotler, the marketing mix is simply: 'the set of controllable variables and their levels that the firm uses to influence the target market', so manipulating the marketing mix is the way in which you balance various aspects of your services in order to achieve the best possible fit between the two.

The controllable variables are the four Ps that we met in the Introduction:

- Product
- Price
- Place
- Promotion.

For service-based organisations the list has been extended to as many as twelve – but at the risk of getting bogged down in theory, we can dispense with most of these. Suffice it to say that the main additional ones of real relevance are

- People
- Processes.

Marketing in its simplest sense, then, involves examining each of these elements in respect of the services you provide, relating them to your internal and external environment, deciding on the 'package' you want to offer and then utilising the appropriate marketing communications tools to promote them. However, in professional services firms the marketing mix is rarely managed in this way and clients are simply presented with a fait accompli – 'this is what we do and this is how we do it' (the 'like it or lump it' bit remains unsaid). When and if elements of the mix – for example, pricing – are looked at, it tends to be in isolation with insufficient attention being paid to what impact any decisions made will have on the overall offering.

One key process which must be undertaken if your marketing mix is to have any effect is that of segmenting your market. This involves sub-dividing your total market into distinct and homogeneous client sub-groups where any subgroup can be identified as a target market to be met with a distinct, tailored marketing mix.

Market segmentation is an area where many firms fall down in as much as clients are defined according to the firm's own criteria, for example, being lumped together as 'employment law clients' (solicitors), 'agency clients' (surveyors) or 'audit clients' (accountants). Although there is some validity in this, to have any real meaning, clients should be categorised according to their own needs – whether these relate to the way the service is delivered to them, the types of services they require in relation to their size and structure, e.g. SMEs or plcs, fee-related factors, or whether they relate to an innate understanding of the client's own business function. See Figure 2.1.

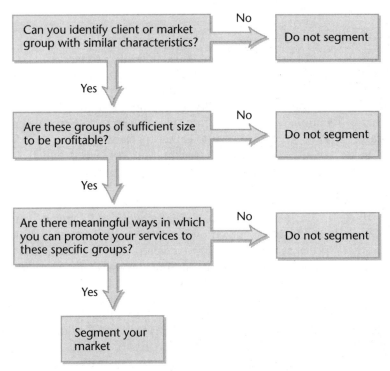

Figure 2.1   Segmenting your markets

A key management role in respect of the marketing mix is ensuring that the process is coordinated throughout the firm so that although different 'mixtures' may be offered to different market segments using different messages and a variety of promotional tools, there is overall consistency. What you should be aiming for is to achieve a wholly integrated marketing campaign for your firm (with the firm's overall marketing plan reflecting the objectives and strategies of the subsidiary team or unit plans).

Integration is vitally important in order to:

- reinforce development of the brand (see Chapter 3);
- ensure that clients and prospective clients are presented with consistent messages in respect of the firm's quality of service delivery;
- assist everyone internally to know what the firm does, how it does it and the strategies and tactics it is using to develop its business – and to be able to assimilate this as a meaningful proposition.

Having defined your relevant market segments, you need to look at what you intend to offer them. We will consider issues relating to people and processes in some detail later in this book, but for now, we will briefly examine some of the issues relating to the first four elements of the mix, with particular emphasis on place and promotion.

Product

For 'product' read 'service'. The key issues regarding service usually concern what services you should be offering, how to deal with those you don't provide and how to balance current client needs against future demand. A common area of difficulty for smaller local or regional firms is whether to remain a full-service firm or whether to drop some of the less profitable services and develop increased specialisms in others. Some firms have benefited either from picking up the work which larger national firms no longer want (e.g. some private client work), or by entering into agreements with larger firms whereby reciprocal referrals regularly take place. A larger firm will refer less profitable work to the smaller firm, which in turn will refer more specialist work to its larger 'benefactor'. Others have merged or taken over smaller organisations in order to extend their specialist knowledge or to develop a ready-made market.

Unlike the consumer or business-to-business products market, new professional services are slow to emerge and apart from those driven by changes coming directly from the profession's legal or regulatory framework, most new services will relate to the way things are done rather than the core content of the service itself. However, occasionally a 'new service' will come on-line and how a firm reacts can often be a good indicator of its fundamental approach to business, its foresight, commercial acumen and readiness to take risks.

An interesting example of a new service which affected all the professions to some degree was the potential year 2000 computer problem. Although with hindsight it proved to be something of a storm in a teacup, at the time it was heavily exploited as a fee-earning opportunity, a chance to build stronger client relationships, and a publicity opportunity by firms of all sizes who were commercially attuned – while those who weren't simply seemed to miss the boat.

The extent to which you should be promoting new ways of doing things relies to some degree on the makeup of your client base and which, if any, segments of your market are 'early adopters' – those who are the first to embrace new ideas – or whether your clients are more conservative and want convincing that something is tried and tested before they will take an interest.

For obvious reasons (i.e. because you have little that is tangible to promote), quality of service and client care are both essential elements of your service offering and we look at them in greater detail later in the book. For now, there are two essential points to remember in respect of your service offering: first, ensure that everyone in the firm understands in detail the *benefits* to clients of the services you offer, not just the features; and secondly, make certain that everyone is also fully aware of the entire service menu the firm can offer (it should go without saying, but unfortunately, too often this is not the case!).

Price

Price goes hand in hand with composition of service offering as the two main areas of focus in most firms' business development reviews. However, price reviews all too often take the form of 'Is it time to put our fees up again – if so, by what percentage?' rather than anything more strategic. Pricing which is driven simply by internal financial factors can result in:

- negative client reaction ('Why are you charging more?' 'Where's the value?');
- poor profitability (you could charge more for premium services or could delegate some of the work to someone less highly qualified and charge a blended rate);
- poor motivation to develop the business (the firm appears to be earning 'more', therefore it doesn't need new business);
- poor return on investment (some areas may generate high turnover but poor profitability).

Due to the varied nature of the work, it is actually very difficult to make price comparisons across professional service firms, unless for a very specific task. Most people are happy to pay a reasonable price and tend to shy away from going with 'the cheapest'. However, people – whether commercial clients or private individuals – expect firms to be open and above board about charging and not to present them with any nasty surprises in respect of fees. You need to make sure – particularly with repeat work from commercial clients – that they are being charged the same price by whoever in the firm they are buying the service from.

Too often, what a client pays reflects the way the firm is staffed, i.e. work is charged on the basis of whether it is done by a partner/director or someone more junior rather than according to the intrinsic value of the work itself. Clients wonder why this should be – and they don't feel they are necessarily getting better value from senior involvement. Although, in many firms partners still prefer to do the work themselves rather than taking on cheaper support staff, and offer 'high levels of partner involvement' as a benefit, the canny client may be all too aware of the downside of this for anything but highly complex matters.

Problems also arise with service delivery in respect of work being undertaken by those outside the traditional professional framework, e.g. conveyancing and personal injury work in the legal arena. Should you try and compete, or should you drop the service rather than face accusations of overcharging from clients or potential clients who have discovered that these organisations offer their services more cheaply? The answer, as most firms have discovered for themselves, is that price is not always the issue and people will pay more for a service if they feel they are getting value for money, convenience and can trust the service provider. However, you need to realise that you are up against aggressive marketing from these suppliers who are keen to break into a new market and although they may be leading on price they will also have an entire client-centred package to offer.

Place

Especially in local or regional firms, the debate over where offices are situated continues to provide problems particularly when – as a result of mergers and acquisitions – a firm finds itself with a string of small branch offices appended to its main city centre practice. On the one hand, there is the very reasonable argument that local clients (especially private clients) want a local service. However, providing it may become increasingly uneconomical when branch office performance figures are expected to fall in line with those of the central office. Branch offices can also provide problems in terms of their isolation, their historical 'self-rule', and often a general reluctance to fall in line with the systems and standards of the main firm.

There is also the debate over whether you should retain traditional 'high street' offices – with a visible physical presence – even though you may suffer from the fact that offices are difficult to access (parking problems) and no longer suitable for the purpose. Client visits are usually only periodic, so in these days of improved communication, the location of your office becomes less important (see Chapter 11 on flexible working). Also, you could consider changing your working methods so that you go to see your clients more often, rather than them coming to see you. In this sense, you can use 'place' as a tool for differentiation – there are still surprisingly few professional advisers who, unless the nature of their particular work dictates it, routinely get out and see their clients on *their* home turf. If you are one of those that do, you are probably pleasantly surprised by how much your clients appreciate and value it.

Many larger, more successful firms have chosen to move to the outskirts into purpose-built offices with designated parking (for both staff and clients) and a less expensive, more adaptable, working environment. Of course, whether or not this is feasible may lie in the nature of your client base – it may be highly acceptable to commercial clients, but less attractive to private clients. As with all else, it is best to seek the views of your clients and other professional contacts rather than relying solely on how you *think* they might react.

Virtual offices have proved to be viable for some firms, and resultant problems are reported to be more internally than externally driven. But if a conventional office is important to your firm, it may be worth considering the option of an additional, less expensive, 'backroom' office at another location, although staff may feel that they are being downgraded and cut off from the buzz of the main office. This can only be overcome if communication processes are streamlined so that everyone is included in them and there is either some form of rotation, or maybe some additional benefits to those agreeing to work off-site. It is crucial to include these personnel in meetings and one-to-ones – both at their office and the head office, to prevent them becoming isolated.

Keeping up appearances

One aspect of 'place' in the marketing mix which is rarely mentioned and often very difficult to deal with, is the issue of the quality and appearance of an office. From our position as consultants, we are ideally placed to comment on the quality of first impressions that many professionals' offices provide. Our first visit to a firm is usually after we have undertaken some background research on them from their literature or website, and how well the firm's offices then live up to the image we have formed of them, can sometimes be quite revealing.

More often than not, with small to medium-sized firms, we see impressive promotional literature and an acceptable website. However, we then go to their offices which can vary from the frankly Dickensian to those firmly trapped in the fifties or sixties. The effect of offices like these is immediately to undo all the good that the previous publicity has done.

Yes, office space is a difficult issue and furniture is expensive – but the problem is that most firms just cannot see the off-putting quality of their environment. As with your own home surroundings, your decor needs updating every 3–5 years and should reflect some elements of current, mainstream taste, even if it is not particularly 'your' taste. If not all the office space can be upgraded then effort must be put into keeping public rooms in immaculate condition and people should use these rooms and not their offices, to see clients and others.

'Cut the clutter' is a modern mantra that we advocate entirely. Try to work to a clear desk policy, which means that papers and files are put away at the end of the day. Not only does this make for improved appearance, but security means you should take this seriously, too.

A bright, contemporary, clean and tidy office can work wonders on staff morale – and it can be worth devoting some effort to this as part of, for example, launching a client care programme. Find out how staff feel about things, what they would like to have, or see happen – even if it cannot all be achieved for financial reasons, some improvements can be made. It may be worth getting people to come in over a weekend to help with a big clear up, on the understanding that they will receive some other benefit later on. Even the simplest things, like providing water coolers/dispensers can have an amazingly beneficial effect on staff morale.

You only get one chance to make a first impression, and in Figure 2.2 we offer some tips for maximum client appeal.

Clean and new	Reception areas, meeting rooms, windows, doors, toilets, furniture and crockery should all be immaculate in condition and spotlessly clean – if in doubt, replace. Ensure paintwork is fresh and non-chipped, carpets are good quality and stain-free and that any exterior or shared areas are kept in prime condition
Tidy	Keep files, papers, and general 'stuff' in appropriate storage containers and streamline your office environment. Working areas should not be an obstacle course
Stylish	Make sure your furnishings and decor reflect your values and brand and reflect some flair
Contemporary	Banish any sign of 'old' – as in old books, old furniture, old pictures – keep up to date
Comfortable	Heating, lighting, furniture should help put people – staff and visitors – at their ease
Commercial	Keep personal effects to a minimum – particularly if they are to be seen by clients

Figure 2.2   Key tips for maximum client appeal

Another aspect worth rethinking is whether you use your receptionist (the person who meets and greets clients and visitors) as your telephone operator. Although on the one hand there is an obvious logic behind this, there are also, we believe, considerable drawbacks. In a busy office, the receptionist may have to juggle greeting clients with answering the phone, which means that one or the other gets insufficient attention. More damaging, however, can be the practice of clients sitting waiting and listening to a number of incoming phone calls and how they are handled. This can highlight the number of callers who do not get to speak to the person they are calling and can also have security implications in terms of confidential or sensitive information which may be overheard.

Aspects of promotion

Promotion – the toolbox of marketing communications activities – is the element of the marketing mix which is often thought of as 'marketing' in its entirety by some professional services firms. We hope that the more you read of this book, the more you will realise that this is far from the case. Numerous books have been written on just about every theoretical and practical aspect of promotion, and specialist support is available from many agencies and consultants, so we will do no more here than glide over the surface of explaining the use and significance of each promotional tool and why some are likely to be more effective in achieving the results you want.

In order to select the best channel and message for promoting your firm you need to understand the function of the type of communication involved. Brand building (which we deal with in more detail in Chapter 3) is all to do with establishing and raising your profile among all your publics – potential and existing clients and others – and should be concerned with such broadly focused messages as:

- the quality of your personnel;
- the range of your services;
- the way you deliver your services;
- what differentiates you from other firms;
- your culture and values;
- and, of course, the overall benefits to clients of using your services.

On the other hand, communication with existing clients should have a much more varied and detailed range of messages, in a way that is:

- tailored and personal;
- regular;

- very focused;
- response orientated.

Before we look in detail at the elements of the promotional mix, it is important to realise that as well as specific market segments you also have different groups within each segment, ranging from prospects to your most important clients. When it comes to promotion, most people – not just professionals – tend to gravitate towards marketing communications which can be undertaken as discrete one-off exercises requiring little personal involvement, but as we show in greater detail in Chapter 4, advertising and article writing will do little to help you win new clients if that's all you do.

Motivation and the marketing mix

The requirement to become involved in marketing is often something which people feel they have thrust upon them. In many firms, someone else devises the marketing mix, writes the marketing plans and produces the promotional tool-kit, and then the whole lot is consigned to the unfortunate partner or fee-earner who is told to 'go and do some marketing'.

Obviously, the above process is far from helpful in engendering motivation in that person, so little wonder that one frequently finds this is the stage at which marketing doesn't happen. In order to get buy-in and ensure motivation and involvement you should, at the very least, ensure everyone:

- understands the entire marketing planning process;
- is required to contribute information and data about *their* clients for planning and analysis purposes;
- has input to shaping the marketing mix with which they must work;
- is involved (as much as is practical) and is kept appraised of the process of producing promotional materials;
- is asked to seek and report feedback from their own clients and contacts on marketing initiatives;
- is asked to monitor continually what other firms and businesses are doing in the market place to promote themselves.

The marketing communications tool-kit

Ask any non-specialist what they understand by marketing and we guarantee they will respond with either 'advertising' or 'selling'. So, for no other reason than that, we will start with these.

Advertising

Let's face it, we are all seduced by advertising. TV, cinema, newspaper/magazine and radio – we are bombarded by it every day of our lives. People see an advertisement – quickly come to recognise the product or brand and have no difficulty with taking on board the idea that advertising works. There are some sceptics – 'I'd never buy something simply because I saw it advertised' – yes, that's true, but advertising will raise your awareness of a particular product or service if you are in the market for buying it, or may go into your memory store for future reference.

So – it's simple – want to sell more? Advertise. Wrong! The most common mistakes professional services firms make in advertising are as follows:

- being overly influenced by what their competitors are doing;
- not being results-orientated;
- being susceptible to advertising salespeople;
- stressing features rather than benefits in advertisements.

Being overly influenced by what competitors are doing: This is reflected both in terms of where firms advertise and in what they say. It is fuelled largely by the fact that advertising – alongside PR – is highly visible. It only needs a partner's mother-in-law to say 'why does such and such a firm have this big advertisement and your firm doesn't?', and the partner/director in question will be making sure his own firm has something similar in future, regardless of the question 'why should we do it?'.

Not being results-orientated: Most advertisements are passive, they are not calls to action. This means that even if there is a response, it is virtually impossible to measure which leads to eventual disillusionment with the medium. It is not the fault of the designer or the copywriter, however, the fault lies in not understanding what the advertisement was designed to do.

Being susceptible to advertising sales people: Sadly, many inexperienced professionals are susceptible to the phone call offering them a deal on advertising space. It may feel as though you're being told you have won the lottery, but you should *never* be seduced into the late availability advertising space offer. For one thing, you are buying something you patently didn't want in the first place (remember your marketing plan), for another, you will probably have to rush around getting an ad prepared, and worst of all, once you have been hooked, the advertising salespeople will be on to you every time. (Even if you place a planned ad, every other related publication will be on to you with frightening speed and intensity.) The answer lies in getting one person to field all sales calls with a remit to say 'no'.

Stressing features rather than benefits: With promotional copy the important thing to remember is the 'so what?' test. If that's the response you elicit from your reader, it means your proposition isn't exciting, doesn't give a reason why it should be taken up, and doesn't spell out the benefits to the reader if they should do so. Remember, you are too close to it. You are involved in producing promotional materials for your firm which you know and probably love dearly. The recipients of your material, however, are used to receiving volumes of such information and have no particular reason to smile kindly on yours. Keep it short, informal, friendly, interesting – and try to engender impact. That's the purpose of what you are doing after all – not to pat yourselves on the back. If you get them intrigued – intrigued enough to read on, ask for more information, or agree to see or speak to you – you are halfway to having them hooked. You won't get there with a 'so what?'.

Selling

Selling is an invaluable and essential part of the tool-kit. Professional services aren't tins of beans or any other product that the consumer can examine and evaluate before purchase. Clients need to be *sold to* – by which we mean you have to guide them through the process of identifying their needs and helping them come to the conclusion that what you have to offer is right for them.

The unpalatable fact is that, despite all your preliminary advertising and promotional material, your services won't sell themselves. At some point, someone has to explain the way you do things, persuade the potential clients to come on board, and see the job through to completion. And that's often where it goes wrong. The job isn't effectively 'sold' until it's completed and paid for, and that can be a long time after the client agreed to purchase, with room for a lot to go wrong in the middle. The gap between promise and delivery is sometimes astonishing – small wonder that the client is disaffected.

The reasons why can be numerous and varied:

- There are no common standards throughout the firm. If the job involves several different people, the client gets different levels of service depending on who they are dealing with.
- A partner sells the firm to the client – but neglects to tell those who will be doing the work what he or she has led the client to expect.
- The firm concentrates on its own way of doing things and ignores the client's own expectations.

Public relations (PR)

The Institute of Public Relations defines PR as 'the planned and sustained effort to establish and maintain goodwill and mutual understanding between an organisation and its publics'. What most people understand by PR, however, is press releases, articles and free editorial. The main difference between PR and advertising is that the former is (more or less) free but you have no control over the printed message (if it gets printed at all), whereas you pay for the latter and thus have complete control over its content.

Effective PR lies in understanding your target markets (your ultimate readership), maintaining good relationships with the appropriate media, being proactive and innovative in issuing a steady stream of material, and responding speedily to opportunities. PR can be handled in-house or through an external agency or consultant, but as with most other aspects of marketing, it cannot be handled *effectively* without commitment and cooperation from those within the firm. The process must be managed and staff must be motivated to contribute and participate.

Print

Never has so much time, effort and money been devoted by so many to the benefit of so few . . . Every firm believes it must have a brochure, but by their very nature brochures are:

- inflexible in content;
- quickly out of date;
- full of generalities;
- virtually indistinguishable from each other;
- a highly expensive means of communication.

Worse, when you ask people exactly what is the purpose of their brochure – printed and stored by the thousands, by and large – they have no idea beyond 'having something to send people'.

The production of printed material is a process that needs careful management. It can be a great opportunity to involve staff at all levels of the firm – and their views should be sought, but you should never let it become 'designed by committee'. No two people have the same taste, and no one person's taste is intrinsically superior to another's. This being the case, someone at the outset has to establish the objectives of what is to be produced, and the values it should embody. The end result should be that which best meets these objectives, rather than the design most favoured by the senior partner's wife, or Monica on the switchboard whom nobody dare annoy.

The one advantage of printed material is that it can visually reinforce your brand – indeed it can show that you are innovative, but unfortunately, it rarely does. Most printed material from professional services firms is virtually interchangeable, in that content:

- focuses on what the firm does rather than on how it does it;
- talks more about 'we' and 'us' than 'you';

- is full of meaningless phrases like 'strength in depth';
- gives very little hard information, guarantees or meaningful promises.

As a general rule, you should look at producing less general, but more focused material, of better quality and higher impact, and in the most flexible manner possible. Leave the lengthy explanations of 'what we do', and 'how we do things' to the face-to-face sales situation and show, don't tell, through use of newsletters, e-mail bulletins and seminars.

CASE STUDY   **'I want it and I want it *now*'**

Marketing plans and promotional strategies cannot be implemented overnight. Promotional material is expensive; it must be integrated across the firm and thought out in fine detail.

Some time ago, we were going through the process of assisting a firm of accountants to produce a new suite of promotional materials to support their new marketing strategy. We had consulted with the partners throughout, kept them advised of what the process involved and how long it would take, and were working with a representative project group on the implementation.

However, for one maverick partner, this obviously wasn't enough. In a burst of misplaced enthusiasm he decided that it was imperative that he undertake a mailshot to the client database to appraise them of some recent financial development and the related services the firm could offer. Without a word to anyone except his immediate subordinates, he had a full-colour brochure produced by 'a printer that his brother-in-law uses'. It cost thousands, looked totally at odds with the new image the firm was about to adopt and emphasised entirely the wrong messages.

Strong words from the managing partner were needed (at the eleventh hour!) to prevent him from sending it out. Had he done so, he would have completely undermined the firm's forthcoming approaches to its client base who, if they had already received the partner's mailer, would have cause to believe they were dealing with a firm where the left hand had no knowledge of what the right hand was doing.

A very common use of print is the external newsletter, which tends by and large to reflect many of the problems outlined above. This is a shame, because a great newsletter can be just that – great – well read, memorable, interactive and even eagerly awaited by its recipients. The way to achieve this is to use the newletter to demonstrate the firm's brand values, personality, character and innovation – through people, interesting information, and an understanding of what makes a good read. Many effective newsletters are produced and distributed very economically by e-mail – although this channel is often better used for more immediate news bulletin style communications whereas a newsletter is something people can take home or read on the train. One particular use of the web, however, is to provide an access portal to fairly dry and technical articles which can then be flagged up in the newsletter rather than providing the major part of its content.

Direct mail

Approach with caution. Direct mail and telesales can be an effective means of selling if first, you understand that they are only one stage of the selling process and are unlikely to sell anything in themselves, and second, you have people who are good at selling and comfortable with using these tools. As this is not the case in most firms, we advise you to steer well clear, or if not, to embark only upon a highly focused, staged campaign which is small enough to be followed up with telephone calls, rather than wasting money on huge mailshots which will inevitably be binned. The other point to bear in mind is that the mailshot must be offering/promoting something specific which respondents can evaluate, e.g. an invitation, or an opportunity to experience something new – the more general 'we're here and we're wonderful' mailers will get you nowhere.

Hospitality

Effective hospitality – a term which we use here to include seminars – is not to do with how much you spend or how often you do it. It's all to do with understanding why you are doing it and tailoring it to the specific preferences of the people you are entertaining and the stage they are at on the relationship ladder (see Chapter 5). The firm's events may be a networking opportunity, a cross-selling opportunity or a purely social occasion but the following tips are useful to bear in mind to ensure that your attendance at them is productive rather than dutiful:

- Think of the type of people you need to meet, as identified in your team marketing plan. E-mail your colleagues and ask them to invite any people they know of that type, or if they have a particular client you want to meet, make sure that client is invited.
- Take a look at the guest list in advance and see who you want to meet – find out who invited them and ask them in advance to introduce you.
- When you meet someone of interest/potential, ask them for permission to make further contact then take personal responsibility for following up – promptly – even if someone else is 'supposed to'.
- If attending a seminar where there may be non-clients among the delegates, identify who they are in advance and split them up between several people from the firm. Be responsible for finding your targets.
- Circulate, circulate, circulate.

- Take junior staff with you – they need to learn these skills before they move into more senior roles, and it can also be a good opportunity for clients to meet some more of the team who do their work in a social setting.
- Act appropriately. If it's a purely social event – sporting, theatre trip, etc. – don't talk business, that isn't the point of it.

The web and e-commerce

Although we are great supporters of IT, personally and professionally, the e-commerce revolution, in some ways, is highly reminiscent of the emperor's new clothes. 'No better, no worse, no change', as Samuel Beckett said, which pretty well sums up the fact that in many firms, the website has now simply taken over from the brochure as the focus for unrealistic and unfocused marketing ambitions and little else has been achieved. Where once the cry would have gone up 'we must have a new brochure', it's now 'we must have a (new) website'. However, the same questions still apply: Why? Who for? What do you actually expect it to do? How will you measure what it's doing?

Realistically, most websites are used occasionally by outsiders to find out more about the firm, and not much else. They can be used for selling, but for various reasons this is not appropriate for many aspects of professional services delivery and besides, most are far away from this in their general approach. Whether or not you already have a site there are a few questions you should ask:

- Do the majority of your private clients have access to the web, and if so, do they find it of use? (If you don't know, perhaps you need to research this with them.)
- Why would companies bother to access your site?
- If they have found it, is there any reason why they would revisit it?

Making the most of your website

Ideally, sites should be:

- short;
- punchy;
- easily navigable;
- quick to download;
- reflective of your general housestyle;
- professionally designed;
- continually updated;
- linked to other useful sites;
- interactive (with a response form at least).

What they shouldn't be is unchanging, out of date and uninteresting. Most firms have invested heavily in their websites. However, for many, the initial high level of enthusiasm for this magical new tool has since worn off and the 'must have' website is now a virtual has-been. Yet as technology and client expectations evolve, a re-examination of the relevance of your site to your current operating procedures, along with periodic updating, can ensure that it continues to generate real results.

Start by asking yourself these questions:

- What was the initial purpose of your site – have your requirements now changed?
- Are you exploiting your site to the full as a tool to improve both sales and service?
- Has the business moved on since your site was first established?
- Is your site now out of step with the image of the rest of the firm?
- Is anyone monitoring who visits your site and how often?
- Do you seek on-going feedback regarding the site?
- If you don't currently use the site as an e-commerce vehicle, is it now appropriate to consider doing so?

The extent to which your site will need revamping will depend on both the nature and evolution of your business, but the following points are worth considering:

1. Redesigning your site. A facelift will give people something new to look at. It will also show regular visitors that the content has been updated (don't ever let it get out of date). Aim for a change about once a year at the least but ensure it continues to tie in with your overall corporate image and sits happily alongside your other marketing/communications initiatives.
2. Making sure your visitors return. Change at least part of the content regularly and think about introducing a sense of ownership to visitors by allowing them to customise it in some way.
3. Checking navigability. Nobody enjoys finding their way around a badly structured website. Sites that have grown organically can often end up overly complex so check that the three-clicks rule applies to your site – can you get anywhere with three clicks?
4. Keeping abreast of the technology (but not getting bogged down in it). Don't be afraid to look at what your competitors are doing. Use the good bits, lose the bad bits, but never forget what your website is there for. And more important than anything, ask your clients what *they* want from the site – you may be surprised at their feedback.

A final word in this section concerns the production of CD-Roms and other cutting-edge new communication tools for promotional purposes.

By all means use them if you have exhausted the possibilities of more conventional channels, can afford to do so and feel that the medium will bring something unique to the marketing process. However, be very wary of being new and different simply for the sake of it – it could cost you dearly and will highlight rather than paper over any cracks in the rest of your approach.

Marketing resource implications

If you are going to get involved in marketing communications, you need someone to do it. But, first of all, you need to decide what you want that someone to do. Don't fool yourself that because you promote a secretary to marketing manager that you'll suddenly have a source of strategic marketing advice. Marketing is a profession too – you should be looking for Chartered Institute of Marketing (CIM) qualifications, on-going professional development and board-level strategic experience. In many smaller firms, marketing is part of the remit of the practice manager and again we would advise caution unless that person has a specific marketing background. Experience shows that many practice managers are excellent at recognising the problems in the firm that could be addressed by marketing, but are often unsure of how to go about it, and how to get the firm's management and staff on-side.

Employing or promoting the wrong people or empire-building can lead to nil profit returns, but equally, firms are often short-sighted in respect of the benefits that can be achieved by employing specialists. In general terms, we advocate the following:

- Employ external consultants for strategic advice.
- Employ professionals for specialist activities, e.g. PR consultants, external designers, web builders.
- Use all available internal resource in terms of secretaries and other support staff for organising hospitality, undertaking mailshots and doing all the other 'legwork' of marketing. Approached properly, they'll enjoy it, they'll get that much closer to their own client base, and it will be cost-effective.

Choosing and using suppliers

Long-term productive relationships with suppliers usually occur where commissioning firms take time to follow a few simple rules of best practice – see the guidelines below. We hope these closely mirror the way you conduct business with your own clients and should not, therefore, involve any unaccustomed amount of time or effort. In any case, time invested at the outset to ensure that both parties have a clear understanding of the project and the processes involved, usually saves time, frustration and disappointment later on.

A common tale of woe we come across when talking to smaller firms is the 'how it all went wrong with the supplier' saga. Closer investigation usually reveals that the project was almost certainly doomed to failure from the outset due to a lack of clarity between the parties as to what was involved. The following guidelines can help avoid this scenario and should be borne in mind when commissioning just about anything.

Preparing an initial written brief

At the outset you should prepare a written brief in respect of the work. This should include an outline of the firm, a summary of what the job entails, some background to the project, your objectives, details of responsibilities, timescales and budgets. If it is helpful, you can also give an indication of what you don't want. Ideally, the supplier(s) should receive this brief in advance of your first meeting so it can then be used as the focus of your initial discussions.

Initial meeting

If possible, everyone who has a key role in the commissioning process should be present at the initial meeting, ideally no more than three people from each side. Where relevant (for example, if commissioning an advertising agency or designer) suppliers will usually bring a portfolio of work – or other evidence of their expertise – to the meeting and you should allow enough time for them to show this to you. At the end of the meeting, make it clear to the potential supplier, if appropriate, when you need to receive further input from them and indicate when you will be making a decision.

Budgets and estimates

It is essential that you indicate to potential suppliers your budgetary constraints in respect of the work on offer. In their response to you following your meeting they should provide you with a clear statement of what the costs will be for each stage, and exactly what these costs do – and do not – cover. If it is not possible for them to provide exact costings at the outset, you must agree how they should notify you of on-going charges and at what intervals you will be invoiced. All initial and on-going estimates provided should be in writing. If in doubt, don't assume – ask.

Timescales

If the work you have on offer is time sensitive, this should be made clear to potential suppliers at the outset. As part of their written response to you, the supplier should provide you with specific or estimated timings for each part of the job and you must jointly agree the consequences if either side should fail to meet these deadlines. Once work has started, if it becomes clear that you are not going to be able to meet one of your deadlines, you should notify the supplier of this as soon as possible and find out from them the relevant implications.

Terms and conditions

Before agreeing to commission work from a supplier, you should obtain – and carefully read – their terms and conditions of business. If you are unclear or unhappy about any points, you should discuss these with them at this stage. It goes without saying, that having agreed to their terms and conditions, you must ensure you work within them. Your own terms and conditions of business should also be made clear to the supplier – if any deviation from them is agreed, this should be confirmed to them in writing.

Commissioning the work and finalising the brief

Once you have seen the potential suppliers, and – where necessary – received their further input and taken up references, you should be in a position to decide which supplier to choose. At this stage, you should consolidate your supplier's detailed proposals into a final working brief and seek the supplier's acceptance before they begin work. This now will be your formal working document (although it can be amended, if necessary, by mutual agreement at any stage). You should now also establish who will be your primary contact(s) at the supplier organisation and provide the names and responsibilities of any other contacts at your firm with whom they will be dealing. The brief should also outline by what means and how often you expect to communicate with the supplier in respect of progress.

Budgeting

One of the most common questions we are asked is 'how much should we be spending on marketing?' In nearly every case, it is clear that our interrogator is looking for a finite, percentage-of-turnover answer so that they can compare their firm's expenditure with their profession's norm. Unfortunately, we don't believe it's that simple, which means our response is generally a whole series of other questions for them.

For a start, much as we often wish otherwise, you are not starting with a blank canvas, so we want to know . . .

How much have you spent in the past?

The relevance of this is that it is a key indicator to what the firm probably 'feels' is the right amount, especially if the sum has remained relatively constant over a period of years. All other issues aside, whoever is in charge of the marketing budget is likely to have a fairly difficult task persuading their colleagues to depart radically from that sum (either an increase or decrease) without intense justification.

Was your past expenditure planned?

This is probably the most crucial issue in effective budgeting. What we really mean is 'is most of it spent in accordance with a marketing plan?' For many firms the answer is 'no', simply because they have no plan. For others a plan exists, but isn't followed. Even those who have a plan and follow it, often don't analyse their past year's expenditure to see how much fell in line with the plan.

What was last year's budget spent on?

Human nature being what it is, it is usually the case that if there is a budget, it will be spent. It is easy to get through money, especially with the increasing number of marketing opportunities available and the natural desire to hold your own against the competition. But without planned expenditure, it's difficult to justify truly why money was spent.

What do you include in 'marketing'?

The whole issue of budgeting is clouded by the question of what exactly should be included in the marketing budget. Some firms include client hospitality, others have a separate pot for this. Many disguise print items in the stationery budget. For others, the costs of website development and maintenance are charged to the IT budget. Frankly, it doesn't matter, as long as someone monitors and assesses the true overall picture of what is being spent on marketing and ensures that every part relates to some aspect of the firm's marketing plan.

What do you want to achieve?

This is undoubtedly the thorniest issue in marketing planning and budgeting. Common responses are 'to grow the business' or 'to increase profits', but you need to focus on specific markets and marketing activities.

Do you know who your key clients and markets are?

Establishing the distinction between potential and existing clients is crucial when considering your marketing spend. What tends to happen in
most firms is that the majority of the marketing budget is spent on the
former market, i.e. prospects, with a much smaller amount devoted to
existing clients. This is often because mass marketing tools, e.g. advertising and print, in particular, tend to be hugely expensive in comparison with other forms of communication. Yet research has shown that it
costs 5–10 times more to win business from non-clients than it does
from existing clients. So it makes sense to ensure you devote the majority of your marketing spend to winning more business from existing
clients, while finding more economic ways of maintaining and building
your profile with prospects. For example, as we saw earlier, PR is a very
cost-effective medium compared with advertising, yet few firms use it
effectively.

What can you afford?

In any organisation, resources are finite, but for some smaller firms, finding the sums needed to make a significant investment in marketing can
be difficult. In this case our recommendations would include:

- to bypass advertising – it's expensive;
- to spend on things that really matter (how important *is* that
  Christmas card?);
- to share costs – look for co-sponsors for publications and events;
- to barter services with clients.

What period does your marketing plan cover?

Having made the point that marketing spend must be linked to a well-
thought-out marketing plan, we recommend looking further ahead than
the current financial year when considering marketing expenditure.
Ideally, your marketing plan should cover a three-year timespan in outline at least. In budgeting terms, such forethought assists in predicting
peaks and troughs of expenditure. For example, in developing a new service area or team, it may be that the first year's marketing will be largely
devoted to research and one-to-one networking activities. Following that,
you may plan to go for a big launch in year two – glossy new brochure,
mailshots, advertising – all violently expensive. However, in year three,
expenditure should drop away significantly – you already have the
brochure and have invested in numerous other 'development' costs, so
regulating the costs of maintenance and steady expansion should be easier
from here.

Have you recently reviewed your current supplier list?

The conflict between client loyalty and price is one which, as a professional services provider, you undoubtedly meet head-on all the time when dealing with your own clients. But ultimately it makes economic sense to compare prices with the quality of service provided and it is an approach you should take with your own suppliers. Although you may be completely happy with the services of your printer, design agency or PR consultant, you ought to review the market every few years. It is easy for both sides to get stale and speaking to other suppliers may spark off ideas about fresh ways of doing things. Even if everything eventually continues as before, a review can be a good opportunity to consider and justify what you are doing and how much you are investing where.

How do you measure the return on your investment?

Although it is often considered 'dead' money, your marketing budget represents an investment in growing your business, and, as such, the return on that investment must be measured and reviewed. However, in professional services firms this is undoubtedly easier said than done. Yes, you can measure what response you get from a mailshot or a direct response advertisement, but the issues involved with those levels of response are considerably more complex than if you were selling products off the page. Even so, it is surprising how many firms still don't ask new clients 'where did you hear about us?' or research with clients whether or not their newsletter is effective in persuading them to use a wider range of services. Although there's no standard formula for measuring marketing results, one standard question should always be asked regarding marketing expenditure: 'How can we gauge the success of this?'.

Who controls the purse strings?

Our work has shown, time after time, that those with the most successful marketing results are those where one person is ultimately responsible for the marketing budget. In larger firms, the overall sum may be broken down into smaller budgets under the control of individual team leaders, but, if so, the marketing plans to which those budgets relate must also be elements of a much larger, overall marketing plan to ensure consistency and cohesion. Plans and budgets should never be so rigid that they prevent responding to an unforeseeable opportunity and a reasonable contingency sum should be set aside for this purpose. The person with responsibility for the marketing budget as a whole should have the sole right to veto such expenditure – and what a responsibility it is! As the time-honoured Micawber principle states: 'Annual income twenty pounds, annual expenditure nineteen

nineteen six, result happiness. . . . Annual expenditure twenty pounds nought and six, result misery'. Keep within budget (but not too under-spent) and you will be regarded as an excellent manager, but exceed it by more than a small percentage and you risk bringing every latent issue and argument about the value of marketing crashing around your ears.

Market research

Although we've left it to the end of this chapter, market research in fact links to an area of activity highlighted at the start – segmenting your market. It is one of the first processes you need to undertake in establishing the marketing and promotional mix for each of your targeted market segments. Before you embark upon any marketing communications programme, you almost certainly need to undertake some market research in respect of the entire market segment (not just your clients) to establish the following:

- What defines market segments that you are currently supplying?
- What are the needs of those market segments?
- How well does your service offering meet those current needs and how well will it do so in future?
- Who else is currently supplying services to that market?
- How does your service offering compare with that of your competitors (in respect of all areas of the marketing mix)?
- What are the current major influencing factors in that market?
- What are the future issues which are predicted to be important in that market?

Although most firms can find out some of this information for themselves, it can be difficult to do so thoroughly and objectively if detailed information is required and it is worthwhile considering retaining specialist advisers to assist. However, meaningful research is dependent on meaningful objectives (what do you want to know, about whom, and why do you want to know it?) and it is essential that these are agreed internally before the advisers are briefed. And, of course, most important of all, you must *do* something with the information once you have received it, or the whole exercise will have been meaningless.

POINTS TO REMEMBER

➤ Managing the marketing mix is your means of manipulating the key variables of your service offering – price, place, people, processes and promotion – in order to best meet the identified needs of your existing and target market segments.

➤ Key market segments should be profitable (actually or potentially) and defined according to their own inherent criteria of differentiation, not simply lumped together for the convenience of the firm.

➤ The marketing mix must be managed across market segments in order to ensure integration and consistency across the firm as a whole.

➤ In order to select appropriate communication tools you need to distinguish between the nature and purpose of broad-based brand-building communications (directed at prospective clients and the market place in general) and client communications which must be much more focused and tailored.

➤ The communication medium to be used will also depend on the stage in the selling cycle you have reached with a particular prospect or client.

➤ Motivation is the bridge between the marketing planning process and making it happen.

➤ Effective communication, clear objectives, and mutually agreed timescales and budgets are essential for success when commissioning external suppliers.

3

Brand building

- What is a brand?
- Why a brand is essential
- Developing your brand
- Managing your brand
- Promoting your brand
- Overcoming barriers to building a strong brand

Think about your firm – do you recognise any of these problems?

	YES	NO
We're completely stumped by the idea of how to differentiate our firm from any of six other similar firms in the town.		
We tried to redesign our logo but none of the partners could agree, so we gave up.		
Which do we concentrate on first – trying to improve 'the way we do things around here', or building a brand – in which case don't we have to work with the status quo?		
Everyone was keen on a new corporate identity until they found out what it would cost – now the idea's dead in the water.		
We know we need to develop at least one unique selling point (USP) – but there's nothing at all we can think of that's unique to us.		
My partners dismiss the idea of developing a brand – they're insulted that we should be contemplating selling ourselves like cornflakes.		

We have partners with wildly differing personalities, simply because our client base has different needs. How do we bring them all under one umbrella as a 'brand'?		
We have branded mousemats, pens, umbrellas and note pads. What more is there?		
I was astonished when one of our clients said to us 'You're known for doing things like that.' It was a positive comment, but I don't think internally we'd ever recognised the fact.		

Assuming you didn't answer 'no' to all the above, then you should read on.

What is a brand?

If you want to get ahead, get a brand. This is not just a suggestion – establishing your brand and being absolutely clear about the values it represents is essential before you can begin to embark upon a meaningful programme of marketing activity. To some this is rather a revolutionary idea – indeed many managers of small to medium-sized firms seem genuinely bemused by the idea that they might turn their rather run-of-the mill practice into a brand. They can understand the significance of brands to large consumer companies like Kelloggs, Virgin, Coca-Cola, Persil, and so on, but are completely unable to understand the benefits that branding may have for their firm, or how to relate the concept to the way their firm operates.

The problem generally lies in their understanding of what a brand is. In the same way that many firms still equate marketing to mere marketing communications activities, most people still think of brands as the tangible representation of the brand: the logo, slogan, packaging and advertising. Therefore, in following that train of thought, if you have no advertising, and no packaging it follows that you cannot have, or hope to have a brand.

Understanding why and how service providers – regardless of their size – cannot only *have* effective brands, but *must* have them if they are to succeed, is reliant on understanding first of all what a brand is, and also, the difference between a services brand and a product brand.

A brand, to quote the Chartered Institute of Marketing is: 'a name, term, symbol, design or some combination, which identifies the "product" of a particular seller or group of sellers and differentiates them from those of competitors'. However, this definition merely underlines one of the biggest differences between product and service brands, namely that service brands are not heavily reliant on the physical properties of the brand. So, possibly rather more helpful for service providers is Ambler and Styles's definition of a brand as 'the promise of a bundle of attributes that someone buys . . . the attributes may be real or illusory, rational or emotional, tangible or invisible'.

The key word in the Ambler and Styles definition above is *promise*. The crucial element in an effective brand is the extent to which that promise is consistently fulfilled by the organisation making the promise – in other words, the extent to which reality lives up to the brand. Because the entire brand therefore stands or falls on that promise and because the delivery cannot be separated from the provider(s) of the service (unlike products), the whole validity of a professional services firm lies in the extent to which the firm's staff – at every level and in every position – visibly and consistently demonstrate the promised brand values. If they do not, the brand will never succeed, regardless of how vigorously it is promoted to the client base.

The following factors explain this further:

- Brands are:
  - a set of emotional experiences/responses;
  - a shorthand way of embodying many different values and strengths;
  - positively recognised by those inside and outside the firm;
  - something which can be spread over varying services or products;
  - clearly perceived by the market place;
  - indicative of differentiation from similar service/product suppliers.

- Brands are not:
  - applicable solely to mass market products or services;
  - independent of the values they represent;
  - dependent on huge advertising campaigns to support them;
  - constantly changing (though they can and should evolve over time);
  - something which only a few people within the firm can choose to support.

In professional services firms, a firm's brand results from its intervention in respect of three factors:

1. Performance delivery (reality versus promised performance).
2. Position (versus competitor firms).
3. Physical image.

When you consider the first two of these – performance and position – you may at first be tempted to think that a 'brand' is only fancy marketing/management speak for 'reputation'. Far from it – in fact, the whole point of a brand lies in the distinction between the two – a reputation, good or bad is what is thrust upon you by others, regardless of what you have or have not done to earn (or deserve) it. A brand on the other hand is a living, managed, created embodiment of what your firm is, and what you want it to be. Although it cannot operate independently of consumer response and reaction, that response is a mechanism for further fuelling the growth of the brand, rather than a barrier to its progress. Let's look in greater detail at why this is.

Performance

Services, by their very nature, are intangible – they can't be separated from the service provider, they can't be stored, and their quality is dependent on the individual or group of individuals providing the service. As a result, unlike product-related brands, professional services brands are concerned largely with intangible elements and offerings.

We have always been baffled by people who say, 'we don't need to market, our marketing is doing a good job'.

- Who evaluates whether or not you've done a good job?
- Who is keeping an eye on what 'a good job' will be by tomorrow's standards?
- Does a full order book equate with maximum profitability?
- Where is tomorrow's work guaranteed to come from?
- How does what you do differ from what your competitors are doing?
- Are you still going to be able to do a good job if some of your staff leave (roughly equivalent to having your machinery break down)?

What these people are actually doing is concentrating on technical capability (the machinery) at the expense of service delivery (the people). The distinction is crucial in understanding the importance of the brand and what it represents. Technical capability (the ability to do the work and get it right) and to do the work at an acceptable price – represents value to the client. However, the service standards of the people doing the work and the culture in which you operate make up your company's values. And it is the combination of value plus values which make up your brand. Concentrate on value in the absence of values and you haven't got a brand, you've got a factory.

Every firm is made up of different people, with different skill sets and personalities, and with individual and shared track records. They all also have a unique set of contacts and these factors together are what underpin your performance and make your brand unique.

Position (vs competitor firms)

Your 'position' is how your firm is perceived externally by the market in which you operate in terms of:

- personality;
- client base;
- key skills.

Some of the most successful firms operating today are not the big, high-earning multinationals, which, although they are the leaders in many areas, are as slow-moving and cumbersome as any huge commercial organisation. In some ways it may be easier for them to reinforce their brand image because of the amount of money they can devote to promoting it. However, the real stars, the rainmakers and the risk-takers are often those where one or more of the partners have broken away from larger firms to set up on their own. Like other small firms, they are desperate to succeed, and have a keen eye for what not to do. In many cases they succeed because their approach is more like an entrepreneurial business than a professional firm. For them, one element of their success is that their values are easier to define because they know what it was that they didn't like in their previous employment, which is then reflected in the way they now operate and what they seek to achieve through their new business.

Even among professional firms which inherently tend to pride themselves on their 'gentlemanly' approach, there are those who take a different stance and do very handsomely from it. For example, in response to a question about which law firm he used and why, a business acquaintance commented: 'I use XX because they're complete b******s and that's why I chose them. If I ever have to go to court I want them on my side, not against me'.

Physical image

This is the most visible and most recognisable aspect of your brand but unlike product brands, is arguably the least important. However, physical image – the use of a logo, design approach and housestyle – is most important when you extend your brand as it helps link the new service into existing brand values. Brand extension has to do with how you stretch your brand into unfamiliar territory (and it is worth considering Virgin as an example of a brand which has done this with wildly varying results). The question of whether you should risk damaging your existing brand by doing so, or leave it to other advisers is one for which there is no 'right' answer. The only true caveat is that – as many have found to their cost – it doesn't pay to dabble.

Why a brand is essential

'We act as though comfort and luxury were the chief requirements of life, when all that we need to make us happy is something to be enthusiastic about.'

Charles Kingsley

A brand consolidates all the positive values of a firm and projects them to the outside world. As professional firms are among the most difficult to market because of the difficulty in differentiating one from another, brands are crucial for achieving and reinforcing:

- differentiation;
- consistency;
- internal and external values.

Differentiation

When we talk to firms about their values and the way they differentiate themselves they frequently say things like:

- 'We do a good job.'
- 'We're more profitable than our competitors – that's all that's important.'
- 'Our clients know the way we work and are happy with it.'
- 'The competition poses no threat to us.'

But when we talk to others in the firm they don't necessarily share this view or reflect it in their conduct or believe that it is in any way important.

So it is obvious that these firms' views are not based on true values. What's more, those views are all to do with where the firm is now, not what it is that is driving it forward. Referring back to our section on strategy in Chapter 1, how a firm differentiates itself depends on:

- the key markets in which it operates;
- the share it has of the market in which it operates;
- the type of services it provides in terms of their value to these client groups;
- the flexibility it can adopt in service provision in order to meet key client needs.

However, establishing and retaining true differentiation in any area – let alone professional services – is extremely difficult. Anything that is truly ground-breaking or revolutionary will soon be copied and you are back to square one. Better then to concentrate on other factors.

Perhaps the most important is signing up to the belief that by definition – because of *your* personnel, *your* location, *your* clients – you are different. The important thing is to look at the strengths inherent in that situation which you can enhance and develop. Marketing theory has it that in any branded situation there is a market leader, a contender, and the rest are just me-too providers. However, there is nothing wrong with that if you strive to be *better* in terms of service delivery than the competition.

Another important point is that differentiation is all about how your clients perceive you, not how you view yourselves. If they don't view you as being different, then frankly, you aren't. Listening to what they want or asking them what they feel is currently lacking in your service delivery or that of their other professional advisers, can provide a great steer in terms of developing your 'differences'.

Consistency

One of the most important management implications of building a strong brand is that it can act as a frame of reference against which the firm can make judgements, decide strategies and set objectives, and do so in respect of strategic and operational decisions at all levels.

> 'Everything we say and everything we do reflects everything we believe.'

> 'To provide unrivalled value to our customers in the quality of the goods we sell, in the competitiveness of our prices and in the choice we offer.'

The former quote is from one of our clients, a small concern who are passionate about what they do and wildly successful as a result. The second is part of Sainsbury's mission statement. What they have in common is an approach which promises consistency. Cynical professionals make tutting noises at this point and accuse us of trying to turn them into automatons without personalities. Not true. Quality of personal service is all, but the most effective personal service is that in which the personality of the individual delivering it is supported by the soul and personality of the organisation they work for.

Why? Because:

- it enhances their own role and provides a backdrop of familiarity for the client;
- it ensures that the client would be willing, should it be required, to transfer their trust to someone else in the organisation;
- it prevents the client being subjected to unwelcome surprises or unexpected, out of character developments;
- in short, it provides reassurance.

One of the guaranteed ways of boosting your brand is to make those brand values a key part of the selection process when employing anyone new, so that you will, over time, end up with staff who are all happy with 'living the brand'. This has to be handled very carefully, however, as there is a natural human tendency to select 'people like us' at interview, and unless you single out very clearly the positive brand values you are seeking, you are more likely to end up reinforcing the negative aspects of your culture. For example, you could end up with a whole firm comprising nice, but introverted individuals who all, more or less, dislike socialising and networking.

Internal and external values

As outlined in Chapter 1, your values relate to your vision and plans for the firm. They are a spectrum reflecting what you and your existing client base regard as important in respect of:

- physical service delivery;
- service range and specialisation;
- balance of power / control;
- team-working and integration;
- sustainability;
- innovation;
- price and value;
- market segments you choose to service.

There are no rights and wrongs in the process – the only certainty is that you can't base a brand around something you are not. It's true that some measure of cultural change can be brought about over time, but it's terribly hard to achieve – and if you simply base the visualisation of your brand round what you wish you were rather than what you *really* are, you're doomed to fail.

CASE STUDY   **Perception and reality**

A man in a hot air balloon realised he was lost, reduced altitude and spotted a man below.

He descended a bit more and shouted: 'Excuse me, can you help? I promised a friend I would meet him here an hour ago but I don't know where I am.'

The man below replied: 'You are in a hot air balloon hovering approximately 30 feet above the ground. You are between 40 and 41 degrees north latitude and between 59 and 60 degrees west longitude.'

'You must be a rent review surveyor' said the balloonist. 'I am' replied the man, 'how on earth did you know that?'

'Well,' said the balloonist,' everything you told me is technically correct but I have no idea what to make of your information and the fact is I'm still lost. Frankly, you've not been much help so far.'

The rent review surveyor promptly replied: 'You must be a selling agent.'

'I am' answered the balloonist, 'but how did you guess?'

'Well,' said the man, 'you don't know where you are or where you're going, you have risen to where you are due to a large quantity of hot air, you made a promise which you have no idea how to keep and, as always, you expect me to solve your problem for you. The fact is, you are in exactly the same position you were in before we met, only now it's somehow my fault!'

Developing your brand

Most people, being social animals, like to belong to a group of like-minded people and feel proud when what they do – personally or as part of that group – receives public praise and recognition. This is the motivation behind brand building. There are many commercial examples of incredibly successful brands which have been built and have flourished on the pride they have managed to instil in their employees in working for and representing that organisation. In the professions the situation is really little different. Employment at highly successful big city firms is sought not just because of the big salaries on offer but equally because of the kudos of working for them. So, a strong brand can provide individual motivation, inspiring employees not only to be content with the fact that they work for a successful firm but also to go on to be a high performer within a winning organisation.

Within the sector of smaller firms it is just as possible to do the same. Numerous examples exist, especially among newly founded breakaway niche concerns of those who had a vision, a passion, and went on to realise it by setting up their own firm. Their enthusiasm and that of their employees is palpable; anyone listening to them describing themselves and their business can hardly fail to be impressed and attracted to them even if their overall profile doesn't fit in with exactly what is wanted.

When thinking at the initial stages about what sort of brand you want to develop, you need to make a definite decision to think outside the box – a process which can often be helped by the presence of an outsider asking what you may think are some bizarre questions. For example:

• If we were an animal what sort would we be?
• What colour best embodies our values and why?
• Which era in history most accurately reflects our style?
• What geometrical shape do we feel happiest with?

- Are we hard or soft or somewhere in between?
- If we were a fragrance, what would it be?

Obviously, this list can go on and on and is probably best reserved for a partners' weekend rather than the regular hour-long monthly partners' meeting. But we hope you can see where it is getting you. By getting agreement on what you represent and what, consensually, you feel comfortable with and taking it to the next stage – how this measures up to what you *want* to represent – you are well on the way to establishing your brand values.

A key advantage of the process in management and motivational terms is that it's also irrefutable later on when you start to hit difficulties with interpretation. For example, when one of the most difficult partners decides that although he quite likes the logo it should actually be in red, you have the perfect ammunition in being able to remind him of the discussion you had which revolved around why the firm fundamentally aspired to being blue (cool, calm, airy, modern, etc.) It goes without saying that you need a good transcript of these conversations for later use – not least because at some stage or other you will find yourselves looking at each other in puzzlement, 'why did we decide we were like kangaroos – can anyone remember?'

Even if you believe you have a high degree of self-awareness and your views are firmly rooted in reality, don't leave it at that. Undertake client research and also ask others in your market place, formally or informally, what they think of your firm. You may be surprised at the answers.

Innovation vs consistency

One of the key advantages of a brand is that it represents shared values and as such challenges a common and serious problem within professional service firms – that of ownership of clients. Time and again we hear complaints about partners treating clients as 'theirs', refusing to share information about them, refusing their partners access to the client directly or 'forgetting' to cross-sell their services, and failing to fall in line with firm-wide standards because 'my clients like things done differently'.

The heart of the problem is insecurity and this must be tackled on a group and individual level before progress can be made on introducing the concept, and then the practice of 'company clients' – whose relationship is primarily with the firm and not with the individual partner(s) with whom they usually deal. Not to take this approach is commercial suicide – the partner who leaves taking 'his' (or 'her') clients with them leaving their erstwhile partners fuming is commonplace. Yes, you can put in place restrictive covenants – they are fine in theory but rarely effective in practice. You can bad-mouth partners for doing it, but it is the firm's fault for letting it happen.

Managing your brand

Because delivery of your services is inseparable from your brand promise, your brand runs through everything you do and it is essential that it is properly managed, developed and implemented. There are three main areas where effective management can make a significant difference to the on-going success and development of your brand.

1. Managing and monitoring client expectations.
2. Implementing clear systems and policies.
3. Enforcing effective quality standards.

Managing and monitoring client expectations

How well your brand fulfils its promise is entirely dependent on how your service meets client expectations. Therefore, it is important to monitor how clients perceive the firm, what they think about the features and benefits of the service they receive and what else they would like to see. You need to do this consistently in order to be able to compare and aggregate results across the firm in respect of different clients. Over time, your clients will, in themselves, become part of your brand in as much as their values will align with your own. Having reached this situation, it is almost certain that you will be in a position where you can enter into mutually beneficial 'partnership' arrangements with key clients both for internal purposes and external promotion.

Implementing clear systems and policies

As mentioned above, consistency is key – the brand promise must be delivered by everyone in the firm to every client. It goes without saying, therefore, that shared systems and policies are essential. The most important thing about establishing a housestyle in conjunction with your brand is that it must be used consistently. You need a housestyle book. Computers can be set up to provide templates for letters and documents. Protocols can be established for just about every activity. However, the key lies in monitoring and managing the process, with penalties for non-compliance. Without this, rules will be ignored and – as so often happens – the result will be that your 'branded' offering will be a complete mess.

Even in small ways, your brand is too valuable to be tampered with. So absolute rules must be put in place to guard against misuse. It is often the little things that count, as Table 3.1 illustrates.

Another important thing to remember about brands is not to tinker with them. By all means review and update them every few years to keep them looking contemporary and fresh, but don't make the common mistake of throwing out the baby with the bathwater and developing

Table 3.1 House style rules

Do	Don't
Use your full name – as you are known – on business cards and correspondence, e.g. John Smith	Put PJR Smith – it's intimidating and unhelpful
Sign your name on every outgoing letter	Sign just the name of the firm or sign illegibly with no printed name
List your direct dial number	Leave it to the client to track you down through the switchboard
Use your client's name	'Sir' and 'Madam' are cold and archaic when you are clearly aware of someone's name
Write letters that reflect some of the warmth of the relationship you should have with the recipient	Use an overly formal 'standard' tone – it makes the recipient feel faceless and insignificant

something completely radical every few years. Remember, it takes years to build up brand recognition and even if your promotional campaign hasn't had the greatest impact in the market place it will still do more for you in terms of recognition and reinforcement than a brilliant, but radically new, interpretation.

Enforcing effective quality standards

Quality is completely down to the perception of the person receiving the service so, having researched your clients' views on quality, you must devise some shared minimum standards of client care for the firm. Don't just stick to the obvious things, for example, time taken to respond to letters – try to develop some quality standards which are uniquely yours. It is one area where innovation could set you apart.

Promoting your brand

The sound of one hand clapping. That sums up the strength of your brand if no one knows about it. Obviously clients will *experience* the benefits – simply because that's the way you do things – but to use your brand to develop your business, you have to do more. Because differentiation between professional services firms is so difficult, apparent differentiation often lies in the physical representation you adopt for your brand, i.e. your logo, the colours and typeface you use, your style of brochure, letterhead, newsletters, and so on. And of course, your slogan – of which countless hundreds of sensational examples exist in the commercial market place.

Visual or words – which comes first – is very much a chicken and egg situation, although it is a fact that you will have to come up with words in order to draw up a comprehensive brief for the designer and copywriter. (But please don't be tempted to write your own copy unless you have someone who is very, very good at it. There is a common misconception that says because we can all write, we can all write persuasive, readable promotional copy. It isn't true. We can all draw, but fortunately for designers it's easier to spot the difference between those who are any good at it and the rest.)

Extend the boundaries of your material: hold a design competition at a local school. Employ the talents of a local artist or photographer. Hold an exhibition of their work at the same time as you launch your brochure. Find an award to enter your brochure for and set out to win. Offer to give money to charity for every response form returned requesting a brochure. Get a foreword written by someone eminent, interesting and known to your market.

Building a brand involves regular communication in order to drive home and reinforce to your clients and prospective clients, your appearance, your approach and what you stand for. Don't expect just to send them a brochure (no matter how good it is) and have them remember you; you need to keep regularly reinforcing the message.

Overcoming barriers to building a strong brand

Professional services firms have difficulties with brand building. The good news, if you can think of it as such, is that they originate from the same issues which create problems in other areas of the firm, for example:

- lack of commercial awareness and business skills;
- adoption of a superior approach when dealing with client companies;
- poor communication, external and internal;
- weak relationships with clients;
- inadequate objective setting;
- lack of cohesion, common goals and commitment throughout the firm.

Solutions therefore lie in :

- training;
- recruiting staff with business development skills;
- establishing objective setting and appraisal systems;
- engendering and enforcing a common set of values throughout the firm;
- improving external and internal communication;

- restructuring if necessary;
- establishing a client relationship management programme;
- introducing a cohesive housestyle and publicity campaign.

Figure 3.1 provides an illustration.

A brand transforms individual partners'
different ways of operating . . .

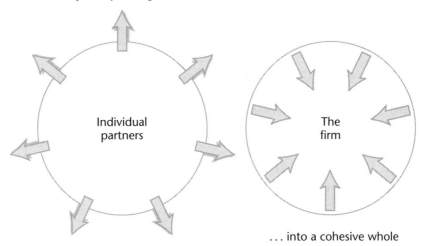

... into a cohesive whole

Figure 3.1   Transforming an uncoordinated approach into a brand

Getting others on board

Professionals are, by and large, mavericks (as many a weary practice manager would no doubt testify) but there's plenty of documented evidence to show they can be brought into line if there's sufficient motivational impetus. Personal objectives should be set in respect of adhering to the values and processes which underpin the brand if this is a problem for some individuals. Training and coaching should also be utilised, especially for those who are having difficulty understanding why a cohesive approach is important.

Another problem with enforcing your brand is that, for a number of reasons, there are those internally who may feel and be less involved with it than others. These are the people who may become disaffected and start to erode the value of the brand. It is important that they are actively involved, the importance of their support role clearly explained to them and ways found of identifying and rewarding the value they provide to clients. Should it not be possible to do so, you might need to consider biting the bullet and dispensing with them and/or their service area entirely.

Promoting and reinforcing your brand is by no means simply an external exercise. You need to make every effort to reinforce the brand with your own staff. Hold training courses to explain the notion of a brand; hold them again to introduce and implement changes. Incorporate physical evidence of your brand into the working environment – displays, posters, computer screensavers are just a starting point. Also, invest in small items that make people feel like they belong – mousemats, pencils, name badges on desks, logos on internal documents as well as external.

Ask for and disseminate feedback from staff at all levels on reaction to the brand image, especially if it is new. What comments have they heard/received from clients or other professionals, do they have suggestions for any new ways of using it, what feedback do they know of from competitor firms?

Live your brand, breathe it, be it. Initial recruitment advertisements, interviews and job specifications at all levels should make clear your brand values and they should be incorporated into your requirements. Induction should also deal with brand issues and values, while your staff manual should make clear reference to housestyle and application.

POINTS TO REMEMBER

➤ Unlike your reputation, which is decided by others, your brand is the living, managed embodiment of what your firm is and what you want it to be.

➤ Your brand is the promise of a bundle of attributes that someone buys – whether real or illusory, rational or emotional, tangible or invisible.

➤ How well your brand lives up to its promise is something which only the external market place (clients and others) can decide.

➤ Brands are crucial for reinforcing differentiation, consistency, internal values and the way they are applied externally.

➤ A strong brand can be an enormous source of motivation for existing staff and a powerful magnet to prospective employees.

➤ A key function of a brand is to act as a frame of reference for management against which to make judgements, decide strategies, set objectives.

➤ Your brand must be promoted internally as vigorously and consistently as it is to the outside world.

4

Existing clients: your greatest opportunity

KEY ISSUES

- Why client care is important
- Understanding client care
- Client care programmes
- Assessing client value
- Client relationship management
- Client research and feedback
- Dealing with dissatisfaction

Think about your firm – do you recognise any of these problems?

	YES	NO
Morale within the firm is low. We work longer and longer hours dealing with more and more complex matters, yet all the clients seem to do is complain.		
We know our most important clients are actively being courted by other firms. We hope they stay loyal to us, but how can we be sure?		
We only deal with one division of a company, we'd love to get more work from the company as a whole but how do we go about it?		
One of our strongest supporters at our biggest client company is due to retire soon. How do we protect our on-going relationship with them?		
One of our partners left recently. Despite all the restrictions we placed on him, he effectively took some of our best clients, because he was the only person in the firm who they had a relationship with.		

We found that one of our clients had gone to a competitor for a particular service. When we asked him why, he said he hadn't known it was something we could do.		
How can we implement client care standards when all our clients seem to have such different ideas of what they want?		
We tell staff that 'the client is king' – and then they get subjected to a load of abuse from some ill-mannered idiot with no understanding of what's involved in doing their work. Surely that can't be right?		
Clients ask for an estimate of fees up front. They get upset when I tell them it's impossible to say at the outset.		

Assuming you didn't answer 'no' to all the above, then you should read on.

Why client care is important

'Many solicitors fail to appreciate that providing a service that clients perceive as excellent is the most cost-effective means of marketing for a firm and the only certain way to retain client loyalty'.

Maureen Miller, Practice Excellence Manager, the Law Society

'Client care' is one of the most overused and under-utilised phrases in the professionals' phrase book. As a concept, it's nothing new and many professional firms proudly tell us that 'our business is founded on excellent client care'. But if you look deeper, this is far from the case – there are no formal procedures at the outset to inform new clients of exactly what levels of 'care' they can expect, no on-going, publicised, standardised procedures and no way of regularly and formally assessing client views on the levels of 'care' they receive.

People talk about it, plan and train for it – but often their actual levels of 'care' change very little. This is more damaging than never having addressed the problem at all as clients are then more aware than ever of the gap between what the firm says it does, and reality. There are several reasons for this, including:

- a misunderstanding of what client care really is – especially the fact that client care by its very nature is defined by the client not the provider;
- the fact that change is difficult. Poor client care has nothing to do with the fact that you are not nice, well-meaning people. It is simply

indicative of the fact that the goalposts have changed and client expectations are higher than ever, which means that you also have to change;

- a failure to appreciate the real benefits that true client care can bring.

Before you can improve client care you need to be aware of what it actually is. Client care, by definition, is concerned with providing services to existing clients – and as such it can be one of the easiest or one of the most difficult areas of business development for professional firms to tackle. As it deals with existing relationships, the skills required for making new relationships and the stumbling blocks associated with the whole process shouldn't be an issue. Also, it is an area where, compared with new business development, risk is low, comfort zones are higher, and the amount the firm has to invest is likely to be less. Figure 4.1 illustrates the elements that make up client care.

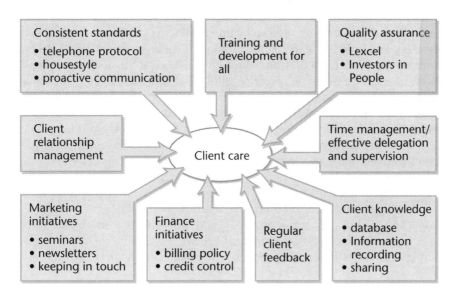

Figure 4.1   The elements of client care

Client care is also deeply interwoven with your whole service offering (see Chapter 3 on service brands). If you sell a 'product' you must expect the type of client response that goes with it – no loyalty, looking for cheapest price, no awareness or interest in added value provided – elements which professionals increasingly complain about in respect of their clients. Yet in order to have your clients demonstrate behaviour which is characteristic of a 'service' relationship – you have to focus on providing a real service, not just the core technical product. See Table 4.1 for the differences between providing a service and selling a product.

Table 4.1 Client care – the difference between providing a service and selling a product

Service:	Product:
Personal relationship	Non-personal relationship
Quality of relationship depends on provider	Quality of product not dependent on provider
Transaction based on emotion and trust	Transaction focuses on physical features
Price usually a secondary factor	Price is key factor
On-going – loyalty	One-off – comparative

Whether you like it or not, the fact is that the quality of the work that you do for a client is not what they appreciate. Research has shown that some 70–80 per cent of perceived value for clients is derived from service delivery and only 20–30 per cent from technical know-how. Yet 70–80 per cent of the costs of operating a firm generally relate to technical know-how, not service delivery. Likewise, allocation of time: rarely is sufficient time allowed for service providers adequately to deliver more than the basic technical nuts and bolts. The implication of this is that instead of providing a service, you end up selling what is, in effect, a product.

What we like about Maureen Miller's comment above is that it succinctly covers three of the key points in the whole process:

1. It implies the firm shifting its viewpoint from what it perceives to be reality, to understanding and responding to its *clients'* perceptions.
2. It shows that quality client care is extremely effective when compared with other business development tools.
3. It underlines that this approach will help a firm retain client loyalty.

The first of these points emphasises the need for the process to be managed, in as much as systems must be put in place for assessing, analysing and monitoring client wants, needs and perceptions and measuring how these are currently being met by the firm. Following on from this, it involves identifying gaps, areas of deficiency, and areas of pre-existing excellence in order to ensure the closest possible on-going fit.

Points (2) and (3) are just two of the key motivators for the process, but motivators which must be writ large and revisited time and again. Providing excellent client care to existing clients also calls into play the selling process to persuade them to trust you with more of their business. None of it is easy, so the answer to the question 'why do we have to do this?' must be constantly front of mind.

Tackling business development through developing the firm's relationships with existing clients can involve a whole spectrum of activities from an overall client care programme for the whole firm addressing service feature issues (e.g. how quickly letters and phone calls are answered) to a key client management programme which concentrates both on gaining maximum benefit from those clients and protecting the relationship against marauding competitors. In this chapter we examine first the implications to the firm of each position on the spectrum, and secondly the importance of management and motivation in moving the firm further towards truly excellent client care.

Understanding client care

What is client care? Quite simply it is:

- shifting your emphasis to the client rather than keeping it on the work you are doing for them;
- understanding client needs and managing client expectations;
- obtaining feedback from clients in respect of their perceptions of the service provided;
- conducting personal, rather than purely technically focused relationships.

'This is a people business and clients are customers. They choose professional lawyers because they want expertise. But they also want efficiency, courtesy, prompt service, to be kept informed of progress and to be charged reasonably, in a way that is no different to the service that they expect from their supermarket or the bank, or an airline. They notice whether their calls are being returned or how long it takes to reply to a letter.

Michael Napier, President, the Law Society

To really understand the importance of client care you have to look right at the heart of human nature.

Research across cultures and societies has identified one characteristic that everyone has in common: we all strive to experience things that make us feel good, and we all try to avoid things that make us feel bad. This behaviour manifests itself in situations where individuals find themselves in the position of being a client (Table 4.2).

From this you can see that client care is largely to do with managing each individual client's expectations – finding out about their needs, wants and preconceptions – and not prejudging the situation.

A common approach to dealing with a client when you are busy is to ask a few leading questions, identify what you think is the problem and offer a common solution. In contrast, the client-centred approach is to

Table 4.2 Clients' emotional drivers

Seeking – good feelings	Avoiding – bad feelings
Security / knowing what's going to happen	Insecurity / wondering what's going to happen
Feeling valued and respected	Feeling unimportant and patronised
Being involved	Being left out
Feeling in control	Feeling manipulated
Having expectations met	Expectations being by-passed
Friendship	Coldness
Trust	Suspicion / wariness
Receiving value for money	Feeling exploited and dissatisfied

help the client identify their problem through asking open questions which enable them to talk freely and from their own perspective. You are then able as part of this process to find out what *they* think and feel would be a desirable outcome – and manage their expectations in the light of what is realistic and possible.

In 2001, the Legal Services Ombudsman, Ann Abraham, said that despite some improvements 'the gap between the attitudes and behaviour of lawyers and the public's legitimate expectations of them is as wide as ever'. The key phrase in this is 'legitimate expectations' – whatever firms think they are or aren't doing, they aren't, by and large, meeting those expectations. Those who can make the cultural leap to a stage where they can and do will be streets ahead of the rest.

Changing the culture of the firm in respect of the way it handles its clients involves breaking down the barriers that say 'we already provide excellent client service'. Perhaps, but on whose terms? The number of complaints being made about professional services firms remains at an unacceptably high level, and despite the fond hope that these are generated by a group of professional complainers about a very few firms, there is no evidence to support this. More worryingly, research shows that most dissatisfied clients don't complain, they either just walk, or put up with things because they believe that no one else would be any better. In the latter case, they will have withdrawn their trust and certainly will not be active advocates for the firm – they are clients who are with you under sufferance only.

Yet every firm we talk to, and nearly every piece of promotional literature we read proclaims 'we're proud of our excellent client care'. Perhaps, some firms are simply not practising what they preach, or perhaps their idea of excellent client care is far removed from what their clients expect – and we're convinced that the problem lies more in the latter than the former.

But why should you change? After all, if so many firms are being complained about, poor client service will hardly make you stand out from the crowd. Try looking at the positive outcome: Simon Woodroffe, millionaire developer of restaurant chain *Yo! Sushi*, was recently quoted as saying: 'Give clients more than they could ever have dreamed of, and certainly more than they are paying for. Out of three clients, one will take advantage of you – in time you can get rid of them. One will treat it as normal. One will be so appreciative that they will never let you go and you can charge them what you like.'

One important thing to take on board here is not to get the values of the firm confused with its service standards. We have had the pleasure of dealing with some extremely 'nice' firms, staffed by decent, genuine, likeable people – and despite this, we've had to conclude that their client care was appalling. It wasn't because they were uncaring, malevolent, disdainful, or any of those other things. It was just that they weren't properly managed and motivated to focus on recognising and meeting the needs of their clients – as people – rather than devoting all their energies to the technical work in hand.

Aspects of client care

There are three main aspects to client care:

- trust;
- understanding;
- value.

Trust is the key factor in successful client relationships and the main area of concern for clients when considering taking on new advisers. Not just trust that you will carry out the technical work, but the trust that you will provide an overall solution and not create more difficulty. Ways of instilling trust involve regular communication, use of familiar language instead of technical terms, a friendly informal attitude and a proactive approach.

There is a particular area of trust which is fundamental to professional services firms and which should act as a prime motivator for a client care programme: cross-selling. Just consider this common scenario. Each partner/director is involved in selling their own services to clients and it is accepted that the client is not buying the services of the firm, but the services of that particular person (and in the best case scenario, the team who works with them). However, what tends to happen in practice is that partners/directors then feel (though rarely openly admit) 'I am reluctant to sell the services of others within the firm in case they give poor service to my client and ruin my good relationship'. Obviously, a client care programme should reduce that risk and put every partner/director in a position where they feel confident about their colleagues and are willing to promote their services.

Understanding your clients' needs and wants is key to meeting those needs and providing satisfactory solutions. It may not be obvious: look behind what the client is actually saying, to what they really want. Taking time truly to understand your client's needs and your client, as a person, enables you to tailor your services to efficiently and effectively meeting those needs. Doing so enables you to provide a high-quality service because quality of service refers to how well and how often your clients receive what they expect from you. *They* decide the position of the goalposts, not you.

Value – research has shown that fee levels are not as important to clients as the level of value they feel they get out of the relationship. So, rather than aiming to be the cheapest, concentrate on being the best. You also need to understand your place in your client's pecking order of significant relationships – your value to them may not be nearly as much as you fondly believe.

Client care, as mentioned above, is often thought of by professionals as a purely positive matter – if not an optional extra, then something which, if not given attention, will only deprive the firm of its positive benefits. However, this is far from being the case, as these facts bear out:

- Most client dissatisfaction is not about technical service it's about issues such as poor communication, unjustified charging, delays and attitude.
- Most clients don't complain about poor professional service, they simply never return.
- Dissatisfied clients will tell numerous other people about their experiences; it's not something they keep to themselves.

Poor or ineffective client care often goes hand in hand with poor knowledge management throughout the firm. When knowledge across the firm isn't pooled or updated, although the firm as a whole should know a lot about their client, this doesn't come across, and leaves the client perceiving disinterest, inefficiency and a lack of care from their professional services provider. Take steps to coordinate the knowledge you have about your clients throughout the firm, keep it in a form that can be readily accessed and understood, cross-reference it to other client or adviser files and update and review it regularly.

An often overlooked area of client care is the issue of confidentiality and the security of client information. Most professionals would be horrified at the suggestion that client information is handled with anything but the utmost care, but unfortunately reality is often far from the truth. Although most firms are effective in respect of IT security and sending and receiving information electronically, it's often the case that computers are left on, or are unprotected by passwords, and subject to being accessed by anybody at any time.

Poor security often shows itself in other more mundane ways. How often are client files left on desks after hours to be viewed by cleaning staff, or subject to being stolen or destroyed? How often do potentially sensitive letters get sent around the office for everyone to read, simply because no one's quite sure who should be dealing with them? Worst of all, how many of your staff hold loud, public conversations with or about their clients on mobile phones?

Think through the potential security risks in respect of client information in your firm and come up with worst case scenarios. Put policies and protocols in place to regulate the handling of data, and communicate these not only to your staff (underpinned by appropriate training), but also to your clients so that they are aware of how seriously you regard the issue.

Client care programmes

Client care programmes are often superimposed by firms on their staff along with re-vamping reception areas. Reasons why such programmes often fail include:

- they are superficial – they deal with the detail rather than core values;
- they are unfocused and uncoordinated;
- they are backed up with insufficient on-going training;
- they lack any form of staff motivation;
- they don't reflect what clients really need and want.

Although there are no hard and fast rules, the following steps are recommended for setting up a client care programme, getting buy-in from all, and achieving results:

1. Set up an initial steering group.
2. Hold internal focus groups. Analyse the behaviours demonstrated by those – internally and externally – who are held to be good at client care. Get feedback from all levels: secretaries and support staff often have a lot to contribute in this area.
3. Ask clients for their views.
4. Analyse 'hard' and 'soft' issues.
5. Draw up a draft programme of general client care standards, circulate and amend.
6. Establish an account management system, by which every client is the responsibility of a named individual.
7. Devise means of keeping in touch with clients in between transactions.
8. Set measurable standards and manage the monitoring and implementation of the process.

9. Analyse training needs – initial and on-going.
10. Build into induction, personal objectives, team plans.
11. Publicise client care standards to clients and others.
12. Seek on-going feedback – internal and external.
13. Communicate feedback – good or bad – to the firm on a regular basis.

Establishing the motivation

Client care programmes are often started in a blaze of enthusiasm and fizzle out under a cloud of embarrassment. This can be more damaging than never having addressed the problem at all – so measures need to be in place to manage the process and motivate staff throughout the firm. If there's initial scepticism there's no harm whatsoever in introducing the 'mystery shopper' process to periodically test external levels of service in areas such as how quickly and in what manner telephones are answered, letters responded to, or voicemails or e-mails picked up. As long as you make it clear to everyone that this is a necessary part of the process, the motivation will be ingrained.

Motivational messages require continual reinforcement and should include such facts as:

- Client care is one of the key means by which a professional services firm can differentiate itself from its competitors.
- Client care shows in the bottom line – a 5 per cent increase in client retention can result in a 50 per cent improvement in profitability. On top of this, excellent client care usually means fewer write-offs and discounts and improved client retention.
- Unlike other forms of business development, client care involves little, if any, financial investment.
- It usually takes no more time to do something well than to do it badly, and it can save enormous amounts of time in the long run (i.e. if complaints arise, or work has to be redone).

The most important thing to remember is to make your programme manageable. Although you can see at the outset the sort of impeccable, wide-ranging, all inclusive client care programme you eventually envisage for the firm, make sure you introduce it gradually, testing and measuring each stage and ensuring it has moved to the level of ingrained behaviour before moving on to the next.

Key tips in respect of client care

Whatever you decide are your own standards of client care, the following points should be borne in mind.

Communicate, communicate, communicate

Discuss with your clients not just what you are going to do, but also what you expect of them. Part of the communication process involves keeping an eye on what's happening in your clients' market place and contacting them with proactive, relevant advice. Most important, whether dealing with private or commercial clients, if there is a development they should know about, don't wait to be asked – circulate them with a news bulletin drawing their attention to it and the relevant services you can provide.

Delight them

To ensure client loyalty, you have to aim not just to *satisfy*, but to truly *delight* them. The dictionary definition of delight is 'intense pleasure': keep this in mind next time you think 'that'll do'. Delight really isn't difficult to achieve – take an interest in your client's business, make an effort every now and again to send them something they'll really appreciate – concert or football tickets, flowers, even a birthday card – and of course, always make sure you do an excellent job.

Along with this you should aim to make the exceptional the norm in your dealings with clients, quality should underpin everything you do. Of course, sometimes the client is willing to sacrifice quality for price, but if so, make sure you have had that conversation with them so they know exactly what to expect.

Demonstrate enthusiasm and energy

Nothing is more infectious than enthusiasm. Some of the most successful people around achieve their results through a combination of overwhelming enthusiasm for what they do, combined with a 'never give up' energetic approach.

Innovate

Making an impression through doing something different is a greatly undervalued marketing tool. Demonstrating innovation in one area, whether publicity materials, hospitality events, or your approach to transactions, bodes well for your creativity in other areas and helps you stand out from the crowd.

Lighten up

Part of the process of delighting your client involves treating them like a valued friend or colleague, rather than just a source of income, so make sure you take time to share a joke and chat about their business and their family.

Ban negativity

Avoid it at all costs. There's a fine dividing line between cautious advice based on your professional view of what would not be desirable, and the impression that you can't be bothered to think through and carefully assess a client's suggestion or proposal which you consider risky, or come up with a slightly unusual, off-the-wall way of handling a problem. Avoid all thoughts along the lines of 'We can't . . .', 'It'll never . . .', 'There's no point . . .' and give it a go even if it's a long shot. Even if it doesn't come off, your client will appreciate your responsiveness and effort.

Actively sell your range of services

'Selling' is a dirty word for many professionals, who prefer a reactive approach to client needs. But nobody minds being sold to when the services in question are something they actually want and need. Frankly, clients won't buy from you if they don't know what you've got on offer, so make sure they are fully aware of your service range, and more important, the benefits of buying from you.

Don't let a lapsed client become an ex-client

Once a particular transaction has been completed and invoiced, don't let the client drift away. Make sure they are on the mailing list to receive periodic information from the firm and put a reminder system in place for an informal phone call, say at six-month intervals just to say 'how are things going?'.

CASE STUDY   **When is a client not a client?**

One firm watched a client (ABC Ltd) grow over many years, and periodically undertook work for them. The firm was disappointed, to say the least, when a new client care programme prompted them to contact the client after some eighteen months' silence. Although the firm still regarded ABC Ltd as a client, the client had in fact undergone a tremendous surge of growth and having being actively courted by one of the firm's competitors, had taken their business elsewhere. When the firm discussed the situation with ABC Ltd they admitted that there hadn't been a problem with the work done, but thought that the firm 'didn't seem interested in having our business'.

Treat them how you would want to be treated

We are all clients or customers ourselves. Thinking about what affects your own experience when you are doing business with a company can be helpful in formulating your own standards of client care. Ask yourself the following questions about your firm from a client's perspective and think carefully about the answers:

- Are you easy to do business with?
- Can clients make contact quickly with the person they need to deal with?
- Do you clearly outline your charges and offer different payment options?
- Do you spell out what's involved in each transaction so it's easy to understand?
- Do you take the time and interest to get to know your clients?
- Do you communicate regularly and proactively, or is it always left to your clients to contact you?
- Do you make provision for not being available – is there always someone else clients can deal with?
- Do you get the feeling that clients are impressed with the quality of the service they receive?
- Do you remember to ask clients whether they have any questions or problems?
- Do you deliver what you promise?
- Do you give the impression of being consistently well organised and efficient?
- Do you keep in contact once the transaction is completed?

When speaking to clients, seek to establish your client's needs and feedback through asking them plenty of open questions using the why?, when?, how?, who?, where? approach, for example:

- What are the biggest problems you/your department/your company faces?
- Why do you think your company is more successful than most of your competitors?
- When do you review your service providers?
- How do you see the market place changing?
- Who are the people who contribute most to the success of your business?
- Where do you see the firm and your own position in five years' time?

CASE STUDY   **'Don't tell me, ask me!'**

The managing partner of a small accountancy firm had long felt there was room for improvement in his firm's relationship with clients. He knew the firm did a good job and their charges were reasonable, but they had difficulty getting close to clients and retaining their loyalty. Having discussed our views on the likely problems and how to go about addressing them, the managing partner agreed to set up a special meeting for partners and all other fee-earning staff where we undertook some role play.

Our 'plant' was a typical small to medium-sized enterprise (SME) client who had come to the practice by way of referral from the local Business Link. The initial interview, conducted by a (brave) volunteer partner was agreed by all to be 'standard' and focused on identifying technical needs. The interview lasted about 20 minutes and:

- was largely conducted through the medium of closed questions – evoking 'yes'/'no' answers;
- involved a response outlining 'suggested' solutions (no alternatives were offered);
- provided an indication of the associated cost of providing those solutions;
- gave the client an opportunity to contribute only by asking, at the end, 'Do you have any queries?'.

We ran the interview again, this time with the pre-briefed managing partner conducting the interview. This time the client was:

- asked open questions – encouraging him to describe his business, his vision and his objectives;
- asked what he wanted to achieve by having the accountancy firm work with him, both in the short- and long-term;
- asked about his previous experiences – including charging – with professional advisers;
- asked how he liked to work;
- asked when the firm could go and see his company in action.

The suggested way forward was then formulated by drawing out the client's assessment of what was required and incorporated flexibility and a longer-term strategy. The interview took 20 minutes longer, but feedback from the client (an actual SME owner) showed that had it been a real situation, he would have bought more services from the firm and was very positively inclined towards forming a long-term relationship with them even at such an early stage.

Assessing client value

A significant aspect of successful client service, is realising that although you need a set of minimum service standards, not all clients should be treated the same. Clients will range from those who are very valuable to you to those who have no value at all. This latter group are your problem clients, the ones who are poor payers and for whom nothing is ever good enough. Bite the bullet, get rid of them and free up more time and resource for those clients you really like, need and want.

At the other end of the spectrum, once general standards of client care are in place for all, you need to consider introducing a client relationship management programme for your key clients. These are the small slice of very valuable clients on whom you should be lavishing maximum effort and energy. For them, standard client service levels are not enough.

Although there are many ways of defining your key clients the 80/20 rule, otherwise known as the Pareto principle, is a good starting point. This is the time-honoured rule which says that in most businesses, roughly speaking, 80 per cent of business comes from 20 per cent of clients. Therefore it makes sense to devote 80 per cent of your business development efforts to your relationship with those clients (hence the importance of client relationship management). Your first job in analysing the worth of your existing clients is to undertake an assessment of fee income over the past three to five years from, say, your top 20–30 clients. This will reveal whether you do, in fact, have a stable core of loyal clients and will reflect the degree of consistency in fee generation year by year. You also need to look at clients in respect of other aspects of the firm's objectives, for example, identifying those who may not be terribly profitable, but are of importance for the firm for strategic reasons.

Client relationship management

Client relationship management (CRM) is the holy grail of business development. In general, it is an approach to building your business through devoting resource to improving the quality of your relationships with existing clients in order both to increase the amount of business they do with you and prevent them defecting elsewhere. More specifically, it means taking an intensely proactive, rather than a reactive approach to your clients – anticipating their needs and managing your relationships with them to achieve the results you want.

Underlining CRM is the fundamental principle that it costs between five and ten times as much to win new business from new clients as it does from existing clients. This is because targeting new prospects involves spending more on publicity, devoting more resource to making contact and relationship building (see the relationship ladder in Chapter 5) and time devoted to setting up and explaining administrative procedures. Recent research has even shown there is a 20–40 per cent chance of winning back business from ex-clients – so, compared with the probability of successfully courting new prospects, CRM makes undeniable sense.

However, next to business development planning, CRM is likely to be one of the most labour-intensive, on-going procedures the firm can introduce, so you need to get it right. Because it is outward facing and involves clients, it is not something you can play at and drop if it doesn't work – once you've started, you must continue. That said, this is an area where, again, you may need to seek external assistance in order to establish the groundwork of your system, to run a pilot programme and establish an on-going periodic source of review, monitoring, feedback and encouragement.

Fundamental to CRM is the concept of account management by which the firm's relationship with the client is actively managed, very possibly by someone other than the person who was originally responsible for winning the client or who has been mainly responsible for doing the work. Two tenets underly this: ownership of the client, which lies with the firm, and responsibility for the relationship and the work, which comes down to individuals.

Other commercial service providers, for example advertising and design agencies, have never had any problem with this concept and have specific account manager roles – people whose sole responsibility is to manage client relationships, working alongside those (e.g. designers, copywriters) who actually do the work. The advantage of their role is:

- they are the prime point of contact with the client and thus the key repository of client information;
- services can be more easily channelled to meet each client's individual needs;
- they are able to coordinate the services of various providers from within the company and ensure consistency;
- they are able to sell in other services as required;
- they are able to assess objectively the work being done in terms of, for example, quality and timeliness.

There's no doubt that CRM programmes involve a considerable amount of on-going effort, but perhaps more than any other area of marketing, the motivation for why you're doing it is easy to see: CRM programmes generate increased profits; effort does produce measurable return. Part of the reason for this is that getting closer to clients, getting to know their wants, needs, goals and desires, makes you much better placed to spot opportunities and benefit from them. But this only pays if you do something about them. Many firms waste huge amounts of resource on trying to win new clients while ignoring the valuable opportunities already staring them in the face.

CRM can be the driver for firms to undertake portfolio analysis of their client base, as mentioned above – analysing clients according to factors such as size, turnover and profitability and, from this, working out realistic profit targets for the firm. Partners can then be set targets which involve increasing profits on the basis of these variables rather than being given, for example, the rather woolly objective 'increase profits by 10%'.

Key elements of CRM

Specific CRM programmes are numerous and well documented and you may choose to follow rigorously one particular programme. If not, there are some key elements you can build into your own programme:

- Ensure everyone understands why you're embarking upon a CRM programme.
- Identify a small number of clients and partners to use as part of a pilot programme
- Set clear SMART objectives in respect of the measurable results you want to achieve from CRM. As ever, if you don't have objectives, you'll never achieve them.
- Ensure support from the very top – ideally the managing or senior partner/director should be closely involved.
- Devise a standard information set to be obtained and updated on all key clients to include such information as their size, turnover, business objectives, competitive position, key strategies, mission statement, future plans, organisational chart.
- Undertake a SWOT analysis of your relationship with the client.
- Analyse all the relationships the firm has with the client and the significance of those relationships. Who are the apparent decision makers? Who are those with 'the power behind the throne'? How are decisions made?
- Pinpoint the nature of your relationship with the client – do they view you as an outsider, supplier, friend or partner?
- Analyse the work done, the client's needs – current and potential – and how much more work could be done.
- Analyse your client's other professional services providers – especially those in direct competition with you.
- Differentiate your own client management roles. Some partners are best at winning work and servicing 'soft' client needs; others are better at technical matters. Appoint the former as your account managers.

- Keep a central data bank on each key client. Make sure everyone knows how to feed information in, and how to access it (remember the security aspects – these are your most important clients).
- Devise an annual plan for each key client – working backwards from what you want to achieve – and build in both 'soft', e.g. tailored hospitality, and 'hard' events, e.g. formal review meetings, proposals, pitches.
- Coordinate your efforts. If your firm has contacts with several different people in a client company, you can dramatically increase opportunities for more business by getting a whole team working on developing the relationship.

The factors listed above are what we call hard requirements – the nuts and bolts of what you should do to set up your programme. But, as ever, to be truly effective you also need to look outside your firm and consider variables such as those below, remembering that, by definition, CRM is all to do with relationships:

- *Make the effort to get to know your client's other advisers* – lawyers, accountants, financial advisers, etc. Being part of your client's advisory team will help strengthen your position, as well as generating referrals from the other participants.

- *Look for the positive measurable outcomes* in what you do for your client and make sure you point them out (e.g. 'this saves you 15%'). Don't leave it for the client to figure it out for themselves – they probably won't! If the success of what's done can be measured, it also provides enormous motivation to keep on doing more.

- *Look for ways to help your client do their job better* and to consolidate the personal relationship you have between you.

- *Work towards establishing a partnership relationship* with your client by benchmarking, non-executive directorships, shared training, reciprocal secondments, familiarisation programmes, and setting up reporting, monitoring and quality evaluation systems.

The fact that not all clients have the same value to you generates an apparent contradiction between setting common standards which apply to the firm's dealings with every client through a client care programme, and tailoring service standards to meet individual client needs. The explanation for this is not simple, but it is broadly that the elements of a client care programme should be the *minimum* standards to be adhered to in every situation. More tailored client care can be introduced for those key clients of particular importance to the firm, so that clients receive a level of care which is in keeping with their *long-term value to your firm*.

CASE STUDY   **You may be my client but do I know you?**

The managing director of a property company was having difficulty persuading a fellow director of the need to take client relationship management seriously. He was adamant that he knew plenty about his clients and that there was little need for him to find out more. After reasoned persuasion repeatedly failed, the managing director decided to call his bluff.

With no prior warning, he called the director into his office and said 'X [one of the firm's other important clients] has just rung and asked me to accompany him on a visit to ABC [one of the director's and the firm's key clients] tomorrow. I've got to go over there in an hour to brief him about the company, so I need some information fast.'

The managing director then reeled off a series of questions, including:

'What are the biggest challenges in their industry?'
'Who are their key competitors at home and abroad?'
'What are their development plans for the next five years?'

There were many more wide-ranging questions, and although the director made a good attempt at bluffing his way through, the gaping holes in his knowledge were painfully revealed.

It took very little more after that to get him on board with the CRM programme . . .

Client research and feedback

Finding out what your clients think is an important on-going process, both in respect of general client care and CRM. The number one rule in dealing with clients, is:

Don't assume. Ask. Having asked, listen. Listen and respond.

Research has shown that across the professions there is still a lack of formal measurement of client satisfaction, with accountants apparently taking the lead over lawyers and surveyors in terms of client management generally. However, there are several advantages to seeking your clients' opinions:

- The very act of asking them makes them feel that you care.
- They are given the opportunity to comment on what they like and dislike about your current service. (But bear in mind that you won't get a common response from all, for example seminar assessment forms often come back with comments that demonstrate that

some people found the room too hot, whereas others thought it too cold!)

- They can be prompted to tell you what they would like to see in terms of additional services, methods of service provision, etc. You will need to distinguish between needs, wants and simply what 'would be nice'.

On-going client feedback

There are no hard and fast rules that will suit every firm and every client about how often and by what means you should obtain regular client feedback. However, you need to obtain it by some means, even if just from a selected sample of clients rather than from every client in respect of every piece of work.

Before you put any system in place, we suggest the following:

- Ideally, get someone independent (e.g. an external researcher or consultant) to talk to your key clients to establish what they consider important.
- Devise a short evaluation form, circulate and get internal approval.
- Establish to whom and how often the feedback form should be sent, or how and by whom interviews will be conducted, and establish a reminder system for doing so.
- Establish who will receive, analyse and act on the responses received.

Ensuring that clients perceive that their input and feedback is valued is all to do with making sure that it results in some sort of change and improvement. This need not involve the specific changes they have recommended, but it should be an acknowledgement that their ideas have been seriously considered and that change is taking place as a result of client feedback. Without this, clients will lose interest, become sceptical and stop responding.

Dealing with dissatisfaction

Despite all the best planned and implemented client care and CRM programmes, there will still be occasions when things go wrong. That's the way the world is, and assuming it is only a rare occurrence, it isn't anything that you should lose too much sleep over. (Don't take it as a signal to throw your client care programme out of the window!)

To take the heat out of the situation, you need to have an effective complaints handling system, make sure everyone in the firm is clear about the procedure, and that it is explained to clients at the outset. If you should then receive a complaint, we suggest the following:

- Apologise immediately – not for the matter being complained about, until this has been investigated, but for the fact that the person felt they had to complain.
- Act and react swiftly – don't give them cause for further complaint.
- Find out from everyone involved the exact details of the circumstances surrounding the complaint and whether it involved the breakdown or circumvention of standard procedures.
- Use the experience positively to mould future practice – whether or not the complaint was justified. Remember, things do go wrong and always will, so use the experience as a building block to build an even better service.

One of the strongest relationships you can have is with a client who has complained, had their complaint satisfactorily dealt with, and still chooses to deal with you.

CASE STUDY   **Delight from disaster**

A client arrived at his accountant's office to find that his appointment had been overlooked and his accountant was actually taking a day's holiday. Understandably, as he had taken time out of his working day and travelled some 30 miles, the client was less than pleased.

However, on receipt of this news from the accountant's secretary, the receptionist knew exactly the procedure to follow. She showed the client into a small meeting room and provided him with coffee. She summoned another partner who apologised on behalf of his colleague, established what the meeting was to have been about and asked whether he would like to see someone else, or reschedule the appointment. As he wished to reschedule, the partner then established times when it would be convenient for the accountant to visit *him* and promised to have the appointment confirmed the next day.

The client was reimbursed his travelling expenses, sent a bottle of champagne and note of apology by the errant partner the next day and was more than happy to see him when he visited his premises the following week. Not only was there a positive outcome for the client but it caused the firm to examine their appointments system and improvements were made to tighten up procedures.

POINTS TO REMEMBER

➤ Client care, by its very nature, is defined by the client, not the service provider.

➤ Client care involves trust, emotional involvement and loyalty – it is the fundamental area of difference between providing a service and selling a product. Some 70–80 per cent of perceived value of the transaction for the client is embodied in the way the service is delivered.

➤ Effective client care means shifting your balance to the client rather than to the work you are doing for them.

➤ Client care programmes need effective on-going management and a high level of motivation at all levels if they are to succeed.

➤ As it costs between five and ten times more to win new business from new clients as it does to win new business from existing clients, effective client relationship management should be one of your key business development strategies.

➤ Effective CRM involves sharing client knowledge, setting goals for what you want to achieve from the relationship, formally planning how to go about it, and coordinating your efforts across the firm.

➤ Regular client feedback is one of the best means of monitoring your service provision and providing new inspiration on how to develop your services further.

5

New business development

KEY ISSUES

- Understanding the relationship ladder
- The role of networking
- Successful selling
- Direct mail and telemarketing
- Proposals, presentations, tenders and beauty parades
- Cost
- Referrals
- Cross-selling

Think about your firm – do you recognise any of these problems?

	YES	NO
It's a waste of time networking – you never come away with any new business.		
We have a poor track record with winning business through beauty parades, but it's difficult to pinpoint where we're going wrong.		
My partners are a selfish bunch. Cross-selling is anathema to them.		
Professionals aren't salespeople, we never will be and should never aspire to be.		
Price isn't an issue. We're not aiming to be the cheapest, so we set our charges on the basis of what we think each client will pay and we tend to gauge this over the lifespan of the work.		
We get very few referrals from people who we know could make them, so we make very few outward referrals ourselves.		

We put a lot of time and money into a big mailshot campaign but the results were rubbish. We got very little out of it.		
There's only one way to develop the business, that's to win new clients.		
Over the past couple of years we've wasted weeks on preparing proposals and tender documents but we never get anywhere. We've no idea why.		
Networking, running seminars, writing articles, cross-selling to existing clients . . . I'm supposed to do all of this and more. But how, and where should I put most effort?		

Assuming you didn't answer 'no' to all the above, then you should read on.

Ask many small to medium-sized firms to describe their key business objective and they will probably say 'to win new clients'. They are not alone; this is probably the greatest challenge facing most businesses, but winning new business – perhaps more than any other area – isn't something that can simply be allowed to happen in a vacuum, the implications are too wide-ranging. As ever, it comes back to managing the process and motivating those involved and for small to medium-sized professional services firms, there are particular problems. These include:

- an inability to easily differentiate their service offering;
- a lingering attitude, especially among older professionals, that professionals shouldn't have to sell;
- generally poor management and poor sharing of client/market knowledge;
- a defensive 'my client' rather than 'the firm's clients' culture;
- lack of understanding of the nature of the sales process for professional services firms;
- inadequate training in all stages of business development.

Winning new business is an area where effective management and appropriate motivation can ratchet up your success rates 100 per cent. However, evidence shows that in most firms the whole area is poorly and inadequately managed, if at all, and there is usually little payoff or recognition for individuals bringing in new business. In fact, in many firms there is a very mixed message about new business development along the lines of 'Go and win new business, get new clients for the firm. But the only thing we'll actually reward you for are chargeable hours and fees, and if you're too successful at new business you'll be despised by your colleagues'. Is it any wonder the average professional keeps his head down and does little more than generate enough new business, through the easiest ways possible, to counteract natural client wastage and meet his fee targets?

In this chapter we hope to give you some helpful tips and pointers on how to manage and motivate yourself and others to undertake new business development and get measurable payback as a result.

When they think of 'marketing', people often just think 'cold-calling' and selling to perfect strangers, and go into a state of rabid aversion. However, 'selling' is actually a process rather than an individual act and cold calling in isolation is something professional firms should resort to only in times of absolute desperation. Telemarketing, which we touch on later in this chapter is, however, a totally different proposition.

Understanding the relationship ladder

The first thing to bear in mind in respect of new business development is that it is a staged process. Marketing doesn't refer to your relationships with only one group of people – at any time the firm, and you as an individual, should be marketing to all those shown in Figure 5.1.

- *Prospects* are those people you have identified that you want a relationship with, but with whom you've not yet made contact.

Figure 5.1   The relationship ladder

- *Contacts* are those people you have marketed to or had some sort of contact with but with whom you're not yet in meaningful dialogue about their needs.
- *Potential clients* are prospects with whom you're in a process of dialogue and need to establish the fit between their needs and how you can meet them.
- *Clients* are those for whom you provide services and with whom you should now be in on-going communication even if you are not currently doing any work for them.
- *Key clients* are clients who for financial or strategic reasons are of vital importance to the firm.

Note that the last two categories also include other professionals and sources of work referrals.

The importance of being aware of these groups is that it will help you decide where to put your marketing effort, bearing in mind that your time is limited and that you are looking for meaningful results – see Table 5.1. The table not only identifies different groups, it also shows the different stage each group is at in respect of its attitude towards the firm. If business development is to be successful, it is important that the firm's relationships are actively managed at each stage in order to keep those individuals interested in the firm and to move them up to the next rung of the ladder.

Table 5.1   How to choose the right marketing tools

Group	Attitude of group	Appropriate marketing tools
Prospects	Neutrality	Profile raising – networking, PR (including articles), advertising, sponsorship
Contacts	Awareness (spectrum from 1% to 100%)	Tailored marketing – mailshots, newsletters, group hospitality
Potential clients	Interest	Capability marketing – seminars, newsletters, focused hospitality, selling, tender submissions
Clients	Decision making	Selling – proposals, presentations, beauty parades, tailored hospitality
Key clients	Advocacy – internal and external	Cross-selling – bespoke hospitality, joint seminars, tailored mailshots, sponsorship

Awareness

This is the stage at which a prospect is made aware of your very existence. This awareness is often generated by use of promotional tools like PR, mailshots, advertising, etc. but the amount of information the prospect will take on board about you and/or your firm will be limited and probably soon forgotten unless reinforced. Realistically, this is the stage you are dealing with at networking functions for example, so it comes as no surprise that people come back disappointed that they haven't landed any new business – the likelihood of them doing so was always very low.

Interest

Interest is generated by demonstrating to the prospect that you can provide something relevant to their needs and wants, impressing upon them the specific benefits of how you will achieve this. The most important part of the interest stage is finding out what the client wants (factors which are desirable and are totally subjective) and needs (factors which are necessary, rational and objective), because until you do you can't present your offering in a way that directly appeals to them.

Desire

This is where what most people think of as selling really kicks in. It's not a process of persuading the prospect to buy something they don't want, but rather of making them aware of and raising their levels of desire for the benefits you can offer them.

Action

This is the decision-making process – the stage at which you finally convert a prospect to a client and from there, hopefully take them on to the status of 'key client.'

The role of networking

In this chapter we deal with two subjects uniformly guaranteed to strike terror into the hearts of even the most hardened of old campaigners: selling and presenting or speaking in public. We have known people go to amazing lengths to avoid either – calling in sick, crying off at the last moment due to being 'too busy', sending the office junior to a meeting in their place – it gets them off the hook in the short term, but it's hardly productive.

Our clients often admit, 'we're not very good at networking and we need help', but frankly, sending fee-earners on a single seminar won't solve all their problems, which include the following:

- People have different personality types – introverts often require more training and coaching than extroverts.
- 'Selling' is a long-haul, stage-by-stage process – you need to understand appropriate tools and behaviour at each stage to be successful.
- The process needs planning and rehearsing and time devoted to it.

Perhaps we should look first at what we mean by networking – which we define as 'establishing a network of potentially profitable contacts taken from a pool of strangers'. Another definition is 'the active cultivation of useful contacts and the use of those contacts, where appropriate, to help in achieving predetermined objectives'. What networking is, therefore, is meeting strangers, creating an embryonic relationship with them and including them in your 'network' of business contacts to be developed into clients, or used in any other way that may be appropriate.

But how do you go about identifying who those people are that you want to make contact with in order to take them up the relationship ladder? This is something you need to think about and discuss internally before you go out into the market place:

- Who are they?
- Where are they?
- What do they need and what you can offer?
- How great is their need?
- Who else is meeting those needs?
- How can you get closer to them?
- Who do they know?
- What are their culture, values and personality?

Having identified the types of people, and specific targets in some cases, that you want to meet, ensure you're also clear about who your colleagues' prospects are – the firm, the team and your own. You may meet someone that your colleague has been trying to make contact with for years – don't let the opportunity slip by.

Practically speaking, networking involves regularly mixing with groups of people who you believe have among them the sort of contacts you want to make, making the effort to assess those contacts, and then making sure you follow them up – thus converting an individual who had been just a prospect into someone you can regard as a 'contact' of yours. And, of course, the process is reciprocal – once you've established contact, the door is open for them to contact you. This doesn't mean, however, meeting a stranger and immediately persuading them to give you some business.

There is an enormous amount to be gained through networking, none of which may be directly related to gaining business from the people you meet. For example:

- It can be a good source of commercial 'gossip'.
- It is a way of gathering information about what's happening in various market sectors or finding out issues of importance to different types of company.
- Through impressing those you speak to, you are building your reputation and creating a positive image.
- It's an ideal means of finding out about your competitors.
- It's the most effective way of making a lasting personal impact.

But perhaps the most important thing to remember is that networking involves *social* not professional skills – it is not the forum to try to impress others with your technical abilities, you'll simply bore them to death. Your focus of attention when networking should be to:

- use open questions;
- circulate;
- obtain permission to keep in touch;
- follow up all pertinent leads;
- try to find ways of doing something for contacts who interest you (e.g. sending them a relevant article, getting tickets to an event, effecting an introduction to a third party).

Research shows that tone of voice, body language and physical appearance make much more of an impression when meeting or presenting to people than what you actually say, so you have to get it right. As in all facets of life, there are those who could be cleaner, neater, and generally more in line with the mainstream in terms of how they are turned out. The trouble is, when you work with people it's easy to overlook their idiosyncrasies, and approaching people about personal matters is delicate and can be embarrassing. But it has to be done. It matters. Much research has been done on the positive and negative impact of appearance and no matter how cerebral you are and feel 'we're above such things' – other people aren't.

More important than appearance is attitude. As they say, 'There's nothing so infectious as enthusiasm – except the lack of it.' This highlights the defining factor for success in winning new business whether you are networking, selling, presenting or creating tender documents. A real sense of enthusiasm and belief in what you are doing comes across as a powerful influencer and is guaranteed to tip the scales in your direction to having other people view you favourably.

Concentrate on generating feelings of reliability and trust, and getting people to like you. At this stage your whole concentration should be on building and progressing the relationship – not what you might get out of it.

Don't let the process focus on *you*. Try to gauge early on the type of person you are dealing with and tailor your approach accordingly. Although this sounds an extreme generalisation, most people fall into one of four different personality types (see Table 5.2) which means they tend to act, react and think in a particular way. Thus people are either task- or people-oriented, and direct or indirect in their approach.

Table 5.2   The four basic personality types

	Task-oriented	People-oriented
Direct	These people are often known as 'drivers'. They tend to be leaders, managers, entrepreneurs – they work alone and like to get on with the job	These people tend to be extroverts. They often work in the media, have a tendency to be flamboyant or artistic, love socialising and aren't interested in the fine detail
Indirect	These people are analytical, like detail, have to be able to see the full picture and are very thorough in their approach. They're often accountants or IT specialists	These people are comfortable only with personal relationships, they like to work in teams and spend time getting to know their colleagues and their backgrounds

Networking doesn't sound difficult, does it? So why do people find it so? A number of common problems can be identified, among which are that people:

- have unrealistic expectations about the role and purpose of networking;
- are not really clear about who they should be meeting or why, and so don't maximise the opportunities. Their networking is unfocused;
- don't really know where to go to network or which invitations to accept or decline;
- simply don't network often enough – this is one area where practice really does make things easier;
- are shy and hesitant about introducing themselves to total strangers;
- don't follow up or keep in touch with useful contacts, so the exercise is wasted;
- don't adopt the '10 per cent talking, 90 per cent listening' rule, so they find out very little about those they meet;
- let their body language reveal their true feelings ('I'm bored/uninterested/out of my depth/nervous and I really don't want to be doing this').

Regardless of your profession or your location, you are almost certain to be surrounded by a wealth of networking opportunities. Some of the more obvious ones, for example Chamber of Commerce events, may not be particularly rewarding because those who attend are not part of your target market (this is where your marketing plan and objectives are important). However, look a little closer and you may find that there are special interest groups, or you could even suggest to the Chamber that you help establish one yourself.

Your local Business Link should be able to help by providing information on networking organisations in your area. You should also find out whether you are able to join and attend the meetings of any particular trade or business associations which you have identified as being important to you. Events held by other professionals to which you are invited are always worth attending provided their client base and contacts are similar to those in which you are interested. If you hear about something to which you would like to be invited in future, why not approach the organisation and ask to be put on their list if you feel there is a good business case for doing so.

Seminars and conferences are good networking opportunities if the attendees are your target market and/or the subject matter relates to the services you provide. Even if these are run by your competitors, remember that the audience is there because they have an interest in the subject. This can be a good chance to get their reaction and to find out how those you meet are planning to have their needs met.

Finally, one of the most important aspects of networking, especially in the early stages, is that it enables you to find out from people you meet what networking opportunities they find valuable and why. This can help focus your own activities – and most people will be pleased to introduce you to a new group. All you have to say is, 'that sounds really interesting, can you send me the details of the organisers or the next meeting?'. And if you come across someone who you think would be interested in a group that you know about (and they don't), then seize the opportunity to 'do something for them', and offer to take them along.

Successful selling

Referring back to Table 5.1, you will see that networking is just the first stage in the overall selling process. It is the first step on the relationship ladder and the 'initial contact' stage in the sales sequence (see Figure 5.2).

Being successful at the rest of the selling process starts with understanding exactly what selling is. Most people think of it as a one-sided process by which one person persuades another into making a decision to buy something they may not necessarily want. If this is what you believe, you won't succeed – it is not about that at all. Although definitions vary, in essence selling is:

Figure 5.2   The sales sequence

1. An exercise in listening.
2. A staged process of moving someone towards making a buying decision.
3. A means of finding out client needs and wants and adapting your offering to them.

Selling is definitely a specialist skill and we cannot do more than just begin to tell you how to go about it. What we would say, however, is that although brilliant salespeople are probably born rather than made, everyone can be trained to be good or at least competent at sales and to become comfortable with the process. It's an area that's well worth investing in. It's also an area where practice makes perfect so it's vital that those people who are trained are encouraged to get out and practise as soon as possible, and to keep refining their skills through continuous practice. Feedback and periodic update training are useful too – it's easy to become stale and to slip into bad habits.

The key aspects of selling involve understanding:

- the sales cycle (which is very similar to the relationship ladder);
- the relevant decision-making unit (DMU) within each target organisation – that is, which individual or combination of people is or

are responsible for making 'purchasing' decisions – and the role and personality of every individual involved in the process;

- the prospect's purchasing criteria and the difference between their needs and wants;
- how to package and present your service range and experience to ensure a close fit between the prospect's requirements and what you can offer;
- what each individual is looking for in a 'good relationship' in terms of emotional factors such as friendship, reassurance and a source of inspiration.

Most important of all is the recognition that selling will only happen if people are motivated to do it. Whether you offer tangible rewards for new business won or not, we believe that personal recognition should be given every time to the person who has done so. It is rarely a case of 'it's easy for them'. Most will have had to have gone through the same difficult process as everyone else, probably suffered rebuffs and numerous frustrations along the way and have spent hours preparing those 'effortless' presentations. (As George Bernard Shaw said, 'I am the most spontaneous speaker in the world because every word, every gesture and every retort has been carefully rehearsed'.)

We believe that anyone seriously attempting to win new business for the firm should be treated with all the reverence and respect of an actor on stage. Yes, what they actually do is dependent on the full panoply of skills of those backstage, but it's the actor who wins the audience over. They deserve everyone's admiration.

Successful selling comes about as a direct result of a combination of attitude and knowledge:

- Attitude

    – reliable;
    – positive;
    – enthusiastic;
    – knowledgeable;
    – determined;
    – helpful.

- Knowledge

    – know your firm and your products/services inside out;
    – know your competitors and their strengths and weaknesses;
    – know your prospect's market place;
    – know your strengths and don't be easily discouraged;
    – know your prospect's expectations of you and meet or exceed them;
    – know lots and say little – knowledge is power.

And finally, remember these other important edicts:

- Never prejudge a situation.
- Prepare as much as possible before entering into any sales-focused situation.
- Think about which stage of the sales cycle you're dealing with.
- Never take rejection personally.
- Remember, as you're dealing with people it is often emotional factors rather than hard facts that influence their decision.

Direct mail and telemarketing

One aspect of selling which is often questioned is the value to professional firms of direct mail and telemarketing. People are often drawn towards them as they seem a cheaper way than advertising for raising profile (this can be true if your advertising is unfocused), and may be more immediate than, say, networking for generating leads (also true).

However, direct mail and telesales which involve contacting a list of 'cold' contacts are therefore, by definition, 'cold-calling'. This rarely achieves significant results mainly because the relationship between the two parties is exactly that – cold. The direct mail industry has undertaken a great deal of research into response rates to business-to-business (B2B) and business-to-(private)-customer (B2C) mailings/calls and this has shown that response rates are low – on average around 2–8 per cent. Much of the problem, particularly for professional services firms, lies in the fact that the mailshot or call has no specific offer for the client (e.g. 'Use our services and save x%'). Instead, firms tend simply to send out a leaflet or letter outlining the services they provide, along with information about certain features of the firm, e.g. 'We've been in business 50 years' or 'We're right in the heart of town'. As you will know from the section on advertising in Chapter 2, this simply elicits the 'so what?' response from the recipient, and the mailshot is at best, filed, more likely simply thrown away.

Even with an attractive offer, a mailshot alone will rarely get you the results you need. The mailshot should be followed up with a phone call – and making those calls is the truly cold (if not downright frosty) bit that everyone hates.

Nevertheless, some firms will directly telephone a prospect in order to make an appointment to visit and tell them about the range of services they can provide and why the prospect should use them. But often they fail to think this through. Why should the prospect agree to give up their time to meet a perfect stranger who is likely to make them feel uncomfortable by having to refuse something they don't want or need? However, if you can focus your script on an 'offer', e.g. 'Can I come and talk to you about how we might help you save XX per cent on professional costs?', they're more likely to agree.

Taken out of context such true sales patter can be very off-putting, which is why you should think very carefully before going down this route and at least try to undertake some rudimentary sales training before you do.

Another way of tackling the problem is to hire a skilled tele-marketer (probably on a temporary basis) to make appointments and/or follow up a mailshot. Properly trained telemarketers can be highly polished and persuasive. They're not there to sell your services, but they can be effective in making appointments for *you* to go and present. They can be a strong selling tool if you are prepared to make the investment and think through the 'offer'.

However, if like most, you have decided to do it yourself, your confidence and success rates can be improved by trying the following:

- Instead of expecting an immediate positive reaction ('please come and see me and tell me all about it'), offer the option of sending for more information, research findings, etc.
- Send regular periodic mailshots, e.g. your newsletter, so that the prospective client can form an opinion of your firm and develop interest gradually.
- Send a short, intriguing mailshot pointing the recipient towards more information on your website. If they're interested, they'll log on and look it up.

CASE STUDY   **The power of a prize draw**

An accountancy firm decided to develop its business by writing an innovative business-to-business letter, introducing the firm and making an inviting offer. Any company putting business with the firm as a result of the promotion would be entered into a prize draw at the end of the year with the winner receiving a refund on fees charged, up to a predetermined value. The promotion was remarkably successful and within a short time, was paralleled by a scheme for existing clients offering a fee rebate for introducing new clients.

Proposals, presentations, tenders and beauty parades

'Failing to prepare is preparing to fail'.

'You have to go and sell and demean yourself' one lawyer recently commented when describing the beauty parade process. His statement summed up why the process seems to be so much harder for professionals than it is for many other types of business, where the beauty parade is simply regarded as a natural part of doing business. For a start it involves *selling* (dirty word) which is viewed by professionals as being *demeaning* – though it's difficult to understand why.

One might have some sympathy if the lawyer had said 'You have to go and sell, which can be difficult for professionals as it is not something we're traditionally used to doing', which is where the real problem lies. But a process which simply means you have to actively compete with other firms in response to a third-party's criteria isn't demeaning. If you think that it is, the answer's simple – don't do it. You may not get the work you want, but if you approach the process with this sort of attitude you probably won't anyway, so stop wasting your time.

Whether or not it is appropriate for professional services to be allocated through the tender and proposal process and subsequent beauty parades is a question that is open to debate and one we are not going to linger over here. Suffice it to say that it happens and it's down to each firm to decide whether or not they want to pursue work through this method. It is worth noting two salient facts. First, done properly, tendering and beauty parades are only one facet of a selection process which should be as much based on personal relationships and market knowledge as any other form of winning work. Secondly, it is a common and successful process in many other industries, e.g. advertising, where the formal 'pitch' is welcomed as an opportunity to impress and make an impact.

Tenders and beauty parades are very much like job interviews and this may be one reason why professionals have so much difficulty with them. Most workers in the commercial market place are more accustomed to changing jobs and throwing their hats into the ring than those in the professions and are therefore familiar with the standard interview process. However, until recently, the professional services market has tended to be quite static, so many partners, in particular, have never been through it.

What that process involves is:

- finding out about the job on offer;
- finding out as much background as you can about the company;
- preparing a persuasive presentation about how good you are;
- matching your specific skills to their needs;

- preparing some intelligent questions to ask;
- finding out how much they'll pay, how you'll slot into the organisation and who you'll be working with and reporting to.

Proper management of the process can make an enormous difference to your success rates. Once you have looked at the initial criteria outlined in the tender document, think very hard about your reasons for applying for the work and whether or not they really make sense. Number one question is 'Does it make sense financially?' Often firms are swayed by the volume of work and the lure of a fixed contract, but if it ends up costing you money to deliver, it could end up being a massive millstone. Of course, there are other reasons for tendering – the client could be a great name to have on your client list, or the work on tender could be a way of potentially securing other, possibly more lucrative, work. The important thing is that the team involved is clear why you're pursuing the work and what's in it for the firm.

Another question to bear in mind is how does the amount of work on offer and your likelihood of getting it stand up against the amount of time it is going to take you to prepare the response to tender? Cost out the hourly rates of everyone involved, and you won't just be astonished, you'll be horrified! It may be worthwhile if business is quiet, but if you have a full order book it's probably going to cost you more than you'll make. Don't let your involvement be a knee-jerk reaction to an invitation – you need to consider how it measures up against your objectives. Why respond if you haven't already identified it as an objective? There may be plenty of other work to be gained through more traditional means of winning business, so why jump simply because you see an invitation to tender being advertised or because you're flattered by an approach from a potential client asking you to participate in the process?

The tender process often involves fairly short timescales for each stage, with rigid deadlines, so being prepared is key. Bear in mind that, certainly in the initial stages, potential candidates will be weeded out largely on price – get this wrong and everything else you put effort into will be a complete waste of time.

We offer below some practical hints for improving your success rate.

Before tendering

- Well before tendering, identify those organisations from which you would like to win work and start to build relationships with them in order to gain insider knowledge of their business, and understand their decision-making processes and key personnel.
- Think about the criteria involved in any work you would pitch for – use that as the measure to judge whether or not to pursue the work. For example, specify type and volume of work, location, frequency of

instruction, etc. and consider what taking on the work would actually mean – dropping other types of work, taking on additional resource, etc. There is a big difference in tendering for work when you're already on the panel and trying to get new work, or if you're trying to hold on to work you've already done, than pitching cold to virtual strangers.

- If you are involved in work which you know will come up for tender either because of a change of policy or as the contract ends, plan ahead. Use all the relationship building tools and techniques outlined in Chapter 4 on client relationship management – and most importantly, ask to circulate all involved people in the client company with a client satisfaction survey a good year or so before the tender comes up for renewal. This should highlight any areas of dissatisfaction and give you time to put matters right.

- If you do want to pursue work advertised as being open to tender make sure that you know where tender invitations are published and that one individual is charged with the responsibility for looking out for them.

- Likewise, ensure that one person in the firm is appointed as the tender/beauty parade specialist. This is another area in which practice makes perfect. Send them on a specialist training course, and make sure they're involved in every pitch – their time will be more than offset by the benefits to the firm of not reinventing the wheel.

- Make sure there is a central repository (ideally on computer) of all previous pitch documents, presentations, references, CVs, financial statements, etc. Tenders mainly require the same sort of information – again it will save you reinventing the wheel. Most importantly, arrange sources of client references well in advance – it can be a nightmare scenario trying to obtain these at short notice.

During tendering

- Set up a timetable – allowing room for slippage at each stage and then stick to it rigidly.

- Go back to the company and find out more information – about the organisation itself, the work, to whom you'll be presenting, who your competitors are, where you'll be in the line-up, what sort of presentation they're expecting. If possible, arrange a meeting with them and ask prepared searching questions about their requirements.

- Set up a team to work on the project with one person in overall charge (ideally your tenders expert, mentioned above). Take care that your presentation team mirrors the size and style of the team to whom you'll be presenting.

- Spend the majority of your time trying to work out what the potential client actually wants – and focus on addressing these wants, not simply selling your own expertise. Couch your approach to each issue in terms of identifying the particular *feature* of the service you are offering and the actual *benefit* to the client that will result. Make your prospective clients feel that they would be really important to you, and that you really want their work.

- Assuming a formal response to tender document is involved, check that you've answered all the points raised in the potential client's documentation and that every problem area has been met with a workable and innovative solution. Also, cover how you propose to work with them – the nature and style of your relationship.
- Make sure you get the document off in good time. It is surprising how many firms end up submitting documents by courier two minutes before the deadline. Your potential clients will pick up on this – so consider what it will say about your general organisational skills and ability to get things done on time.
- If asked to present – rehearse, rehearse and rehearse again. And don't be shy: get an (internal) audience together and ask for their feedback. You are far better off finding out how boring or incomprehensible you are from your own colleagues while there is still time to do something about it, than watching your potential clients' eyes glaze over on the day.
- A common problem at pitch meetings is that the presenter talks incessantly yet is not focused in what they're saying. Rather than considering: 'how do we tell them what we do?', what you should be analysing at the outset is: 'how do we find out more about their needs and how can we best present our view of the solution?'.
- Be innovative. Advertising and design agencies, in particular, expend an enormous amount of effort and ingenuity on making sure they stand out from the crowd. This needn't cost a lot and should be polished and professional but can be the one thing that sets you apart from the rest.
- Make sure you establish when you can expect to hear the outcome and by what means.

After tendering

- Hold an internal debriefing – look at the good points and bad of how the presentation went and any areas you feel you need to feed into the process for next time. Don't simply look at what the prospective client did or didn't do (e.g. they didn't know what they wanted), try and look at where you might have gone wrong (e.g. 'we ultimately failed to understand their needs'). This really works in understanding why you might or might not have won the business. Try it.
- Write and thank the prospective client for having seen you.

- If you are not successful, contact them to find out why and keep persevering until they tell you.
- Make sure any feedback is noted and acted on next time (again, your tenders coordinator is the central repository for such information).
- If you are successful, don't forget to let the rest of the firm know of your success, and issue a press release if your client agrees.

Because of the direct and concentrated 'cause and effect' nature of the tendering process, the motivational aspects can be high. People often feel energised and even elated during the preparation stage – and even more so if the business is eventually won. Even if the bid isn't successful, individuals tend to feel that they gave it their best shot and are willing to try again, more so than in less formal sales situations. This being the case, it is worth trying to recreate this motivation in respect of other attempts to win new business. For example, setting clear objectives, focusing on the needs of your prospects rather than the services you have on offer, undertaking a timebound sales push and then reviewing your performance and feedback as a group, can all generate feelings of camaraderie, elation and real achievement. This is likely to be far more effective than leaving people to embark upon 'selling' by themselves with little feeling of support or interest from others.

Cost

We discussed pricing as part of the marketing mix in Chapter 2 and, obviously, how you set your prices and at what levels is something to be decided internally before you get in a sales situation with a potential new client.

However, it is important that costs are discussed in detail at the outset of a client relationship, so that the client is aware of exactly how you charge, what they can expect to get for their money and when they will be billed. In respect of this, you should attempt to find out at an early stage how your client (assuming it is a commercial client) charges for *their* services and on what basis, as well as establishing their broader feelings about cost. For example, a firm told us about one of their clients who disliked being charged for 'input time' (meetings, research, etc.), but was quite happy to pay very high rates as long as they were directly related to specific outcomes. Fortunately, the firm discovered this at the outset. The firm then had to do a lot of unpaid work in areas where there was no 'output', for example, deals which fell through, but made a great amount by charging maximum fees in those areas where they were able to assist the client take a deal through to conclusion.

Usually, in a pitch situation, you will have had to have given an indication of price in your initial submission and you will have been included or discarded from the presentation stage on the basis of this. Assuming you haven't been discarded, you should be able to take it as read that your prices are acceptable. Remember that imaginative proposals for pricing and charging have often been proven to win the work.

When discussing charges with a new client it is, of course, important to consider a number of factors including:

- the client's long-term value to you;
- the strategic importance of winning that client's work (taking into account future cross-selling opportunities);
- the level at which the work can be carried out (the sort of blended rate that will be appropriate);
- the short- to medium-term workload of those who will do the work (will it damage other client relationships if those who are to do the work are already under pressure?).

Referrals

Referrals of work from other professional firms have traditionally been a major source of work and continue to be for most firms. However, despite its importance this process is often woefully badly managed and as a result, most firms are not getting as much work from this source as they could.

Firms should consider referrals as one of the most important marketing and sales tools at their disposal, as compared with many other ways of winning new business it's both easy and non-threatening.

It's easy because:

- Other professional firms (in related disciplines) are familiar and comfortable with the concept;
- There is potentially 'something in it for them';
- It can enhance the service they offer;
- It's quick and easy to establish and maintain.

However, it can go badly wrong if referrals are not reciprocated, the referrer's client is given poor service, or the referrer forms a bad impression of your firm for some other reason. You'll then have a very hard time winning back their trust.

To prevent this happening and to maximise the business you get from referrals, take on board these points:

- Analyse within your firm your sources of inward referrals and the destination of outward referrals over the last three to five years. Look at the types and volume of work involved and calculate the value of each firm to you.

- Compare past referrals with marketing objectives. Do you want to continue to receive referrals from those sources? If you want to develop strengths in other areas of work where would these referrals come from? Will courting these other firms cause conflicts? What referrals will you be able to make back to new firms?
- Establish a central referrals register to which everyone can contribute and see where referrals are coming from and going to. Ideally, ensure that one person is in charge of referrals for each area of work so that appropriate reciprocation takes place.
- Visit or phone your sources of referral specifically to discuss the referral process – or if they are a big source of business for several teams, organise a get-together between the two firms. Make sure they are fully aware of all the services you offer, changes in key personnel and any other developments and ask them to keep you updated about their services. Put them on your mailing list for newsletters and seminar invitations in particular.
- As referrals must be reciprocal, you must take into account the problem of spreading yourselves too thinly if you haven't much to offer in return. If direct reciprocal referrals are in short supply, it's worth looking at other ways of cementing your relationships with the other firms from whom you regularly receive referrals – for example, hold a joint seminar, or have their leaflets in your reception area. However, be aware of the signals this will give to their competitors who may move you down their list as a result.
- Make the effort formally to thank the source of the referral and if necessary, extend hospitality as a further sign of your gratitude. Also, if you have put forward the name of another firm to a client, phone and tell them that you have done so. Otherwise, they won't necessarily know, and the value of the referral will be lost.
- If you are seeking new sources of referral, decide which firms may be able to help you and suggest a get-together. These can often be very successful – but they can be completely non-productive unless you make it clear what you want and make definite proposals about how you might work together. If possible, get the ball rolling by putting a referral their way; if this isn't possible, look at other ways of cementing the relationship and working together in future.
- Look more widely than other professional services firms. Depending on the type of work you do, advisers such as Chambers of Commerce, Business Links, recruitment agencies, management consultants, etc. can all have a part to play as well as, of course, Citizens' Advice Bureaux and other consumer advice centres.

Asking existing clients for referrals is an obvious but much neglected source of new business. When we ask clients how much business they get this way, they often say 'not as much as we'd like'. When questioned whether they positively ask their clients to refer them to others, they often say 'no'. The problem is not that clients won't – usually it simply doesn't occur to them, but if only 25 per cent of your clients came up with one positive new referral each year, you'd have 25% more clients!

The past few years have seen the growth of networking and referrals clubs, set up with the primary objective of generating business among their membership. A typical club allows only one member from each profession, e.g. accountant, solicitor, etc. to join, with the club holding weekly or fortnightly meetings which members are expected to attend. At the meetings, members are invited to make short presentations about themselves and their business.

Each member is required to give a certain number of leads (usually two or three) per month to other members and should receive leads back in return. These clubs can work effectively for professional members, so if there isn't one in your area (or there are no vacancies in existing clubs for your profession), you could consider establishing one yourself as a way of generating new business and cementing relationships.

Cross-selling

Finally, cross-selling to existing clients is an area you also need to consider as part of the sales process. Especially when dealing with larger client organisations and maybe approaching people on their side who are not familiar with working with your firm, you should handle the cross-selling exercise with as much care and preparation as a cold pitch. It may take place in a different situation, for example over lunch, and it may involve developing the sales pitch alongside people on your side and theirs who already have a strong working relationship, but in essence it is the same as if you were selling to a non-client prospect.

There are a number of scenarios which equate to the cross-selling opportunity, all of which have somewhat different repercussions on the way the situation should be handled. For example:

* The client deals with someone else in your firm for one type of service but has asked to make contact with you as they have a need for your particular service.
* The client and his colleagues deal with several other people in your firm who provide them with a range of services, but have asked to make contact with you as they have a need for your particular service.
* You have recognised that the client fits the profile of a potential client for your services and you approach the person/people within your firm with whom they currently deal in order to obtain an introduction.

In all of these situations, the main element of the cross-selling process is establishing what the client's needs are in relation to your services so that you can tailor your offering appropriately. However, in the third example above, there may be an extra step involved in the sales process in as much as you will have to sell the idea of approaching his client to your colleague(s) – which can sometimes be harder than selling to the client.

Many cross-selling opportunities of this type fail because those seeking the opportunity to meet an existing client are fobbed off with excuses. Your colleague says 'Yes, fine – I'll mention it to them' and nothing happens. You remind them, and they say 'Yes, of course, I'll set something up'. Still nothing happens and you slink away, defeated. The only effective way of tackling this is to make cross-selling the responsibility of the individual who has the main relationship with the client and to build this into personal objectives and client relationship management plans. The onus is then on them to appropriately sell as wide a range as possible of the firm's services to their client over time. If this is the situation, it goes without saying that if/when you are then asked to present to that client, it is imperative that you make it a priority to respond.

Whatever has driven the cross-selling opportunity, the key thing to remember is that the person (people) you are attempting to sell *your* services to may not know *you* at all. Even if they have met you and know you slightly, they still won't yet be in a position to trust you or the way you deliver the service(s) you offer in the way that they trust your colleague(s) who currently service their needs.

There are some specific tips you should bear in mind in respect of this (remember, too, that cross-selling applies equally to private clients):

- Find out in detail about the client and their company – not just the part(s) your colleague(s) deals with, but the company as a whole.
- Find out who they currently retain to do your area of work, and why they might want to change.
- Find out whether any other areas of your firm are interested in work from the client company. The worst case scenario is a series of uncoordinated approaches from different areas of the firm, so try to consolidate your approach.
- Prepare what you want to say – features and benefits, as well as questions to ask.
- Find out whether they want a 'pitch' or just a conversation, and prepare accordingly.
- Run through what you're going to say with your colleagues who already work with the client – whether or not they're going to be present at the meeting. A rehearsal may reveal some glaring misconceptions, errors or omissions.
- At the end of the meeting, agree what the next stage will be; don't just leave matters hanging.

Cross-selling is one of the most obvious areas in which a firm can grow its business, yet for many the problems caused by poor management of the process combined with lack of motivation of all parties involved mean that it is often relegated to the 'too difficult' pile when the firm considers its marketing opportunities.

POINTS TO REMEMBER

> Marketing involves forming and developing relationships with different groups of people with different levels of awareness and interest in the firm and moving from the bottom to the top of the 'relationship ladder'.

> Networking often fails to be successful because people have erroneous ideas about why they are doing it and unrealistic expectations of what it can achieve.

> Successful networking involves social not technical skills – dramatic results can be engendered by having a real sense of enthusiasm and belief in what you do.

> Selling is a two-way process. It is heavily reliant on establishing personal relationships with the prospect and understanding their needs and wants and how the buying process operates for them, or within their organisation. Ultimately, it is about helping them find solutions to problems, not bombarding them with information about how *you* do business.

> Tendering for work is time consuming and can be non-productive. It's essential to implement a streamlined system for dealing with it, to manage the process and to decide on your initial financial criteria for pursuing the work.

> Because the motivational aspects of tendering can be high, it is worth trying to recreate them in respect of other areas of business development by setting clear sales objectives, undertaking a timebound sales push and reviewing performance.

> Referrals are a traditional source of work for most firms and effective management can dramatically improve performance and consolidate relationships.

> Successful cross-selling often results from putting the onus for selling additional services to a client on the person who already has a relationship with them, rather than the colleague who is seeking to sell them their services.

Management

Strategic management and structure

KEY ISSUES

- What is management?
- The importance of strategic management
- Structural issues
- Why have teams?
- The decision-making process
- Choosing leaders and managers
- Partners and their roles

Think about your firm – do you recognise any of these problems?

	YES	NO
Dealing with management problems was proving too time-consuming, so we have taken on a practice manager to do all that for us.		
Running a tight ship and keeping a close eye on the bottom line – that's what successful management is all about.		
The hardest part of being managing partner is dealing with all the partner politicking – it's no mean feat trying to keep the peace.		
Yes, I would have to admit that we have a couple of partners who just coast along – but we can't get rid of them and they won't change the habits of a lifetime, so we just have to work around them.		
The real power base in our firm lies with the head of the litigation team – his department earns the most fees.		
All our partners are made responsible for some aspect of management. The junior partner ended up in charge of marketing because no one else wanted to do it.		

We've grown so big, we probably need to restructure but we don't know how.		
As the partnership has grown, it's become almost impossible to make decisions on anything – everyone has an equal vote and wants to have their say on how things are run.		

Assuming you didn't answer 'no' to all the above, then you should read on.

What is management?

> 'To manage is to forecast and plan, to organise, to command, to coordinate and to control.'
>
> Henri Fayol (nineteenth-century theorist)

Reams have been written about management – style, approach, responsibilities and so on – and there are many books that are well worth reading. What we want to focus on here is why management is particularly important, yet often especially complex, for professional services firms and offer some practical guidance on issues to consider and how you should go about instilling an effective management process in your firm.

Many professional firms confuse administration with management and argue 'we've never needed management in the past, why do we need it now?'. It is invariably these firms – which fail to distinguish between strategic and purely operational management – that struggle to develop their business.

Management, in essence, is a *series of interventions* which, together, govern the way a firm is run – how its people behave, how services are delivered to its clients, how it reacts to change, everything from crucial strategic issues down to who orders the paper clips. But of course, there's a fine line between management and interference: achieving the balance between 'letting people get on with it' and guiding, chivvying, encouraging and leading them to perform – and taking action if they don't – may feel like an almost impossible task. In the next chapter, we shall deal with some aspects of this type of day-to-day operational management. This, however, forms merely part of what must be considered here – namely, *strategic* management of the firm as a whole.

Strategic management, particularly in the context of professional services firms, breaks down into a number of 'hard' and 'soft' elements as shown in Figure 6.1. Each aspect of management influences and underpins the others. Table 6.1 shows the range of matters to be addressed under each hard and soft element – undeniable evidence of the exceedingly wide spectrum of issues which come under the umbrella called 'management'.

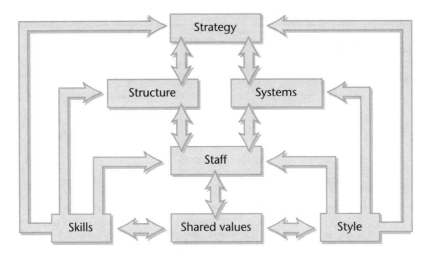

Figure 6.1 Elements of strategic management (adapted McKinsey's 7-S framework)

The importance of strategic management

Poor management – both of strategic issues and people – emerges as one of the biggest causes of complaint in staff surveys. Part of the problem is that many partners still do not regard managing as a skill in itself, requiring training and aptitude, and/or they simply don't feel that most issues within the firm need managing. Whilst it's true that if things are left to their own devices, *something* will eventually happen, the invariable result is muddled or non-existent strategic management, inefficient administration of the business and disaffected staff.

Where management is concerned, three common misconceptions abound in small to medium-sized professional services firms which add up to what is perhaps their biggest barrier to progress:

1. Management is something that just comes naturally.
2. Management is something which can be 'fitted in' around 'proper' work.
3. The management function is inherently inferior in nature and importance to 'real' fee-earning work.

Any firm brave enough to tackle these issues and take the risks needed to turn them on their head will have tackled one of the most fundamental obstacles to its future success.

Table 6.1 Management orientation, focus and task

Management orientation	Management focus	Management task
Hard	Strategy	Defines and champions firm's vision Takes and maintains an overview of resource implications Assures implementation of business plan Ensures unity of direction and purpose Reviews progress and seeks adjustment as necessary
	Structure	Acts as authority figure, providing stability and order Ensures appropriate division of labour Implements appropriate balance of centralisation and decentralisation of tasks
	Systems	Oversees administrative order Facilitates appropriate vertical and horizontal channels of communication Monitors financial and other measures of performance
Soft	Staff	Motivates workforce Facilitates good employee relations Champions initiatives Ensures appropriate remuneration and fairness
	Skills	Ensures every level of workforce has sufficient resources and training to carry out their tasks
	Shared values	Identifies and upholds firm's values
	Style	Balances individual aims with group goals and needs

The role of management

The role of strategic management can be defined as follows:

1. *To coordinate the effort, talent, product and purpose of the organisation.* Good management can turn the organisation into an identifiable entity with a collective sense of where it wants to go, instead of being a group of unrelated individuals each with their own agenda.
2. *To provide reassurance.* One of the key roles of management is simply to 'be there', to be seen to be there and to be involved. Human nature dictates that people hate to work in a vacuum – and with something as long drawn-out as delivering professional services, often client feedback isn't regularly forthcoming. Management can provide the reassurance that someone is there, taking an interest, monitoring

progress, acting as a source of information, praise and even punishment. As with small children, being ignored or feeling that no one is in charge is also most adults' worst possible emotional state!

3. *To be the guardian of the firm's culture and to articulate its values.* Culture is what people pay attention to. It includes the firm's spoken and unspoken rules – what is accepted or rejected, what is rewarded or punished and all formal and informal communications.

4. *To provide a framework for leadership throughout the firm.* No matter what level of leadership a person is able or empowered to exert, or what style of leadership they adopt, they will be directly influenced by the manner in which the firm's senior management body – whether this be a sole managing partner and/or a management board or committee – conducts itself.

Those charged with strategic management of the practice must aim for maximum effectiveness on all fronts in order to prosper and grow – mere operational efficiency will not be enough to prevent the organisation from gradually losing ground and declining – see Figure 6.2. It used to be the case that all a manager needed to know was more about the work than those who they managed and, for this reason, there was a certain logic in appointing partners with seniority to management roles. However, the world has changed and this requirement, although still useful in its place, is no longer enough. Good managers need to know more about management than those they manage. It's as simple as that.

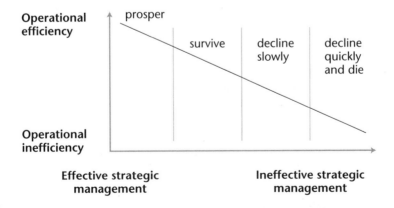

Figure 6.2 Operational vs strategic management (adapted from Christopher et al.)

Management and marketing

Management is particularly important in the context of marketing which is defined by the Chartered Institute of Marketing as 'the management process responsible for identifying, anticipating and meeting customers' needs profitably'. Note those words – 'management process'. They mean that, by definition, marketing is inextricably bound to management and must be subject to all it entails.

As you will have seen by now, effective marketing involves going through the sequence illustrated in Figure 6.3. All of this needs managing. There are more examples in professional services firms than perhaps any other market sector of those who naively hoped the process would happen by itself without management intervention – and were proved horribly wrong.

Often marketing failure can be put down to misunderstanding about roles and, frankly, passing the buck by those who should know better. For example, recognising a need for improved marketing performance, the firm appoints a marketing assistant or manager to 'manage' marketing. However, the person appointed has neither the strategic skills nor the professional experience to do so, nor are they given the level of authority or influence they need to be effective. What they are really being asked to do, therefore, and all they can do, is *administer* the tactical marketing programme – a vastly different exercise from strategic marketing management.

Management and motivation

'Effective managers are people who are able to see what the world looks like from another person's point of view.'
Nigel Nicholson (*Managing the Human Animal*, Texere Publishing, 2000)

By definition an organisation cannot manage itself. Management involves getting things done through others and there are two important implications of this approach:

1. You need those you manage more than they need you (they're actually coming up with the goods).

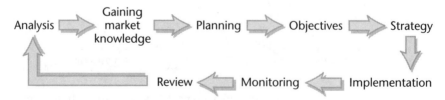

Figure 6.3 The marketing sequence

2. Your success and remuneration is dependent on what they do, not what you do (they're earning the fees).

In professional services organisations, the product itself (legal/accountancy/surveying services, for instance) is only ever deliverable through people. This means that, in determining strategic direction and approach, it is vital for senior management to ensure that the workforce is also on board and fully motivated. If the staff of an organisation are demotivated to the point of apathy or rebellion, then no matter how dynamic and customer-focused the management board may be, their best-laid plans will be doomed to failure.

Just in case you still need to be convinced of the link between management and motivation, consider the connection which has been discovered in recent research between a happy, motivated workforce on the one hand and higher profitability and more satisfied clients on the other.

Why is it so difficult to manage professional services firms?

The reason is quite simple and it boils down to the fact that professional services firms operate (as a rule) as partnerships. The partnership is a peculiar beast, not respecting of conventional corporate rules and discipline. Its essential characteristics are these:

- It comprises a unique set of separate powerful personalities.
- Professional services partners tend to be analytical, critical and somewhat sceptical individuals (qualities instilled by their professional training, no doubt).
- Several giant-sized egos and possibly one or two conflicting private agendas may be involved.
- Partners are each other's peers – this makes it very difficult for them to agree on, let alone ever apply, sanctions against each other.
- The above problems are self-perpetuating. There is always the next generation waiting to become partners who emulate the bad behaviour of their superiors because they believe this is what is expected of them.

If professional services firms are to prosper and grow in today's market, they must overcome these problems – perhaps by starting to operate along corporate lines. Discipline and accountability must be instilled within the management body itself and these rules for implementation of an effective management programme followed:

- *Rule One.* Aim for operational ease – straightforwardness and simplicity are the key.
- *Rule Two.* Achieve firm-wide integration – effective team-working and cross-team benchmarking will ensue.

- *Rule Three*. Focus on staff ability – properly trained and motivated staff of the right calibre are essential.
- *Rule Four*. Set clear objectives – aim to arrive at a shared understanding of what the firm as a whole and each individual within it are trying to achieve.

Structural issues

There is no right way to manage. To quote Raymond Miles and Charles Snow: 'Efficient organisations establish mechanisms that complement their market strategy'.

There are countless theories of management out there, resulting in as many different ways to manage as there are people and situations to be managed. But, while theories are fine in management textbooks, it is in trying to make them actually work that one can run into difficulties.

In determining the right way for your firm, regard must be had to the defining characteristics of your organisation and the defining characteristics of the market place in which you operate. The needs, aspirations, skills, values and cultural norms and attitudes of the people involved – both as individuals and as a group – must be taken into account. Together, these aspects produce your firm's culture and it is culture which intrinsically influences one of the critical considerations of management – how your firm is structured.

Structural implications

Although there is no uniform ideal for professional services firms, structure has implications. As professional services marketing guru, David Maister points out (*True Professionalism*, The Free Press, 1997): 'Firms are free to make whatever choices they prefer, as long as they acknowledge the trade-offs involved. If a firm cannot make a policy to which everyone must adhere, it will be literally impossible for the firm to develop a firm-wide reputation, a brand image or a common culture.'

So no matter how a firm appears to be structured, its real modus operandi will be reflective of its underlying culture. That said, however, it is possible to identify certain structural types which commonly feature in the professional services sector.

Feudal

Many firms operate as a loose association of fiefdoms. There will typically be a number of individual departments based on work type, each one classed as a separate profit centre and headed by a partner who rules it as their own separate little state. This structure by its inherent nature, works to make management a chore – everything needs general consent, subterfuge, pressure and ceaseless negotiation in order to achieve coordinated effort. In terms of efficient operating procedures, service standards and staff satisfaction, it can be a massive millstone. To the outside world and particularly, say, to a client who utilises the services of more than one department in the firm, the resulting fragmented picture is a marketing disaster in terms of trying to present a cohesive brand image.

The way forward is to put the existing hierarchy on the back burner and introduce a more appropriate operating structure, which sees work teams focused around external needs, and leadership delegated according to ability rather than lust for power. You'll find it works – some of the most successful businesses around are those who have cleared the status hurdle and now concentrate on how best to get the job done.

Anarchic

Although many firms proudly proclaim they are democratic, in reality they are anarchies. They undertake strategic planning, create teams, and set up monitoring and review systems, but what they actually achieve is dependent on the inclination of each individual partner to deliver the goods. The majority do not, so, in effect, anarchy rules.

Turning an anarchic culture into something more positive and productive can be difficult but, essentially, it will depend on taking a firm line on non-compliance and introducing both incentives for good behaviour and some meaningful sanctions for those who refuse to play ball.

Dictatorship

In this scenario, real power is in the hands of a single individual or a small and, usually, close-knit group. Information is disseminated on a need to know basis, decisions are taken without consultation and the whole operation is generally ruled with an iron fist (although the 'dictator' in question would probably prefer to term it 'strong leadership'). The news isn't all bad though – dictatorships can be highly effective and some of the most dynamic commercial enterprises have thrived thanks to the initial vision and energies of one individual or minority group. However, the growth of larger partnerships driven by the need to provide a wider range of services, the realisation that effective group dynamics are necessary to achieve goals and the unacceptability of bullying has led to the downfall of the old commonly recognised benevolent dictatorship. Although such a structure or style may survive for a while, particularly in a falling market, the inevitable result is that those over whom the dictator rules will eventually revolt – back to the motivation factor. Recognition of effort, individual advancement and involvement in decisions and intitiatives are not really on the menu for most dictators. However, in the absence of such motivating factors, most minions will sooner or later move on to more democratic climes.

Democracy

The essence of a democracy, according to Maister is that: 'issues are broadly debated, consultation is extensive, a majority position is identified, and (here's the defining moment) if a new policy receives majority support, it becomes law and everyone must conform to it'.

To succeed in today's fiercely competitive market place a firm must agree, consensually, where it wants to go and how it is going to get there and allocate tasks to ensure this happens. It sounds logical and is something with which most commercial (i.e. non-professional) organisations – with their hierarchical structure, and culture of accountability – don't have a problem. However, professional partnerships continue to struggle, reinventing plans and procedures rather than tackling the real problem which prevents them moving forward – non-performance and non-conformity.

To be a truly successful democracy the firm must devise acceptable means of exercising social and financial controls against those who fail to comply, and be prepared, if necessary, to exercise sanctions against those who still follow their own agenda. Not to do so, through poor monitoring or management cowardice, undermines the whole democratic basis of the practice, demotivating those who *have* performed. If your partnership follows this pattern, you are allowing your rogue partners to win every time simply because, by not taking action, the rest of the group is effectively endorsing their behaviour.

Ironically, arriving at true democracy is often harder for small and medium-sized firms than it is for the larger organisations. In a smaller partnership, styles of management are likely to be deeply entrenched and there may be no clear route to dealing with partner performance or under-performance.

Choosing a structure

Usually, of course, structure is not chosen – rather, it will be the lot of the hapless, newly elected managing partner to inherit a structure which was probably devised when the firm was a tenth of the size and which is now loaded down with cultural and political baggage from the past.

How your firm is physically organised, however, is one of the key considerations when looking at implementing effective management systems.

The first thing to think about is that, whatever structure you choose, it should be relevant to and should be aimed at facilitating the external and internal marketing ethos and efforts of the firm.

The vast majority of firms we see persist in grouping their people together according to work type – thus, in many law firms, there will be a department which deals only with wills and probate, one which handles personal injury matters, one labelled residential conveyancing and then the 'star' department which deals exclusively with corporate work and whose clients are so important and sophisticated that their identities must (seemingly anyway) be kept secret from the remainder of the firm.

It seems there is almost a theory in these firms that too much contact with fee-earners from another discipline will lead to some sort of natural erosion of specialist abilities and knowledge. Perhaps none of the above would be so bad if only the different departments got together and regularly shared knowledge about their respective clients, prospects and contacts. The trouble is, this tends not to happen and the work-type structure simply becomes a barrier to:

- delivery of service to existing clients;
- marketing efforts in respect of new business development;
- internal communication and motivation.

Clients are individuals first and foremost – someone who comes to a law firm as the representative of a business client will perhaps mainly deal with the head of the corporate team. However, in an individual capacity, they may well at some stage decide to make a will, or suffer an accident in respect of which they want to seek compensation, or want to move house. If the physical structure of the firm and its resultant underlying culture mean that the corporate client in our example and those providing private client services are never introduced to each other, valuable marketing opportunities will have been lost.

The word 'clients', at grass roots level, means 'people' and every firm, no matter how big or small, must manage itself in such a way that clients are treated as such and that their multiplicity of needs across different disciplines and practice areas is catered for in a way which is relevant and convenient to them. A client-facing structure addresses these issues by basing itself on what clients need.

Although it is tempting – because it is what we are familiar and comfortable with – to perpetuate the status quo and stick with work-type organisation (in other words, structure according to function), it is worthwhile taking a moment to consider the relative merits and disadvantages of each structural option as summarised as in Table 6.2. There is, of course, no perfect structural blueprint for any organisation, certainly not for professional services organisations where the nature of the product and the medium through which it is delivered are highly intangible concepts.

Probably the best approach in practice is to aim for a mixed structure – a sort of matrix management system which takes a client focus as its principal foundation but then allows for a mixture of purely client sector or service groups and work-type teams to overlay it.

Table 6.2 Client-facing vs functional structure

Structural option	Advantages	Disadvantages
Client-facing/ service-based structure	Focused marketing decisions Improved client relationships (because structured according to client needs) Improved cross-selling opportunities Aid to positive team working and internal communication Tends to increase market/client knowledge Vehicle for creativity	Can lead to duplication of effort Increased structural complexity (e.g. if individual's expertise is required in more than one team)
Function/practice area structure	Logical and familiar therefore may be simpler to manage Aids clear allocation of work according to specialism Can facilitate/promote increased specialist knowledge in areas of expertise Financial profitability of work types more visible	Leads to poor internal communication Tends to inhibit creativity Limits cross-selling Client needs become an incidental rather than the central focus

CASE STUDY **Divide and rule**

Law firm XY & Co has grown considerably over the past few years and the new managing partner thinks it's time for a restructure. But how, he wonders, to go about this? In a full service firm, the permutations are endless. Having recently attended a seminar on marketing awareness, he decides to start by dividing the firm into two broad groups, representative of its main client profile – business clients and private clients.

'Good,' he thinks, 'in fact, excellent – the word "client" actually features in the name of each department which will help focus the internal mindset of the firm on our most important asset.'

The private client group naturally includes the residential conveyancers and family law practitioners as well as the probate lawyers. Likewise, in the business sector department, the commercial property lawyers could be placed in small, market-facing teams catering for the firm's retail clients, industrial property clients, and so on. A recent contact with the local Business Link was producing regular instructions from those setting up new enterprises so the managing partner forms a business start-up team.

'But what' he ponders, 'am I to do about the employment lawyers?' Their area is one of specific expertise but they have both corporate and individual clients. He doesn't want to break the team up, but should they go into the business sector department or the private client group?

Finally, after much agonising, he remembers something said at the end of the seminar – don't get hung up on the structural detail. 'That's it' he decides, 'it doesn't matter which group they belong to internally. What's more important is that they stay together as a team and they will have to work extra hard at communicating with every other team in the firm.'

Why have teams?

Several in the services professions would no doubt argue that their best work is done in splendid isolation. Working in groups is all very well they say but, as there is less room for error in the legal/accountancy/surveying world than in other walks of life, it pays – in terms of helping to protect the insurance policy – for one fee-earner to have complete care and conduct of each particular matter. Consequently, while many firms consist of a number of work-type departments, these tend to exist primarily for reasons of financial and administrative convenience.

While administrative convenience is a valid and common reason for the existence of teams (even in small and medium-sized firms, breaking the organisation down into a number of subgroups will tend to aid day-to-day management and financial control), many firms never get beyond this elementary level of justification and fail to appreciate that team working, provided it is pursued and developed properly, can lend an added dynamic to the internal functioning and external output of the firm. More importantly, the team is the vehicle through which the firm can deliver a truly market- and client-focused service. The specific advantages that a team can offer include:

- defining and upholding shared standards and procedures;
- effective means of delegation and balancing work-flow;
- peer pressure in respect of group performance;
- substitution – resulting in being able to provide a seamless service.

Although teams consist of individuals, the contribution of a good team will always exceed the sum of its parts. The essence of good team working is:

- to recognise that every individual has a contribution to make in the nature and quality of the service ultimately received by the firm's clients;
- to assemble or restructure the team in such a way that the right mix of personality types is brought together;
- to ensure that the appointed head of the team has the appropriate style and skills to be able to positively develop the particular team of which they are in charge.

A team is a collection of individuals bound together by a number of unifying threads (see Figure 6.4) in order to form a cohesive whole, including:

- unity of purpose;
- a set of recognised objectives;
- a mix of complementary skills and abilities;
- a sense of collective responsibility and accountability.

Building the team

In a professional services organisation, many individuals will simultaneously be members of a number of different teams of varying sizes and these can be either formal or informal. A fee-earner, for example, will typically belong to a main work/service team or department and, at the same time, might be a member of a temporary client project team within the department, part of a newly convened marketing focus group which meets intermittently and captain of the firm's football eleven.

Whilst the significance of informal teams should not be overlooked as an aid to staff bonding and motivation, what we are concerned with here is how to build and develop formal teams.

Teams form naturally around a common purpose. The trick – which has been learnt by the successful firms – is, first, to recognise that this is the case and, secondly, to know how to foster and promote team conception and development in such a way that the marketing and management of the firm are improved and internal motivation levels are boosted. See Table 6.3.

Figure 6.4   The unifying elements of a team

Table 6.3 Implications of the team

Motivational aspect	Marketing implication	Management implication
Team has unity of ideas and purpose and decides on clear roles and responsibilities	Team is able to implement and achieve focused marketing strategy	Effectively functioning teams means more efficient and devolved management style

The functions of teams

How many and what sort of teams you should have in your firm will depend on the features, nature and size of your organisation. Clearly, there will be a need for a number of work teams and, as already touched on in this chapter, it is recommended that these, as far as possible, are given a client or service focus.

But it is also worth considering whether other – non-work – teams can be formulated: they can often be a distinct aid to management and motivation as well as helping with the implementation of the firm's strategic marketing plans.

Although large firms often have in-house 'experts' in charge of core functions such as marketing, IT, training, HR, and so on, smaller firms typically won't have these. In many small firms, the managing partner is expected to be in charge of and actively involved with all of these areas while carrying a pretty full fee-earning caseload. Even in larger organisations, senior management can quickly find themselves drawn into the nitty-gritty of non-strategic, sometimes inconsequential issues. Consider setting up a management team with a member of staff in charge of day-to-day operational management of each area (for example, a partner or senior fee-earner might head up the marketing, training and HR functions; maybe a senior secretary could be placed in charge of the IT team). Each team should report on a regular basis to the managing partner or management board, freeing them to direct time and attention to areas of more strategic importance and concern.

Marketing focus teams can be set up as a vehicle for concentrated new business development. They might be of only temporary duration (depending on objectives and whether/at what stage the objectives are met) and might not need to meet as frequently as work teams. Rather than tackling new business development through work teams, marketing groups are an ideal means of reaching over work ('product') boundaries and drawing together relevant personnel from different disciplines, which can provide a tremendous boost to cross-selling, creativity and ideas.

Another form of occasional team is the special project group. You might set one of these up if, for example, the firm decides to apply for a quality award or invest in a new IT software system. Rather than expecting a single person to take on the responsibility for the project, a team consisting of members who represent all areas and levels of the firm will stand a much better chance of gaining commitment and cooperation from all concerned, meaning, in turn, that the project itself has more prospect of success.

The decision-making process

> 'The best thing you can do in my organisation is to make the right decision; the next best thing is to make the wrong decision. What gets you fired is to make no decision.'
>
> Percy Barnevik, Swedish CEO

Management consists basically of getting things done through others so, by definition, it is all to do with delegation, which the dictionary defines as, 'entrusting or committing to a subordinate'. In the case of strategic management of a professional services organisation, 'subordinate' will actually mean the firm's managing partner, practice manager or management committee or board.

In a small firm, for instance one with only three or four partners, the senior management team responsible for taking decisions will usually comprise the whole partnership who take decisions on the basis of a majority vote; many firms get by very happily using this arrangement.

Larger firms, however, would find their management efforts severely hampered if full or even majority consensus of the partnership were to be required for every aspect of running the practice. Where the firm has grown to a certain size, therefore, it becomes more appropriate to devolve functional power and decision making to a smaller group which, in turn, might delegate a degree of authority to a single person.

What's crucial – if the firm is to operate as a democracy as we have suggested it should – is that the management structure and its decision-making procedures are transparent and clearly defined and that its outcomes are regarded as obligatory for all.

It will be the task of the other key component of effective management – the role and ability of the managers themselves – to ensure that this happens.

Choosing leaders and managers

> 'A business short on capital can borrow money, but a business short of leadership has little chance of survival.'
>
> John Adair

Throughout the professions and even the wider commercial world, managers tend to be chosen according to how well they have performed in their field of specialisation, whether it is technical or service based. Although this has some validity for purely supervisory roles, where the manager generally needs to be familiar with the work their team is carrying out, once you get to the level of strategic management an entirely different skill set is required, and the person most suitable for the job may not necessarily be the one who has the greatest amount of technical ability. Alternatively (and probably even worse) in professional services firms, just having been around for long enough – the seniority factor – will be sufficient to merit election to the higher echelons of management.

Often management is viewed as a poisoned chalice and the person who ends up in the role is there by default.

In fact, because of all that effective strategic and efficient operational management entails, the personal qualities of the manager are crucial in achieving results. Essential qualities include:

- vision – both short and long term;
- knowledge of the market place within which the firm operates (though this can be learnt);
- ability to motivate;
- ability to listen;
- ability to make decisions and stick by them;
- an understanding of the role of communication;
- a sense of accountability.

In addition, a good manager must pay attention to the following key aspects of the managerial role:

- *informational* – the manager must collect, coordinate, monitor and disseminate information and act as a spokesperson;
- *inter-personal* – the manager must fulfil the functions of figurehead and ensure liaison between groups and individuals as well as providing coaching and mentoring when necessary;
- *decisional* – the manager is a negotiator, responsible for allocation of resources, for settling disputes and setting priorities;
- *entrepreneurial* – the manager is a provider of new ideas, ensures action and acts as a source of motivation;
- *leadership* – marketing and management guru, John Kotter, wrote in the *Harvard Business Review* that 'leadership and management are distinctive and complementary systems of action'. The role of the leader, he argued, is highly strategic – it is to determine direction, to communicate that direction to the organisation and to motivate and inspire people to follow it ('What leaders really do', John P. Kotter, *Harvard Business Review*, June 1990).

The nature of the job involves fragmentation of activities, frequent inter-ruptions, variety, challenge and, usually, a frenetic pace. A lot of time will be spent in meetings, in liaison with internal and external contacts and in one-to-one motivational, review or problem-solving discussions.

CASE STUDY   **A leap of faith**

One of the most worthwhile risks that a firm can take if it wants to move for-ward is to try allowing the managing partner to drop all fee-earning work during their period of office in order to give them the time needed to take the firm forward.

The reason why many dare not do this is that the managing partner is often one of the highest fee-earners in the firm (high fees = high clout) and the firm is (naturally) unwilling to lose those fees. Evidence has shown, how-ever, that with proper delegation and management the managing partner's work can be done by others so that the fees need not be lost.

This can also be a good strategy to pursue when a firm doesn't have enough work. The managing partner passes their workload to another partner, and devotes 100 per cent resource to managing the firm and undertaking new business development. This does, however, mean that barriers and issues regarding trust and ownership need to be resolved at the outset.

Charisma and energy are key attributes. And remember – the most effective manager is unlikely to be the firm's highest fee-earner since the personal attributes required for each role in professional services firms are often incompatible.

Indeed, the lack of recognition of the importance of full-time, on-going management roles within professional services firms and the failure to appreciate exactly what they involve is one of the biggest handicaps that small and medium-sized firms face in becoming commercially competitive.

In smaller firms, those who produce the business must also be the managers of it and do dozens of other tasks that would and will be dele-gated as soon as the company starts to expand and prosper. In profes-sional firms, however, support staff, IT staff, administrative staff, HR and marketing staff are all much higher on the list than the management function per se. This is a short-sighted policy. The more those ranks grow, the more management is needed, therefore the pressures on beleaguered working partners to manage, in addition to their fee-earning jobs, gets worse and worse. More ends up being invested with very little of the potential output of the situation realised – simply because the firm is unwilling to acknowledge the true role of management.

Think hard about taking on the services of one or more non-executive directors. Their commercial nous and contacts can be invaluable; their ability to bring a fresh perspective to what you are doing – whether or not you agree with them – can be incredibly helpful when seeking to resolve internal issues. Professional paranoia and pride often prevent partnerships going down this route – it's almost as if they fear being found out, while the idea that someone else could have anything useful to say about their business is anathema. Once again, however, it is common commercial practice. Stop and think why.

Similarly, examine the role of non-core personnel in your organisation, by which we mean the likes of financial, HR and marketing professionals. Although it is more common for the former to have a place on the management board and (almost by definition) a finger in most pies throughout the firm, the skills and experience of the other two are often ignored. Research into the roles of HR and marketing professionals within the professions reveals that:

- they are often treated as second-class citizens;
- they are not consulted on wider issues affecting the firm, for example, restructuring, mergers, and so on, even though these have enormous implications for their area of specialisation;
- they are usually not party to the firm's business plan so have only an incomplete picture of what the firm is attempting to achieve;
- they are usually utilised for their day-to-day tactical skills rather than for strategic advice and implementation.

Yet, to hark back to the obvious again, most commercial concerns have these people on their management committee – and for obvious reasons. Their experience and skills are perceived as being worth the value that is invested in them.

In smaller firms there may only be a practice manager to undertake all of these roles but, if so, choose someone with one key strength (e.g. finance) and the ability to recognise what is needed in external advisers.

Outsourcing can be a good way of working, especially for firms which are not large enough to carry the continuous overhead of an HR professional or marketing expert, but if the relationship is to succeed, you have to be focused about what you want to achieve and succinct in your dealings with the service provider. Internally, make it very clear to everyone that they are dealing with an expensive commodity which can provide real added value to the firm.

Succession issues

Many firms think of succession issues purely in terms of the most senior roles within the firm: who is retiring or stepping down and when and who will be the next managing partner, chairman, and so on. What is often overlooked, however, is who would succeed in any one of a number of other circumstances – the sudden death or serious illness of a leading player, a sudden defection – or similar circumstances affecting if not the key players then those on whom they rely heavily. For example, consider those who deal with practical matters in the office – accounts, facilities management, HR issues, marketing – what would happen if anything happened to them? Do they have a good system of records and guidance notes, or is it all kept in their heads? When do they plan to retire and who will take over from them?

Valuable time can be lost when a comparative newcomer has to start from scratch in any job – far better that they can learn alongside the present incumbent, even if the intention is that they should eventually do things entirely differently.

An effective management solution when things are not running as smoothly as you would like due to the dyed-in-the-wool ways of the person currently carrying out the job, is to take on their successor at an early stage. Those who are having to endure the less than perfect service can see that the end is in sight, while the person who is to take over has an opportunity to work with them and canvass their views from a very early stage about how they would like to see things done in the future.

Partners and their roles

As we have already mentioned, many of the difficulties in running a professional services firm stem from the fact that, usually at least, it consists of a partnership.

The very term 'partnership' implies a level of parity – partners own the business between them; they share its client base and profits; and collectively suffer its problems and losses. In the professional services sector, the partners and those employed by them are the medium through which the firm's services are delivered. The relative success or failure of the practice will be directly linked to the nature, extent and quality of the contribution made by each individual.

On the other hand, the partners are also the stakeholders of the business – it is they who have invested in the firm and they who therefore expect a worthwhile return.

The trouble is, the contribution made by each partner will not be equal for the simple and rather obvious reason that everyone has a different set of skills and level of ability in any particular area.

We shall look at how disparate offerings should impact on the question of partner reward later. The immediate question is how differing personal skills and qualities can be harnessed by firms into filling the myriad roles that feed into its strategic management scene.

Horses for courses

A wise old managing partner held the view that partner roles should be allocated on a 'horses for courses' basis. Not everyone, he maintained, could be equally good at exactly the same things. This didn't matter as there was a great range of different tasks and roles within management, so it was simply a matter of matching roles to relevant talent.

Long before a certain management guru coined the phrase, he said that those in professional services organisations generally fell into one of three categories – finders, minders and grinders – and that people should be given freedom to concentrate on whichever one it was that they were good at. They should work at improving in that area rather than waste time and risk losing morale by trying to become something which it was not in their nature to be.

There is a lot to be said for this approach.

Some people are naturally gifted at getting out and about, making new contacts, pursuing leads and extolling the virtues of the firm. These people are the finders. Make them responsible for developing new business but give them, first, the freedom (that is, time) to do it by reducing fee-earning commitments or relieving them, where necessary, of other tasks. Secondly, give them the motivation by recognising and rewarding their business development effort and results as much as you would bottom-line financial performance.

Others, unable to handle the pressure of making completely new contacts with all its associations with cold-calling and the like, are much better at developing and maximising existing relationships. Such people are the minders – the champions of the firm's service quality. Put them in charge of managing key client relationships and monitoring competitor activity to ward off poaching attempts by other firms.

Then there are the individuals whose love in life is to churn out the work, lots of it, consistently and well. Frankly, without the grinders, the firm will not have any product offering. Take grinders away from the sharp end of business development – they hate it and are not often particularly good at it anyway.

This view of things does not mean there is never a role for grinders to play in marketing – get them to write an article about the latest hot topic in their area of practice as a contribution to the firm's promotional activities. Nor does it mean that finders and minders should not have to do any fee-earning work. What it does mean is that it is worth paying attention to what your people are naturally good at and feel comfortable with before wasting time and effort trying to force square pegs into round holes. It also means deciding exactly how important you think each type of contribution is to the operation and development of your business and then actively valuing that contribution accordingly. Consider closely, however, what you want the future structure of the firm to look like and, if you know that you need to have people with different qualities, take them on – even at a fairly junior level – and resist the temptation or pressure from others to perpetuate the status quo.

Although partners are the business owners, they are also a fundamental part of its resource. Applying the horses for courses philosophy to the selection of partner roles is a means of managing that resource.

Partner performance

Given that partners' contributions across a range of issues will not be equal, how should firms deal with assessing partner performance – should they assess it at all? And how should they approach partner reward or, in some cases, sanction lack of performance?

Traditionally, partner progression and reward has operated on a lockstep basis – the more senior (that is, long serving) the partner, the further up the ladder to full equity they moved. An individual would only make it to junior partner if their face fitted, and in the less competitive market place than today's it meant that once you were in, there was no need to do anything other than turn up, do some work and wait for time to do the rest.

More recently, rising levels of competition within and between the professions and, it has to be said, increasing awareness and ability amongst the younger generations of professionals in respect of business development techniques, has meant that in order to become a partner, it is necessary for an individual to demonstrate that they can add value to the business.

The problem in many firms is that, whilst the young guns are obliged to rise up the ranks the hard way having constantly to prove their rainmaker abilities, the partnership is still being run on a traditional lockstep basis and there may be several within it who are content to take the same share of compensation without making any more of an effort than they ever used to. To say that this leads to friction and fall-out is an under statement. As one partner put it: 'lockstep is a great strategy so long as everyone is pulling their weight'.

Recognising that such systems are anachronistic, some of the larger firms are either completely changing their compensation structure or – because full meritocracy is still generally regarded as rather too aggressive – are, at least, introducing a performance-based element to partner compensation.

Introducing a merit-based system of reward is not necessarily as easy as it sounds though. As we saw earlier, different people are good (and not so good) at different things – for example, when it comes to business development skills, most would agree that there are very few who are naturally excellent marketers.

Also, it is easy to measure performance which comes with tangible indicators – someone who is good at churning out bills, accurately recording time, keeping on top of credit control. With other skills, such as managing people, networking, giving presentations and so on, it is not so easy to measure success. The difficulty in measuring intangible outcomes makes it hard for firms to assess just how important each attribute or contribution is to them.

Firms must sit down and find a way to do this, however, if they are to harness the improvement and benefits that are there to be realised in a merit-based culture of partner performance. Assuming that merit-based reward is the way forward for all modern partnerships, there are some rules to be followed when evaluating partner performance:

- Define, clearly, the criteria for good performance. Remember, people have ability in different areas. You need to rate each type of contribution according to how much value it adds to your firm.
- Introduce an even-handed, open partner appraisal system. This must follow the usual rules for conducting effective appraisals (which are discussed fully in Chapter 10) and should be an interactive forum, giving the partner concerned the opportunity to demonstrate why they should continue to enjoy such status.
- Ensure everyone knows the agenda and the rules – what will happen in the case of good or high performance and what are the sanctions for lack of it.
- Aim to instil a culture of performance in your partnership, not an annual day of reckoning which is then put on the back burner for the rest of the time.

Most firms, if they are honest (and even if they only have an unspoken, mental rather than formal set of criteria on which to judge) can quickly identify at least one or two partners in their organisation who are 'coasters' or 'passengers' or 'letting the side down'. The question is, what to do about it?

The first step is to consider why there is a problem:

- Is the under-performer approaching retirement? Would early retirement and a move into part-time consultancy be the answer?
- Is the under-performer suffering stress or illness? Consider whether workloads and responsibilities need to be adjusted or reduced.
- Is the partner concerned an inherently poor manager of their own time or unsure and unpractised in business development skills such as networking or selling? Here, providing coaching and training may

be all that is required to get the problem sorted and the partner back on track.

Occasionally, the poor (or non-existent) performance is habitual and may even be deliberate (we've all come across a total maverick from time to time). In such cases, for the greater good of the firm, there is nothing for it but for management to get tough. Some firms operate a yellow card/red card system where one or two offences merit a warning but anything further results in dismissal or removal. Other possible sanctions include de-equitisation and/or withholding an element of partner reward.

POINTS TO REMEMBER

➤ Successful management entails looking at the 'hard' elements of strategy, structure and systems and the 'soft' aspects of staff, skills, style and values and recognising the ways in which these impact upon each other.

➤ Management does not happen all by itself – it requires positive intervention at numerous different levels.

➤ Management is an essential process in marketing and – since it involves getting things done through people – is inextricably bound up with motivation.

➤ Power politics, powerful personalities and personal agendas can prove some of the hallmarks of professional partnerships but can present major barriers to the implementation of effective management.

➤ When choosing an internal structure, professional firms should consider what formation will facilitate their marketing aims and objectives, such as service delivery and client relationship management.

➤ A team must have unity of purpose, shared objectives and a sense of collective responsibility.

➤ Teams can be used to fulfil other functions beyond production of the work itself – operational management teams, marketing focus groups and special project teams will all assist with effective management, achievement of marketing strategy and can help boost internal motivation.

➤ The best managers and leaders will be those chosen on the basis of their management abilities not merely according to rank or seniority.

Operations management

Think about your firm – do you recognise any of these problems?

	YES	NO
Looked at on paper, the firm's very profitable. But if you look at how much we have to write off, it's a totally different story. How can we improve?		
Clients love to complain about everything, but my only genuine complaint about clients is that they don't pay their bills!		
I don't hold with delegation – if you want a job doing properly, do it yourself I always say.		
We all know we ought to be doing more marketing – but it's a matter of finding the time.		
There's nothing wrong with our appraisal system – but most of the managers just never get round to carrying them out.		
We all thought that installing an impressive new IT system would solve problems – instead of which it seems to have created even more.		

By now we had planned to have a fully integrated case management system, but some of the partners just won't change their working practices.		
We seem to spend huge amounts of time in internal meetings but I don't know that we achieve much in them.		
Benchmarking sounds fine in theory – but how do we go about it in practice when other firms won't release information on what they do?		
I have no problem scheduling the things I need to do into the working day, it's all the interruptions that make time management impossible.		
We don't have difficulty managing the work, it's managing all the other issues like client care that we struggle with.		

Assuming you didn't answer 'no' to all the above, then you should read on.

Managing for profit

> 'Money is better than poverty – if only for financial reasons.'
>
> Woody Allen

Ask people why they work and their initial response will be 'for the money', even though if they gave a considered response, they would usually tell you something else. Research has shown that money is not the prime motivating factor in a work situation and that other variables tend to be more important, including:

- quality of life;
- relationships;
- job satisfaction;
- recognition.

However, most managing partners of professional firms tend to put these second in priority to financial factors (often a very long way behind), for the following reasons:

- The firm will go out of business without proper financial management (but so it would without a workforce).
- Finance involves hard black and white facts, unlike 'airy fairy' human issues.

- The gap between cause and effect is usually less clear and much harder to influence with human issues than it is with finance.

Anybody managing a firm will be well aware of the key distinction between turnover and profitability, and of the importance of return on investment. Key indicators for these are regularly published in respect of the professions and freely available from financial advisers. However, as with all else, industry norms can sometimes disguise key issues under a cloud of 'that's the way we do things'. For example, how many firms take work billed but not paid for into account when considering their annual turnover? All well and good, but how much of that work is actually ever going to be paid for? At what stage should it be written off, and more importantly what can be learnt from the writing off exercise?

Financial analysis ought to be fairly easy yet it is hampered by a number of common factors and these are where the 'softer' human issues start to creep in. The problems are all to do with management and motivation (or lack thereof) of people:

- Financial information is often not up to date – therefore any financial snapshot will not be accurate.
- Formal procedures to do with notifying clients about billing and issuing bills are not upheld.
- Billing and other financial matters are left to partners and fee-earners when they could be better handled by dedicated accounts staff.
- Credit control in terms of chasing non-payment is left to partners – again this could be better handled by accounts staff.
- Internal systems allow billing to be left to the end of the year, or some other significant period, with the result that resource is over-stretched and mistakes are made.

Too many firms still concentrate on doing the work rather than getting paid for it, with the unfortunate result that they end up carrying out an alarming amount of work for free.

One way of getting a true financial picture is to adopt a 'balanced scorecard' system – whereby a number of factors relating to a team's financial performance are regularly considered by management in parallel with those of other individuals/teams. For example, regular reports might be prepared by team leaders and submitted to management in respect of work in progress, unbilled time, overdue bills and write-offs. Regularly focusing on these ensures that everyone maintains concentration on all these key variables and any one area is not allowed to get out of balance and lapse below an acceptable level.

Our clients are often bemused when we refer to financial procedures as one of the essentials of client care and effective client management. Yet although it may seem to have little to do with marketing, it is in fact one of the most important areas for clients in terms of their satisfaction with the services you provide. Taken at its simplest – the whole transaction has to do with their feelings about what they got compared to what they paid. Basically, if they paid nothing, they would probably be pretty satisfied with your services, no matter how underwhelming they actually were!

Client care and management in respect of costs involves:

- giving the client a realistic indication of how much they are likely to end up paying;
- letting them know what exactly they will be paying for (ensure you mention disbursements and any other extra costs so they don't receive nasty surprises);
- ensuring that they will be able to pay for your services (carry out credit checks if necessary and put in place a system for taking fees on account if appropriate);
- agreeing how often they will be invoiced and ensuring that they are invoiced in accordance with that agreement;
- providing an itemised bill which gives them a clear indication of what they are paying for;
- enforcing rigorous credit control (if they know you won't chase a bill for six months, why would they choose to pay it sooner?).

If financial management has been somewhat lax in your firm, a burst of concentrated effort to tighten up procedures, chase unpaid bills, bill all outstanding time and undertake realistic write-offs, can be a great motivator in terms of showing that management and action do actually work. If you are planning a period of concerted change in other areas, such as marketing or client care, this can be a worthwhile exercise to undertake before you do so. It will improve motivation and underscore the fact that people are capable of achieving measurable results if they know what to aim for and are allowed to devote time and effort to doing so.

CASE STUDY   **Calling a truce**

In common with almost every professional services firm, some of our clients report a problem with the regular build-up of unbilled time which the management team suspects is likely never to be billed and which simply clogs up the accounts system and distorts the true work in progress picture.

We asked them to think hard and talk to their fee-earners about why the build-up was happening. It soon transpired that internal procedures to enable 'dead' time to be written off were, in fact, quite cumbersome, involving the fee-earner having to give a detailed explanation and seek the authority of several partners before each write-off request could be dealt with.

One or two took our advice of introducing an annual amnesty in the run-up to the firm's financial year-end during which write-off requests would be actioned, with no questions asked. The results were amazing – not only did the managers end up with far more realistic financial information than they had ever had before but the fee-earners were extremely motivated by the exercise and took the opportunity to 'spring clean' their filing cabinets and weed out dormant files, which led, in turn, to noticeably greater operating efficiency.

Delegation

> Give a man a fish and he can eat for a day. Teach him how to fish and he can feed himself for life.
>
> (Chinese Proverb)

Often referred to as an art, delegation is a management tool which should and must be used by all who are in a position to delegate in order to:

- most effectively manage personal time;
- assist in training and developing less experienced staff;
- ensure that clients receive best value (they should not have to pay the rates of a senior fee-earner when a more junior person is capable of doing the work);
- look after the bottom line – the firm will not be profitable if too much work is too often done at the wrong level.

It is not uncommon for professional services providers, perhaps because there is a perception that they tend to work in high-risk areas, to display a general reluctance to delegate, the principal barriers being:

- a feeling of loss of control ('it's easier and quicker if I do it – at least I know it'll be done right');
- a fear of being usurped by the assistant ('he might do a better job than me – the client might prefer him to act in the future');
- knowledge that if they do delegate they will have to do something else with their time – marketing and management being top of the list – and produce measurable results.

If this is the case in your organisation, try following the golden rules of delegation set out in Figure 7.1.

Step one:	Set the scene	Give your assistant comprehensive but relevant background information and explain the nature of the task to be delegated.
Step two:	Set the rules	Agree precisely what the assistant has to do and within what timescale. Make it clear when and in what circumstances it is acceptable for him or her to seek supervision, clarification and assistance
Step three:	Let go!	Allow the assistant to get on with the job without interfering beyond the extent of the agreed supervision.
Step four:	Review	Once the task is complete, examine – together with them – how the project and the delegation exercise went and whether either could have been handled better. Did the assistant cope with the level of the task? Could he or she handle more responsibility next time? What did delegating this task enable you to do instead?
Step five:	Feedback	If the assistant performed well, give praise and encouragement – the motivation part! If problems arose, tackle them honestly, fairly and constructively. Remember – mistakes are an opportunity to learn not to apportion blame.

Figure 7.1   Rules of delegation

Time management

'Time is money' is one of the greatest truisms for any professional services organisation. What this boils down to is that improved financial performance, for one reason or another, depends on improved time management and ensuring people create sufficient time for winning new business, carrying out existing business, or reviewing what has gone before.

The most common excuse heard in response to any new initiative is, 'Yes, love to – but where am I supposed to find the time?'. The syndrome is known, for obvious reasons, as 'being too busy fighting alligators to drain the swamp'. However, human nature being what it is, there will always be things in the working day that we don't want to do and these are what tend to be submerged in the 'too busy' swamp. Logic says to do the things you hate first, to get them out of the way (often the feelings of dread and loathing clutter your approach to other tasks and drain you of energy), but like most 'ought to's' this is usually easier said than done.

For most people lack of time is an excuse. We nearly all have peaks and troughs in our workflow which means that everyone at some stage will be genuinely busy. However, if this is an on-going problem with some individuals it can mean that:

1. There is a genuine lack of resource, in which case you need to take on additional help.
2. Being too busy is used as an excuse not to undertake unpalatable tasks.
3. Time is not being well managed.

The long-hours culture is an indication of any/all of these – and, in summary, is a game. Although it is reasonable for everyone to put in some extra time other than their contracted hours (even if only thinking about their job) – persistent long-hours working in most firms is a power game. The only exception is in some industries and top firms where employees are paid astronomical salaries and are expected to carry a workload to match. In that case, you've made your choice – money or moan – you can't have both.

Time management is a circular process: effective time management comes down to planning (see Chapter 1) – but the key to planning success is effective time management. Similarly, successful time management results in improved effectiveness and efficiency (see Table 7.1) – leading to improved productivity, requiring even tighter time management! Figure 7.2 illustrates this.

There are no right answers in respect of the way people organise their days, but you must make sure their approach is constructed around the legitimate needs of others – colleagues, clients and family – not just their own preferences. For example, partners may decide not to accept

Table 7.1 Improved effectiveness and efficiency through time management

Effective working	Efficient working
Development of range/depth of skills/ knowledge	More delegation/involvement/ specialisation
Focus on meeting client needs	Improved client communication
Management of team to meet objectives	Team working and collaboration
Time spent building the business	Smooth workflow patterns
Learning and development	Continuous assessment of process and results

Figure 7.2 Improved productivity

calls for the first two hours of every day in order to have a period of silence and carry out desk work even though clients expect them to be instantly available when they call. This is not an insurmountable problem if it is explained to clients, and partners ensure – every time – that someone deals sensibly with their call, and it is followed up as soon as possible.

Similarly, if someone regularly needs to leave the office by a certain time for family reasons, this is not a problem as long as everyone is aware of it, and knows the procedure for contacting them.

Analysing and improving your allocation of time

Time-recording in respect of hours spent 'doing the job' is still driven in professional services firms by the need for accurate and accountable billing. However, for the majority, all time outside this is simply dumped into 'admin', 'business development' or 'other', or simply left unaccounted for. But, if you want to improve time management – your own, or that of the firm as a whole – you first need to know how time is currently spent.

One approach is to call for exact time-recording for every category – which can be extremely easy if you are working with some of the more advanced IT case management systems. However, it is not that difficult even without IT. Use job descriptions and current personal objectives as an aide-memoire and also take into account all the key roles you have within the firm. If you are on various teams and committees the time needed to serve on them must be taken into account.

You can then draw up a chart – for a week or month, whichever fits most comfortably with your task allocation – and work out exactly how much time (percentage-wise) you spent on each area. The key process then is to compare this with how much time you feel you ought or want to be spending on each, and if there is a shortfall, where the extra time is to come from. An example is given in Table 7.2. This is where things will start to get difficult for, unless you have very few demands on your time, you will now be facing the thorny problem of setting priorities and devising the means by which you will adhere to them.

Table 7.2   Improved productivity through time management

Function	Time spent per month (current)	Time that should be spent
Fee-earning – billable time	65%	30%
Client meetings/calls/CRM (non-billable)	5%	20%
Meetings – internal	15%	5%
Research/keeping up with developments	5%	5%
Staff management/supervision/training	5%	25%
Business development/networking	5%	15%
	100%	100%

To assist their time-recording, some firms have (bravely) adopted a process of 'shadowing' where someone fairly neutral (HR, training, IT manager) actually sits with each person for a period to record how exactly they spend their time. This shows up any number of areas where time is wasted, for example on family calls, internal meetings or simply trying to find things.

A key factor in reallocating your time is to analyse how much of your time is controllable, that is, where you can predetermine how much time you will spend on the process (e.g. time allocated to preparing a report), and how much time is responsive time (e.g. dealing with client calls or employee/colleague enquiries). By its very nature, the time spent on the latter will be to some degree out of your hands, but the important thing is to remember that in your overall schedule, all the former activities will need to be fitted in around the latter.

The benefits of time management

The motivation and overall benefit of improved time management for both the individual and the firm as a whole is that it allows you to 'work smarter, not harder'. However, as with every other aspect of analysis and planning, your ultimate effectiveness will hinge on the goals you set in terms of what you want to achieve. For maximum motivation the answer may lie in a mixture of personal preferences (spend less time in meetings) and corporate objectives (spend more time marketing the firm).

Although time management can only be implemented at the level of the individual, it is, nevertheless, worth looking at periodically for the organisation as a whole. The old, factory-related 'time and motion' studies may have been largely discredited, but the thought process behind them is still sound. Where can time be saved by the organisation as a whole? What procedures can be put in place across teams and departments in order to bring about improved efficiency and effectiveness? Remember, for example, that the entire point of team working is that the productivity of the whole should be more than the sum of its parts.

One of the most effective maxims of time management is 'spend to save'. For example, when working with firms, we often come across the situation where people have spent only the minimum time needed to become familiar with their IT system – perhaps just to the stage where they can send and receive e-mails. The rest of the system remains a mystery to them simply because they have chosen not to spend more time in finding out how it works and the benefits it could bring them in respect of their clients, their work systems and their working day.

Time management is largely to do with habit and good time management is a discipline. It is worth referring to it as such, as very few professionals like to be thought of as undisciplined. Table 7.3 illustrates this.

Table 7.3 Personal qualities reflected by time management

Good time manager	Poor time manager
Disciplined	Undisciplined
Meticulous	Sloppy
Reliable	Unreliable
Punctilious	Casual
In control	Unable to cope
Respected	Tolerated

In respect of formal time management training, numerous systems are promoted, none of which is necessarily any better or worse than the rest. However, should you be thinking of investing in such training it is worth bearing the following in mind:

- Ensure that more than one person undertakes the training. The ability to practise in pairs or groups thereafter is the best possible way of keeping each other on the straight and narrow.
- Follow up internally to see that the systems are being implemented – i.e. that learning has actually taken place. As with many training courses, the most common response is to say 'great – in theory' and then within a day or two, to return to doing things the way you've always done them.

Managing time

Time is not an amorphous entity. There are numerous aspects to it within the professional services firm which need to be taken into account when considering improved time management.

Managing people time

In a service business, managing people and their expectations is the very life blood of success. Earlier chapters have dwelt on the importance of allowing time to get to know clients and to get to the bottom of their needs, above and beyond the technical time required for you to do the job. The importance of allowing time to keep in touch and develop relationships with contacts and potential clients in order to move them up the relationship ladder and win their business has also been examined.

Chapter 6 deals with team working – which, internally, involves effectively communicating with your colleagues. And, from a management perspective, managing people, appraisals, and coaching and mentoring are covered in Chapter 10. All of these take time – and a regular input of quality time at that. The number-one rule in managing people is to make them feel that they are important and that their views and actions (positive or negative) matter. Frequently, systems and procedures are undermined because managers don't allow sufficient time to support them. For example, appraisal systems may be fine in themselves – but they can become discredited in employees' eyes if their manager does not keep to the agreed timescale or carry out their part of the process.

Managing management time

Remember planning, monitoring and reviewing – all those things that go hand in hand with business and marketing planning? Well they won't happen by themselves – they need time. Schedule in formal meetings with employees and colleagues well in advance and insist that such meetings (with very few exceptions) are not to be moved. Block out times for informal management matters in your diary or planner. Even if that time has to be rearranged, it will have been flagged up that it needs to be done – and another time set should it have to be postponed.

Managing meeting time

'Don't shoot the messenger' is the key maxim which should be applied to meetings. People often complain about time wasted attending meetings, when what they should be complaining about is the way the meeting is handled, a lack of clarity about the objectives of the meeting, and a paucity of preparation by those involved. There are times when only a meeting will do – and it's usually the case that the shorter they are the more effective they are.

Regular, formal team meetings are essential both in a professional and administrative sense and from the point of view of boosting and maintaining motivation levels. Moreover, they are something which all team members should attend. Remember, though, that meetings should only be held where they serve a real purpose – for instance, it just isn't necessary (and is tremendously inefficient in profitability terms) for the whole team to be assembled for a couple of hours whilst the team head goes through each individual's current workload, transaction by transaction. The most important function of meetings is that they can be the communication bridge (see Figure 7.3) between client and service provider, a chance to share knowledge about client needs and an opportunity to work together to provide imaginative solutions.

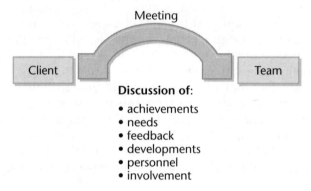

Figure 7.3   The meeting as a bridge

Managing thinking time

Formal brainstorming sessions aside, the normal work environment usually isn't conducive to thinking. The shower, the traffic jam, the middle of the night, the Sunday afternoon walk are all far more likely arenas in which to reflect on problems and challenges and come up with some bright ideas. However, in order for this to be productive across the firm you need to have mechanisms in place to communicate to people the current challenges facing the firm, (e.g. 'what do you think we ought to do about...?', 'how can we best tackle...?') and some formal means of feedback, positive expectation and reward to ensure that people actually do give such problems some serious thought.

Managing 'doing' time

When delegating, simply moving your unrealistic workload in its entirety onto someone else is not going to solve the ultimate problem. Delegation relies on effective time management. It is much like the above example of IT training – it takes time to teach someone how to do something and supervision time may initially be heavy, but following that, you will be freed up from doing some particular task even though the responsibility may still be yours. (Being responsible for something doesn't mean doing it all yourself.)

The difference between people and machines is that people suffer differing levels of productivity depending on their mood, their state of health, their feelings of worth and their attitudes towards the world around them. Therefore you have to build these highs and lows into your working week and recognise that there's no point in punishing yourself or others for having one non-productive day. Just accept the fact that tomorrow will invariably be better.

Managing marketing time

For our purposes, this is perhaps the most important area of operational management that you need to consider. As you will have seen in earlier chapters, there are many different components and areas of activity to be considered in marketing, whether marketing planning and review, contributing to and implementing various aspects of the promotional mix, or undertaking networking or CRM activities, including visiting clients. These are just a few of the demands on your time, but what they have in common is that they must all be done regularly and consistently. You must make them a priority and ensure others do too. If not, if you wait until you have the time, it will never happen and you will constantly undermine and damage your own and the firm's efforts to develop the business.

Internal systems and procedures

Every organisation will have some sort of operational systems and procedures even if only of the most rudimentary kind. Unfortunately, many professional services organisations have a considerable element of 'that's the way we've always done it' in their operating approach – and often state that the reason they're unable to evolve is that 'XX [individuals or groups] would never agree to change'. However, as the world, technology and client expectations change, your operating procedures need to change too in order to keep pace.

The operational management structure

Operating procedures can be divided into two different groups:

- 'hard' – standardised systems involving forms, reports, paper- or IT-based systems which are associated with specific outputs and processes, usually involving numbers;
- 'soft' – operating procedures which involve dealing with people, communication, etc.

As you will realise, the key to effective and efficient operating procedures is to ensure they are properly managed, and as these areas are often concerned with a very high level of detail, this is where delegation plays an important role. Problems often occur because processes and procedures are expected to be managed through the firm's existing management structure which is probably based on the fairly natural breakdown between work types or groups.

The disadvantage of this, however, is that the focus of each team or group in this hierarchy is primarily doing the technical work – all other processes such as client care, marketing, IT development, knowledge management or whatever, are very much secondary to this and tend to have only lip-service paid to them.

Although we would be the last to suggest installing over-complicated or unwieldy management systems to counter this tendency, generating a matrix management situation in doing so, it is worth looking at how you might manage these issues separately. As shown in Figure 7.4, it can be worthwhile taking representatives from teams and forming them into an alternative system whose focus primarily is to develop these soft areas.

(a) Operational management structure (technical)

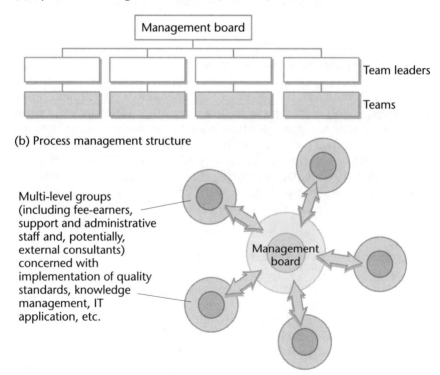

(b) Process management structure

Multi-level groups (including fee-earners, support and administrative staff and, potentially, external consultants) concerned with implementation of quality standards, knowledge management, IT application, etc.

Figure 7.4   Hard and soft management structures

The simplest process to adopt when considering any refinement to your operating procedures – hard or soft – is as follows:

1. *Examine*: how does what you currently do relate to your objectives in respect of quality control and client care? What do your customers expect? How do they want things done? What do they say you currently do well or badly?
2. *Analyse*: the client value chain (see Figure 7.5 as an example) in respect of the service you provide. Which areas of service do clients perceive as being the most valuable? What are those areas of service which are important to you but have little or no effect on the service you provide to your clients?
3. *Standardise*: agree current best practice in respect of key systems within your organisation and make this the basis for standard firm-wide operating procedures. Doing so will afford clients consistency of

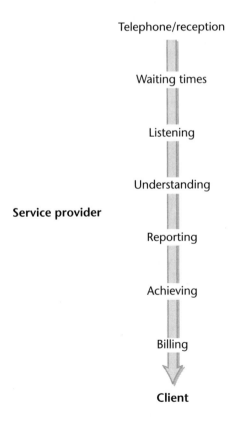

Figure 7.5   The client value chain

approach regardless of who they deal with within the firm, and will also make internal operations and cross-team working more efficient.

When contemplating changing or introducing systems and procedures there are three further things to bear in mind:

- *Consultation*: ask for input, both internally and, if appropriate, from clients, remembering that you don't have to implement all of what has been suggested.
- *Explanation*: explain clearly what has been decided and why.
- *Enforcement*: ensure that the new system is rigorously enforced to the stage where it becomes second nature.

Change for change's sake?

One stunning area of waste in operational systems change is in respect of IT investment, where the majority of firms have ploughed considerable resource into introducing and updating IT systems over the past 10–15 years. When asked why, most would answer 'to improve efficiency', yet few have any measurable results of the financial benefits to them of that improved efficiency or have even made any attempt to measure it.

What has happened is that the investment is made, both in terms of hardware and software and supporting personnel, a certain amount of time is given to training, then life goes on the same as before – with no improvement in service and with staff seemingly following Parkinson's law, ensuring that their work expands to fill the time available. The staff have said, 'if we had such and such our lives would be transformed, we would be able to work more efficiently and the firm would benefit'. Eventually they get their new photocopier, fax machine, scanner etc – yet no attempt is made to hold them to their side of the bargain!

As we can see, change for change's sake is not necessarily productive or beneficial. So how do you best decide what changes to implement? One of the most effective ways is to consider benchmarking – which means comparing the way you do things against the way others do them in order to seek ideas and avenues for improvement.

Benchmarking

Benchmarking, like most other technical terms, has numerous formal definitions, but basically it is a means of setting standards to monitor and control performance through identifying, monitoring and applying best practice from other organisations. In short, it means aiming to be the best through emulating the best.

In its 1995 publication *Best Practice Benchmarking*, the Department for Trade and Industry identified the following key elements of what benchmarking involves for organisations:

- Establishing what makes the difference, in their customers eyes, between an ordinary supplier and an excellent supplier.
- Setting standards in each of those things, according to the best practice they can find.
- Finding out how the best companies meet those challenging standards.
- Applying both other people's experience and their own ideas to meet the new standards – and, if possible, to exceed them.

The DTI report continues:

'[Benchmarking] . . . is not about aiming to clone the success of other companies, or indulging in industrial spying. Nor is it measurement for measurement's sake. The real goal is to build on the success of others to improve future performance. By benchmarking on a continuing basis, you are always researching current best practice, not dated ideas. Benchmarking is always carried out with the goal of putting improvements into action.

Companies world-wide have found that there are very significant gains to be made from benchmarking. Among them:

- better understanding of their customers and their competitors;
- fewer complaints and more satisfied customers;
- reduction in waste, quality problems and reworking;
- faster awareness of important innovations and how they can be applied profitably;
- a stronger reputation within their markets;
- and, as a result of all these, increased profits and sales turnover.

Benchmarking helps achieve all of these benefits by giving you a disciplined, realistic approach to assessing the performance you should expect in critical areas of your business. It also helps you learn from the experience of others – saving the cost of making your own mistakes.'

This sounds great – but how do you go about it, bearing in mind that most of your competitors are unlikely to share the secrets of their success with you out of the kindness of their hearts? There are a number of potential avenues, depending on what you want to measure, and the strength of your relationships within each:

- very similar organisations who for whatever reason (usually different physical location) are not direct competitors;
- similar organisations from a different professional area;

- similar size/turnover service businesses in the commercial sector (e.g. advertising agencies);
- client companies/organisations;
- benchmarking groups made up of organisations in any of the above categories.

Within each of the above the key point to remember is reciprocity – organisations will want to be assured that there is something in it for them and that you can be trusted to be as open and reliably forthcoming with your information as you are expecting them to be with theirs. In studying the most effective benchmarking processes, it is clear that motivation is of vital importance – you have genuinely to want to learn and improve. If what you really want is to ascertain how much better you are in some areas than other organisations, and to find ways of justifying why you don't need to improve in others, you may as well forget it. The whole exercise will be a waste of time.

Yes, benchmarking is a risk, but it is also a very sound and productive means of generating change and engineering continuous improvement. And, of course, the knowledge that you do perform well in certain areas compared with your competitors is an enormous source of motivation.

The benchmarking process

1. Set up an internal project team. Identify and understand the processes involved.
2. Decide what to benchmark and which firms or companies to match.
3. Collect comparative data.
4. Establish comparative performance and identify gaps.
5. Set improvement targets.
6. Plan and implement improvements.
7. Monitor progress and fine-tune as necessary.
8. Formalise the improvements into the firm's systems and procedures.

Although it takes time to set up and even more time – usually – to overcome initial internal misgivings, the process can be fairly painless thereafter and to quote the DTI report again: 'the relatively small amount of time and effort involved is repaid many times over.'

The report identifies the main requirements as being:

- a strong commitment from top management to act on any major opportunities for improvement that are revealed;
- a small amount of training and guidance for employees who will have to gather the information needed to identify and analyse best practice;

- authorisation for employees to spend some of their time on bench-marking activities.

It continues, 'Of these, the most critical is top management commitment. To prevent benchmarking becoming an academic "snapshot" of how you are performing, senior management needs to own the process and be seen to be steering it'.

Using consultants and in-house advisers

One approach to change which has the additional benefit of inbuilt benchmarking is the use of external consultants in areas such as management training, marketing, and change management. If chosen carefully, they will – by their very nature – have built their business on dealing with similar organisations to your own and will provide you with 'best practice' advice based on their own benchmarking observations across firms and markets.

Discussions with managing partners of many smaller firms have shown that taking the leap of faith involved in seeking specialist advice (whether from consultants or by taking on permanent in-house support) is a recurrent and tricky problem. Deciding on the type of advice needed, finding a source of supply, and managing internal expectations are all key issues. On top of this, firms of all sizes struggle with the best way to set budgets for such assistance and ensure they are spent wisely and productively.

Help! But what type?

Consultants or employees? Practice managers or management practitioners? Fundamentally it's a matter of:

- *the size and nature of the problem* (do you need strategic advice or on-going implementation – consultants tend to be cost-effective for the first, but can be expensive for the second);
- *risk* – consultants are easy to part company with, employees generally are not;
- *clarity about your requirements* – although you need a detailed brief to get the best from a consultant, it's nevertheless reasonably easy to switch to a different type of adviser if you find after a while that your problems are not what you thought they were.

What type of in-house employee you take on, if you decide to go down this route, comes down to the difference between a generalist (often with a particular strength in one area, e.g. accounts or HR) and a specialist who deals only with their area of expertise, e.g. marketing, HR, training – although they all may be able to extend their skills to managing and developing other areas. Apart from very small firms, most professional services firms will at the very least have a practice manager to relieve them of some of the day-to-day administration. The decision to take on in-house specialist support beyond this then comes down to a number of factors and it's crucial that you decide and debate them internally before you take matters further. Ask yourselves:

- Are you seeking administrative or strategic support? (See pp. 120 for the distinction between the two in marketing terms.)
- Do you know enough about the person's abilities to know whether they could be kept fully employed, or alternatively rushed off their feet?
- What can you afford (specialists, like professionals, don't come cheap)?
- Are you expecting them to achieve the unachievable?
- Do you want them to do things for you which only you, the professionals, can actually achieve?
- Who will they report to and what will be their position in the pecking order?
- Are you prepared to take their advice or are they expected to come in and do things the way the firm wants to?
- Is there general recognition and acceptance of the fact that the specialist will be focused on and expecting to generate, change?

Chalk and cheese, or yin and yang?

Deciding whether to take on an in-house specialist with professional services experience who may have fallen into the 'can't see the commercial wood for the professional trees' trap, or someone from outside who may have fresher ideas but a steeper learning curve in coming to terms with how professional services firms generally do things, is a tough decision to make. Our advice is not to specify – interview some of each and choose the best contender based on a number of other factors.

However, one thing you must be absolutely clear about in advance if you have any chance of living happily ever after is the amount of power and status the person will be allowed. Often this is where external consultants win hands down over internal employees as the latter unfortunately are never regarded by professionals as 'one of us' and are often thought to be inferior. The idea that they might sit on the firm's management board and take an active role in running the business, is anathema to all but the most enlightened firms, who often expect their specialist employees to somehow achieve miracles while giving them no power or influence to do so.

The damage to your firm if you allow this to happen will be greater than the damage to the employee who will often put it down to experience and get another job – outside the professions. Internally, you will then be faced with another 'marketing didn't work' situation (this applies equally to whatever other discipline the employee may have specialised in, such as IT or HR), together with cynicism and disaffection from many within the firm, and greater hurdles to overcome next time you set off down this route.

Living happily ever after

Whether employing a consultant or taking on a specialist employee, bear in mind the pointers given in Chapter 2 about choosing and using suppliers. Be absolutely clear about what you want the person to achieve and do, before you go looking for candidates. Make sure their values align with those of the firm, look for signs of innovation, and ultimately make sure you choose someone with whom you personally can work.

POINTS TO REMEMBER

➤ Managing for profit means shifting your focus from doing the work to ensuring you get paid for it.

➤ Client care is deeply embedded in the financial aspects of the transaction – ultimately it comes down to the client's feelings and level of satisfaction about what they got for the money they paid.

➤ Delegation is a management tool which not only makes the best use of managerial time but also helps train, develop and motivate team members.

➤ Effective time management involves looking at what you currently do with your time and planning how you *should* be spending it, building both controllable and responsive time into your new schedule.

➤ Time allocation involves managing various aspects of time in different ways and by doing so, creating the motivation to ensure it happens.

➤ Team meetings can be an ideal communications bridge between service providers and their clients.

➤ Operational management structures need to look at managing the soft aspects of a firm's procedures as well as the hard technical process.

➤ Benchmarking is an effective means of setting standards to monitor and control performance through identifying, measuring and applying best practice from other organisations.

➤ Effective use of external consultants or in-house personnel for specialist management support is heavily reliant on having clear objectives, allowing sufficient time and other resources in order to meet these objectives, and bestowing sufficient status upon them to be able to operate effectively in the professional environment.

Knowledge management

Think about your firm – do you recognise any of these problems?

	YES	NO
We're a million miles away from a 'paperless office' – e-mails and shared files seem to generate more paper than ever.		
We seem to be driven by what the technology can do rather than what we want it to do – how can we change the balance?		
We've invested huge amounts in technology and support staff over the past few years yet we're no further ahead in process terms than when we just used typewriters.		
One of our clients has suggested that we look into allowing them access to their files through an extranet. Although we're horrified at the idea, we're going to have to respond somehow.		
Some of our fee-earners think it's demeaning for them to amend their own documents on the system; we need to persuade them otherwise if our investment in IT is going to pay off.		

We thought technology would revolutionise our working practices, but we still have a ratio of one secretary to one fee-earner.		
Some staff seem to spend hours every day doing 'research' on the Internet; what's the most effective way of controlling and coordinating this practice?		
It's a circular argument – people won't take client databases seriously if they don't contain valid, up-to-date information, but if they don't take them seriously, they don't input the information!		
All the knowledge about our IT systems is held by one member of staff – if anything happened to them our business would pretty well collapse.		

Assuming you didn't answer 'no' to all the above, then you should read on.

The role of IT

Information technology (IT) has progressed from the stage of being a mechanistic *process enabler* to a business development and communications *facilitator and generator*. The change is significant and is reflected in the fact that appropriate platforms are now referred to as ICT (information and communication technology), rather than just IT. Whereas in the past, technology was simply used to support existing work processes – as first word processors and then PCs were used for typing, document storage and simple databases – now entire work systems are driven by what the technology can provide.

However, although IT (or ICT) is now one of the biggest overheads most firms carry, most still struggle with maximising the full potential that their system can offer. Firms are making inroads into more effective use of ICT in various ways, with results which vary from incredibly impressive to fairly disastrous. Two areas of under-utilisation are very common yet ought to be easy to rectify:

- PCs are still used as glorified typewriters and to send and receive e-mails. Little use is effectively made of the potential of the entire ICT system in terms of case management, communication, data sharing and analysis.
- Insufficient use is made of the web or in-house CD-Rom-based systems for research, training, and technical information-gathering and updating, with most people still relying heavily on paper-based documentation. (Time savings through improved web use can easily be costed and can result in impressive savings across the firm.)

To improve this situation, both of these areas require attitudinal and behavioural change, the latter of which can be brought about fairly easily through training. However, these changes won't take place without sufficient management and motivational support.

There is another area which is in itself more complex and with which the majority still continue to struggle – this is the concept, and application of, effective knowledge management.

Technology-driven knowledge management is one process that will enable your firm to 'work smarter, not harder' both technically and in business development terms, but problems of implementation abound. Turning data into knowledge involves selectively analysing, adding value to, and interpreting information and data – which isn't easy if the quality of the data held is patchy and incomplete. Associated problems often have little to do with technology and more to do with the way the firm has always operated.

Traditionally, knowledge within firms has been held (and is in some cases, jealously guarded) in small disparate pockets around the firm and prising it out can be a significant management problem in itself. So it's easy to see that if a firm has never been able to create a knowledge-sharing culture pre-IT, the advent of a facilitating system isn't necessarily going to make it happen automatically.

Increasingly, as firms turn their focus towards their competitive position and business development, this situation is one which must be tackled. For example, when working with firms, one of the biggest problems we face is that the client firm knows about their business and what they want to achieve, while we know about business development and how to make it happen. But who really knows about the essential missing link – the firm's own clients? As we have stressed, if you don't know about your clients and their needs, you have little hope of marketing to them successfully. See Figure 8.1.

Added to this is the problem that, after gaining support for the *idea* of knowledge sharing, in order to achieve a situation where IT can deliver real benefits and save you time, you will have to expend a significant amount of time in setting up and testing systems and entering initial data.

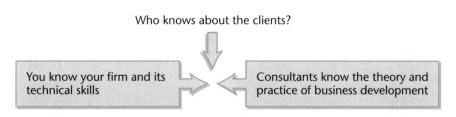

Figure 8.1 Client knowledge – the missing link

So, is effective utilisation of ICT worthwhile for most small to medium-sized firms, or is it something which should by and large be left to the big firms with their big budgets and pools of financial, advisory and staff resource? There is no reason why ICT and knowledge management cannot be as workable in smaller firms as large ones; it's one of those areas in which size doesn't matter.

In fact, it can be considerably easier to develop ICT systems for a small firm than for a large one which will involve potentially huge amounts of data and the cooperation of a large number of people with disparate attitudes. The issue is how you can best adopt a manageable level of IT expertise and supporting systems and utilise them so that they are a beneficial tool for your firm rather than a millstone around your neck.

Most small to medium-sized firms have now crossed the threshold and invested heavily in systems – but it is what they do with them then that counts – and that seems reliant on the enthusiasm of one or two individuals.

Drowning in paper appears to be an affliction for which there is little or no cure in professional services offices. Despite their considerable investment in IT, the spectre of the paperless office still seems as unattainable as in pre-IT days. Yet although both practicality and human nature mean that a certain amount of paper will always be needed, why have things progressed so little? We believe that it comes down to lack of management process to move things forward, and suggest that to do so, you should adopt the following approach:

1. Draw up a plan outlining specific objectives the firm needs to achieve in respect of its knowledge management and utilisation of ICT systems.
2. Discuss the concept, objectives and measurable benefits which will be generated through the plan with everyone in the firm and ensure you have their feedback, input and buy-in before you attempt to take matters further (this may be a lengthy process!).
3. Introduce the plan, stage by stage, giving named individuals specific responsibility for seeing that project through, on time and on budget.
4. Don't attempt to move on to the next stage until the previous stage has become an ingrained process, and be constantly alert to slippage and reversion to bad habits.
5. Continuously feed back to the firm the outcomes of behavioural change through new processes – how much is the firm saving in terms of time and money, how much is efficiency and effectiveness improving, what do clients think?

Use of ICT systems is one area in which the M^3 model – marketing, management and motivation – is highly relevant and all three aspects must be looked at in detail before embarking upon investing in IT , or reviewing your current use of IT prior to upgrading. Consider some of these specific issues in relation to your firm.

Marketing:

How can you use ICT to:

- manage potential client leads;
- identify, and meet the needs of existing clients;
- cross-sell;
- manage client relationships (enabling you to take a proactive stance and anticipate client needs);
- improve speed and efficiency of communication with clients;
- improve competitiveness?

Management

How can you use ICT to improve:

- HR management;
- workflow patterns;
- flexibility;
- financial management;
- technical information storage and retrieval;
- time management?

Motivation:

How can you use ICT to underpin:

- added value services for clients;
- benefits for internal users;
- measurable improvements in communication and morale;
- the overall win-win situation for the firm as a whole?

What is knowledge management?

ICT consultants van der Spek and Kingma, writing in the CBI publication *Liberating Knowledge*, (CBI in association with IBM, 1999) have given a commendably pragmatic view of knowledge management: 'Knowledge management is not rocket science, it is about smart ways of working and smart businesses.'

Although some within professional firms use the term 'knowledge management' in a very narrow sense to relate specifically to shared know-how (e.g. precedents), we use the term here in its widest sense to cover all the knowledge a firm has, has had and needs in the future in respect of its:

- financial operating procedures;
- personnel records;
- technical expertise (know-how/intellectual capital);
- quality control protocols;
- client companies – potential and current;
- individual contacts within client companies;
- information about other professionals and contacts;
- market sector information;
- marketing information (including research channels and data);
- monitoring and review mechanisms;
- training and development opportunities and programmes.

The advantages of maximising the use of IT for managing this information are powerful and persuasive, yet often firms have either chosen not to develop them, or have dismissed the issue as 'too difficult'. However, there are three main advantages which we believe are incontrovertible: the management of data, the manipulation of data and improved communication.

Data management

The greatest advantage of IT is the freedom it brings the individual from the responsibility for managing all the data they might ever need to refer to (apart perhaps from accounting records and a few books in the library). Instead of each individual having to keep their own files and records according to their own filing systems and procedures they are simply responsible for entering, reviewing and updating their own data in the overall knowledge bank. Figure 8.2 illustrates this.

Data manipulation

ICT systems provide the ability to structure and sift large amounts of data. These days we are all in danger of drowning in information. A good knowledge management strategy and platform allows you to know what to keep, where, how to access it in future and when to delete it.

Management and marketing information which can be mined from a good system is virtually limitless and includes:

- cost of acquiring clients;
- cost-effectiveness and profitability of various business areas;
- fee income patterns;

- client profitability;
- write-offs, discounts and lost fees.

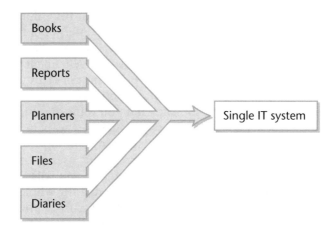

Figure 8.2   The rationalisation of data through use of ICT

Improved communication

Shared knowledge can lead to dramatic improvements in proactive communication – both within the firm and between the firm and the outside world simply because people start to realise the benefits it can bring. People complain that e-mail, and technology generally have simply added to the amount of information they have to deal with – whether technical, or one-to-one communications – but in terms of speed, convenience and coverage, it represents an incredible step forward. Like voicemail, associated problems are usually down to those using the system and related psychological variables rather than the technology itself.

Key issues in knowledge management

There are a number of key issues in respect of knowledge management which you will need to consider if you are to make any headway. Although this is by no means an exhaustive list, it covers a number of the main points.

What benefits do you want to generate?

Like anything else, you will only get out of your ICT system what you put into it, and what you put into it should relate specifically to the needs of your firm – not simply the recommendations of your IT supplier, the use your competitors make of their systems, or the well-meaning advice of others. The only area, perhaps, where you should look carefully is in respect of benchmarking partners (see Chapter 7) as the use of IT is an excellent area for comparison.

In deciding how best to develop IT within your firm, don't concentrate on what your current system – or indeed the latest tempting system on the market – is *capable* of doing but look instead at what you would *like/want* the system to be able to do (see Table 8.1). What it all boils down to is how does your firm, or how could your firm, use IT to improve its effectiveness and efficiency internally and externally.

First of all you will need to look at what you want to achieve and set some SMART objectives. Consider using some of the points outlined under the three areas of marketing, management and motivation above as your basic list and add any other areas or specific uses or benefits that you feel are particularly pertinent to your firm and your client base. The basic question is: which areas of knowledge – across the whole firm – are the most relevant to you and, from that, establish a list of priorities.

Never lose sight of the fact that the prime benefit of improved IT must be increased profits – not just through cost savings in business efficiency, but also from increased work effectiveness. Although the investment you may have to make on an initial and on-going basis may be high, you have to work out how and when you will reap this benefit if the entire exercise is to have any meaning or rationale.

Table 8.1   Identifying the benefits of improved ICT

Current situation	Wish list	Benefit/objective
Finding information takes too much time	Want to find information easily and quickly	Improved efficiency
Information is often out of date and unreliable	Data has to be kept up to date through operating constraints	Improved confidence
Not sure what information is available	Menu of directly accessible and updated information	Improved information tool-kit
Information currently available only in particular formats	Want to be able to manipulate and analyse data in different ways	Improved flexibility
Information has to be specifically requested from individuals	Data should be available in a shared repository	Improved accessibilty

What data and how much?

Just because the knowledge is there, it doesn't mean that you have to record, store or analyse it. It's easy to drown in data, so carefully assess what you need the data for and what the benefits to the firm will be of collecting and storing it. If the effort involved in doing so over time – once the system is established – isn't dramatically outweighed by the demonstrable benefits to the firm then you should question its validity carefully, but do not fall at the first 'too difficult' hurdle. Basically, the criteria you should work to are that the firm's knowledge should be:

- up to date;
- relevant;
- meaningful;
- concise.

This requirement is arguably even more important in respect of information which is monitored and stored about the outside world – whether relating to specific clients, client groups, market sectors or statistical data. As with researching on the web, too much information can be self-defeating, so it may be better simply to record a reference of where data can be accessed rather than storing the data itself. This, in effect, means creating your own internal library system on-line, probably through use of an intranet.

One of the biggest problems you will have to face initially when inputting data to ICT systems is de-duplication and data cleaning. Often the problem is not the identification of duplicates but the issue of who should decide which is the correct data if details differ, and who should be given the responsibility of physically rectifying incorrect or incomplete data. The size of this sort of task is why it's often worth running a pilot project with a data sample to enable you to work out at the outset the extent of the problem and the resource which will be required. It can be an area where it's worth taking on external help, e.g. to input data, but only if everyone is on-board with the idea of assisting in the fulfilment of the project.

Who is responsible?

The whole debate over who 'owns' data has raged for years in many firms, since the introduction of the first shared systems. One of the most common problems has occurred where work-related data is kept up to date, but data for marketing purposes (kept on a separate system) is not. Similarly, for example, accounts data can be so jealously guarded by its 'owners', the accounts team, that management is unable to access meaningful up-to-the-minute reports without their permission.

Added to this are self-defeating arguments about who ought to have done what, and why, in respect of data input and management, and possibly, as a result, a feeling that 'the system is rubbish' which diverts attention from the real issues involved. The crucial fact is that along with its people, a firm's data is its most valuable resource and too important to be left languishing and largely unusable for many purposes, while individuals hide behind excuses of 'too difficult' or 'no time'.

Every item of data on a system which is out of date, incomplete or incorrect is a complaint or a disaster waiting to happen. Slightly less dramatic, but equally important, is the fact that missing or incomplete data generally means poor communication – internally and externally – lost opportunities, and incomplete information on which management can analyse the firm's position and plan for the future.

Having looked at a number of systems and processes – technical and human – it seems that the only sensible answer to who should be responsible for data is that it should be an individual responsibility – 'your clients, your responsibility' – the execution of which, in terms of data entry or amendment, can be delegated on an individual or team basis to a secretary or assistant, as appropriate.

How to get everyone on board?

Knowledge management is an area in which it is crucial that everyone understands the importance of the systems in operation, how to use them and their own individual responsibilities in respect of them. It must be seen to be led and supported from the top – as the most common cause of failure is that 'they' (partners or directors) refuse to fall in line and commit to using systems. However, as with any major change involving the entire workforce, you should get together a working party or advisory team at the outset to contribute representative ideas, inspiration and 'reasons why not' – from their particular perspective.

Thorough consultation, explanation and training is, as always, the main way to generate buy-in and support. Identify those people, at whatever level or function, who are personally interested and enthusiastic about IT and use them as standard bearers. Step up your internal communications programme in respect of IT developments – make it clear to people on a daily basis if necessary, not only what you are currently aiming to achieve, but what they might expect to have go wrong as part of that process. On the other hand, don't be too downbeat – keep stressing past achievements and future benefits and be prepared to take an approach which says 'if you don't feel the pain, you won't feel the gain'.

A distinction must be drawn between the 'can'ts' and 'won'ts' with those who are trailing behind. With the 'can'ts', training is obviously key, but training support must be flexible and open-ended – people learn at different rates, especially in respect of technology, and a single session or series of sessions on how to do it, just won't be enough for some people. Especially for more senior (in age and status) members of staff, their reluctance to use the system may be shielding their embarrassment at their failure to grasp how.

The 'won'ts' pose a rather more difficult problem. A combination of carrot and stick is probably the most effective approach – first of all demonstrating the system's specific benefits to the firm and the way it will help them improve their own operational efficiency. If this fails, it may be necessary to make participation mandatory with pay reviews or similar being dependent on the individual having contributed the required levels of knowledge or data to the system or provided proof that they are using it.

The most persuasive means of getting people on board and keeping them enthused and participative is by designing the system so that it produces tangible benefits in their own working lives. Even if these can't be achieved immediately, it is helpful and motivating if people have a clear idea of where their current efforts are leading – and when they can experience the pay-off.

CASE STUDY   **Incomplete data – taking matters to the edge**

Taking matters to the edge is one of the most effective means we have found of improving data input and sharing.

Take the example where one of the key objectives behind developing a particular database of client information is to assist with marketing planning and the generation of future marketing initiatives. This has been clearly explained to people and the benefits and importance of the system reinforced, yet still some mavericks are refusing to devote time and effort to updating and completing the data for which they are responsible.

Knowing who the offenders are, once the system has been established and the deadline for the initial input of data has passed (or updating data in an on-going system), we take action. We ensure that the non-conformers will be directly involved in implementing the future strategy and reinforce how much decisions which are about to be made will be heavily dependent on statistical data analysis, e.g. correlating nature of business, size of company, fees earned.

Then we explain to everyone involved that the data as it stands will have to be used to underpin all hypotheses and premises as we can wait no longer. Actually being able to see what the consequences of non-contribution will be usually generates quiet requests along the lines of, 'could you just give me a week or two to update my data before we take matters forward . . .'.

How to go about choosing a system?

What system, at what price, and from whom is something you need to take specialist advice on. Due to lack of space and constant new developments there is little else we can say here by way of guidance, except for the following few points.

Don't reinvent the wheel. Unless you are doing something amazingly revolutionary, it's a sure bet that as a small to medium-sized firm, the system you need is already on the market and has been tried and tested by many other firms before yours. So don't risk calling in developers to design you something bespoke unless you have stretched the most similar existing product to the limit and even the developers admit that it's a worthwhile and innovative challenge that – astonishingly – nobody previously has required them to do. (If this is the case, they are probably going to be able to market the outcome for profit – so they should be willing to invest in the development themselves.)

Look around. There are numerous exhibitions and trade fairs focusing on ICT within the professions – so organise a working party to go and visit several (once you've decided on your objectives). Professional and representative bodies can also be of considerable assistance, whether for your profession, or more general, such as Chambers of Commerce, Business Links, etc. – so seek their advice, too.

Don't start off being too ambitious. Just because you need a system to be able to do a number of things *eventually*, doesn't mean you either want or need it to do them all at once. Work out a reasonable timescale with suppliers – they should know from experience how long it takes, on average, to establish workable procedures (it's usually the human input element that slows things down). It may be that by the time you reach the end of your wish list the system you're investing in will have been upgraded anyway.

And until you have got the basic normal processes in place (case management, database, etc.) you are probably best steering clear of anything too fancy. For example, you may be approached by various companies (or other professionals) who have developed, or are promoting, software packages which aim to take the pain out of planning and analysis by utilising various business models and outcomes. The systems sound like a dream but we would advise smaller firms to be wary of what they will actually achieve through using them. It is often in the area of people – management and motivation – that firms struggle, and these packages won't help with these. Used correctly, however, they may be a tool which the firm itself could use in assisting its own SME clients – though proceed with caution unless your baseline use of technology is well developed.

How to get from where you are now to where you need to be?

Whatever you want to do and whichever stage you're at, the following are some useful pointers to ensure that the process is ultimately successful:

- Obtain specialist advice.
- Work out who will manage and support the project.
- Look at what's on the market, what's possible, and what others are doing.
- Ask your clients for input about their needs.
- Allow for ongoing day-to-day technical support and training.
- Look at what you want to achieve – in the short, medium and long term.
- Aim to start small and run appropriate pilot projects for each stage.
- Set up a working party and consult.
- Devise SMART objectives and an IT plan.
- Set and monitor budgets and timescales.
- Get appropriate buy-in through effective management.
- Review the measurable benefits and publicise them to the firm.

What about data security?

Unfortunately it is all too easy for data to be destroyed, corrupted, or illegally distributed or leaked. Even if the actual damage done isn't that great, the embarrassment to the firm and your reputation can be immense. So it goes without saying that all knowledge management systems should be surrounded by strict usage protocols which are rigorously enforced. Although not all data will be personal data, you must ensure that you have notified the Data Protection Commissioner's office of your use of data and that someone within the firm is formally charged with responsibility for data protection. Personal data aside, the principles of the Data Protection Act, which state amongst other things that data should be kept secure, up to date, and kept no longer than is necessary (don't clutter up the system with information you no longer use or need) are sensible guidelines to follow in respect of *all* data you keep.

Document and case management systems

Whereas document management can be taken to mean, more or less, the electronic storage and retrieval of documents, case management is much more and refers to the electronic management and progression of all stages of a transaction, from beginning to end. Case management systems can provide automatic generation of documents and letters, automatic date or diary prompts and timetabling, and a comprehensive listing of the standard steps to be followed in each transaction – helping to save time, avoid errors and prevent the all too familiar time-waster of reinventing the wheel.

For obvious reasons, document management systems are of relevance to every firm whatever their exact nature of business. However, the scope, nature and applicability of case management systems will vary according to the type and volume of work to which they can be applied. As always with ICT, it is important that your current needs and those of your clients drive the development of the system rather than having a less than perfect system dictating what you can and can't do. Quality of input dictates the likelihood of high-value output, so there are some issues you will need to look at carefully and spend time developing manually before you go anywhere near the ICT system. These include:

- Quality of documents – are yours routinely monitored for accuracy of content and consistency of style?
- Flexibility of output – can your system produce reports and information in the format and at the frequency you and/or your clients require?
- Standardised procedures and protocols – are your document and case management systems standard across the firm or does each department 'do its own thing'? Do you have an appointed member of staff responsible for policing and ensuring firm-wide consistency?
- Access and authorisation levels – document templates and precedent materials should be clearly marked as such and, ideally, should be 'locked' in the system so that only authorised personnel can amend, replace or remove them.

Case management systems often carry with them inherently large amounts of change in respect of the way people work and the services you can offer. Undoubtedly, over time, this will be beneficial but, in the short term, you may encounter resistance from those who dislike change and will dwell on initial bedding-in problems and other negative aspects. This being the case, it is best to start with a pilot project, if necessary run in parallel with the existing systems of working. Although this may lead to accusations of time wasting, there are two benefits:

1. Data won't be lost or service levels downgraded if there are problems with the new system.
2. It makes it easier to measure new ways of working against old and identify the benefits to the firm and the individuals involved.

Obviously, the benefits to be derived from the system are what will provide the motivation for people to take it seriously and apply themselves to making sure the change actually works. These benefits may not be immediately apparent, so it's a good idea – both at the outset and on an on-going basis – to talk to others who have installed the same or a similar system and benefit from their experience. This is an area where benchmarking may be useful in driving levels of competence and commitment to the system.

Case management systems can be highly rewarding because they enable you both to offer new technology-driven services (e.g. e-conveyancing) at highly competitive prices, and also to charge premium rates for added-value services the system allows (in terms of speed, accuracy, coordination, for example). However you choose to develop your services, you must ensure that you keep your existing clients fully informed and spell out the benefits to them both in terms of cost savings (if any) and also any other services that you can now offer, or perform better. By communicating with your clients from the outset, and perhaps also working alongside them in developing particular services, you will also ensure that they have been alerted to any glitches that may occur while the new systems bed in.

Case management systems are particularly beneficial for firms with a number of branch offices which in the past have tended to do things their own way. Not only will the system produce uniformity across the firm but it should make it simple to access case-related information and files from numerous locations. Effective systems, with their intrinsic reduced supervision levels and greater availability and immediacy of information, also make them an almost indispensable feature for underpinning effective flexible working practices – more of this in Chapter 11.

Intranets

An intranet is an internal electronic network set up by an organisation to allow staff access to commonly required information. The system is driven by Internet software and operates in a very similar fashion. Items which might commonly feature on an intranet system in a professional services firm, include:

- staff handbook/manual;
- daily schedules/fee-earner appointments;
- internal systems and procedures (how to book rooms, taxis, etc.);
- internal and external communications, e.g. newsletters, fact sheets, etc.,
- firm-wide CVs (biographies and photos);

- referrals register (inward and outward);
- external supplier details;
- case studies and precedents;
- research data – as appropriate;
- lists of books, CD-Roms etc., held by the firm;
- lists of memberships of associations, networking groups, etc.;
- quality and client care standards and procedures;
- information for use in tenders and pitches.

As with all else, responsibilities must be allocated and procedures put in place for updating and controlling the content of the intranet, and most important – as with all aspects of ICT systems – there must be readily available and highly competent support for when things go wrong (nothing is guaranteed to put the cause and development of ICT back by years than a series of poorly-handled system crashes!).

Practice management and client information systems

A true practice management system contains information about clients, work in progress and work history, time and billing information and contact data. Depending on the underlying requirements of the system, it can also include marketing information about clients, potential clients and other contacts including databases and client reports. Also, it will handle information *for* clients such as may be provided through regular e-mailed reports, newsletters or through use of an extranet – a separate secure external website, or a secure, restricted access section of your existing website allowing clients direct access to their files.

Information for clients might include:

- work-related information – progress of matter, billing record, etc.;
- case studies;
- on-line fees.

Information about clients might include:

- relationship management information – knowledge about contacts and details of who within the firm knows the client;
- details of work in progress;
- historical snapshot – work undertaken over past several years, broken down by work-type and fees earned;
- information about the company itself and the market within which it operates;
- information relating to the company's other advisers;

- account planning information;
- client contact reports, client evaluation or feedback forms.

A good client information system is essential if you are to undertake effective client relationship management and information in such files should include:

- contact names;
- composition of relevant DMUs;
- client's other advisers;
- company profile;
- competitive position;
- plan for developing the relationship;
- contact reports;
- record of hospitality extended, and other contacts made.

As much of this information will be highly sensitive, access must be carefully controlled, although not so tightly controlled that it defeats the object of the exercise (information sharing).

Whatever area of the practice management system you are looking at, two fundamental points should be borne in mind if the system is going to improve your firm's effectiveness and efficiency:

1. Staff should be discouraged from maintaining parallel, paper-based files, unless for documents which cannot be held on the main system. To do so for all documents simply wastes paper and time, and leads to doubt about which system is the most up to date and correct.
2. Fee-earners at all levels should be encouraged to access, amend, review and send data without their secretary's assistance. Although this is not generally an efficient way of working for inputting large amounts of text or complex formatting, it can save enormous amounts of time when making small amendments or corrections. However, the greatest benefit is the freedom it gives fee-earners to be able to work independently and not have to rely on support staff, especially for urgent matters, or work done out-of-hours.

Whatever systems you currently use and however you choose to make use of ICT at present, the fact is that the whole area of ICT is crucially important and will continue to be so because it represents the way the world in general is moving. Professional services delivery will never be entirely technology driven, but clients – commercial and private – will nevertheless be increasingly demanding more ICT-driven systems in those areas where they can see they produce increased value.

The challenge now has changed from what it was some years ago. It is no longer a matter of simply having the hardware and software, it is keeping up – and ideally, keeping ahead of the pack – in terms of the use you make of it, to the advantage of your clients, staff and the business as a whole.

POINTS TO REMEMBER

➤ Effective knowledge management is not dependent on having sophisticated ICT systems. If a firm has never been able to create a knowledge-sharing culture pre-ICT, the advent of a facilitating system is not going to make it happen automatically.

➤ It can be considerably easier to develop ICT systems for a small firm than for a large one. The issue is how to adopt a manageable level of ICT expertise and supporting systems and utilise them as a beneficial tool for your firm rather than an unwelcome infiltrator that you struggle to control.

➤ The three main benefits of effective knowledge management are: improved data management, data manipulation and communication. However, it's easy to drown in data so it's essential first to assess what you need the data for and what specific benefits it will create.

➤ When considering installing or upgrading a system, don't be too ambitious: draw up a plan and progress from one stage to the next. Just because you need a system to be able to do a number of things eventually, it doesn't mean you need it to do them all at once.

➤ Your priority in holding data is to ensure that it is all up to date. Old, incomplete or incorrect data represents a complaint or a disaster waiting to happen. It can undermine confidence in the system and demotivate people from supporting it.

➤ Knowledge management must be seen to be led and supported from the top. Consultation, explanation and training is the main way to generate buy-in and support as well as using people who are personally interested and enthusiastic about IT as standard bearers.

➤ The challenge of ICT in business no longer is being able to demonstrate that you have the hardware and software, it is showing that you can make effective and innovative use of ICT-driven processes for the benefits of clients and your firm.

Motivation

9

Internal communication

Think about your firm – do you recognise any of these problems?

	YES	NO
In the old days we just used to talk to each other, now we've grown bigger no one ever seems to know what's going on.		
It's certainly the mushroom syndrome here unless you're a partner.		
Yes, we communicate quite well about work-related matters, but there's no feeling of camaraderie outside that – people are quite insular.		
Someone in the firm once won an award for bravery – although some partners knew, no one said anything internally – we had to read it in the paper.		
The partners are the worst. They're always too busy – so things like minutes from meetings don't get written up or they come out so late as to be virtually useless.		
We tried an internal newsletter, but it folded after the first few issues as no one contributed much.		
We talk about service standards but nobody is ever clear exactly what we should or shouldn't do.		

All the staff are happy to communicate by e-mail – it's only the partners who refuse.		
They wanted us to trust in a new climate of openness, but then I found out that a problem I'd spoken to my manager about in confidence had been widely discussed outside of that relationship, against my wishes.		

Assuming you didn't answer 'no' to all the above, then you should read on.

What is communication?

Many dictionary definitions of 'communication' refer to giving, transmitting or imparting information, and to judge by what, when and how they communicate, the management of many firms would seem to go along with that. However, for the purposes of effective management and motivation, this definition is far too narrow. Communication is as much to do with the receipt and understanding of information by the receiving party – active listening – as it is to do with transmitting it.

Communication isn't really complete until it has been acted upon by the recipient as proof that it has been received and understood, although, of course, there are many instances where that's difficult to gauge as the communication may not include an obvious call to action. Often the communication process is not complete until the recipient has responded with their own views and ideas and a conclusion mutually agreed, which results in a final version of 'the communication' which may or may not be identical to the original information or edict.

Without this process, information is worthless. A common comment from a disaffected employee is, 'Yes, they said we had to do it another way. But I'm not going to.' Without the process that seeks dialogue, confirmation of understanding and commitment to action, *effective* communication hasn't taken place. And if it's not effective, it's useless.

The importance of communication

Management and motivation can only be engendered through communication, so by definition, internal communication is key to effective external marketing. Although in this chapter we are concentrating on internal communication, it is important not to forget that marketing, as a process, is all to do with identifying, anticipating and meeting client needs, which is impossible to do without effective communication – much of which in a professional services firm needs to happen inside the firm itself.

Internal communication is important because it is a real motivator, something about which, you – as a manager – can do something. Communication can create energy, which comes from employees feeling involved, committed and informed – it gives them the confidence they need to feel good about themselves and the firm. That energy is the one element that can make a real difference in setting your firm apart.

Through communication you not only share information, you bring about *change* (see Figure 9.1). All your values, vision, objectives and plans count for nought if they are not effectively communicated to your workforce and acted upon.

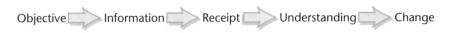

Objective ⟹ Information ⟹ Receipt ⟹ Understanding ⟹ Change

Figure 9.1   The process of change

Even in the smallest of firms, internal communication can be truly appalling. And in some firms with the most impressive and effective external communication programmes, internal communication is not regarded as important. Yet in staff surveys of professional services firms, communication is usually the second most important factor to people after good management (which are both way above salary). This is not surprising: people are social animals and although each one's position on the spectrum between introvert and extrovert will vary, people view themselves first and foremost as individuals – operating against a background of the group/work environment (see Figure 9.2).

This means that how we each interpret the world around us depends on the information we receive. In many firms, information is filtered,

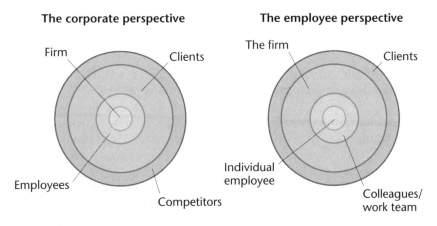

Figure 9.2   The corporate vs. the employee perspective of the firm

patchy or second-hand, causing people at all levels to feel excluded, undervalued and out of touch. Little wonder that they have limited enthusiasm for any task outside the confines of their own job against which, ultimately, they feel (probably correctly in many cases) their performance will be measured.

Studies have shown that fundamentally people want to work hard and do a good job. Although there are exceptions, it is not human nature to want to do otherwise. Yet many firms seem determined to prevent this from happening through not bothering to communicate effectively with their most valuable asset – their employees. The lack of a properly considered communications strategy can be compared with the lack of a servicing plan for machines in a factory. It's no good just putting them in there and hoping they'll keep running without regular maintenance.

Unfortunately, a lot of the problems regarding internal communication within professional services firms are driven by the on-going hierarchical structure and partner paranoia. The upstairs/downstairs atmosphere is still commonplace. Older partners, in particular, have lived through such a regime themselves – however, most will realise that life has moved on. Sometimes, a minority view (and it is usually only a minority) can prevent others from implementing a policy of openness and equality, but this is a situation which must be managed if communication is to improve.

Most would agree that on a personal level, matters of finance, i.e. personal finance relating to the individual, should remain confidential, as should sensitive matters relating to conduct and performance. However, beyond this, there is very little information that cannot and should not be common knowledge around the firm, the exception being truly sensitive information capable of damaging the business or its prospects if leaked.

At the outset of any new internal communications campaign it can be a good idea to have someone come in to talk to the whole firm about the legal implications: slander, racial or sexual harassment, data protection, etc. Without this the potential for embarrassment and real damage can be high.

These issues aside, there are several other factors to take into account when considering your internal communications policy:

- Information tends to leak out via the grapevine. The downside of circulating news in this way is that a reasonably innocuous piece of information can end up fuelling damaging and incorrect rumours because of the 'Chinese whispers' effect.
- People's paranoia increases if perfectly innocent information is kept from them. They fear there must be something sinister or worrying about the information, otherwise why wouldn't they have been told openly?

- The majority of employees, if given the privilege of being entrusted with sensitive information about their firm, will keep that confidence and will be far less likely to pass on information than if they had found it out illicitly. They will respect the trust that has been placed in them and feel personal ownership of the information and increased loyalty to the firm.
- It is relatively easy when disseminating sensitive information, e.g. related to finance or a possible merger, to make it clear that anyone leaking it will be subject to disciplinary action.

The recommended route for improving internal communication is to start by asking employees how they feel about the present level of communication and how they feel it could be improved. It is best to keep this process as neutral as possible, and it may be beneficial to employ an external adviser to whom people would be willing to give truthful and frank responses.

When we go into firms to carry out an audit we often receive some interesting input from staff at all levels regarding communication. This can be the one area which gives a true indication of the overall culture and levels of satisfaction and contentment throughout the firm.

Typical comments from partners include:

- 'I don't know what my colleagues are working on half the time, they keep matters very close to their chests.'
- 'We have partners' lunches but we just tend to sit around and talk about football and holidays, there's not much point to them really.'
- 'I don't know what some people in the firm actually do.'
- 'If you gave us a list of company names and asked which ones were clients of the firm I don't think many of us would know.'
- 'I can't keep pace with who the support staff are. I've never even met some of them.'
- 'Which other professionals are most important to us in terms of referrals? I don't think any of us would agree on that.'

Other professional staff are likely to say:

- 'It would help if we were told how well the firm was doing. Good or bad, we never get to know so it's difficult to know whether you should be working harder or whether everything's fine.'
- 'We were never told anything about the merger until the day before it happened. Of course there'd been rumours, but it was a bit of a shock, to put it mildly.'
- 'Our team leader comes out of his office every few days, fires off instructions like bullets and then retreats. If you don't get him then, you have very little chance to ask any questions'

- 'We never get told where the business as a whole is heading. We all know people and have contacts, but I just don't know whether it's worth trying to get business from them or develop them, so what's the point?'

Comments from support staff include:

- 'Do we have an IT policy? I don't think so. They seem to spend a whole load on new equipment every now and again and then just dish it out to those who shout the loudest.'
- 'As I don't work for any particular partner, I don't know anything about the clients or who the important ones are. I see some of them quite often so I suppose they must be important – but no one ever says.'
- 'There's no system for making suggestions and having them taken seriously, which is a shame. People have lots of good ideas but they never get further than the person they sit next to.'
- 'Who are our competitors? I have no idea.'

Developing an internal communications strategy

Like marketing, internal communication is an evolutionary process and firms which may feel that they are good communicators may in fact still be at the bottom of the scale. As Figure 9.3 shows, it is all to do with the amount of employee involvement in the process – are you just telling them, or are you listening to what they have to say and truly involving them?

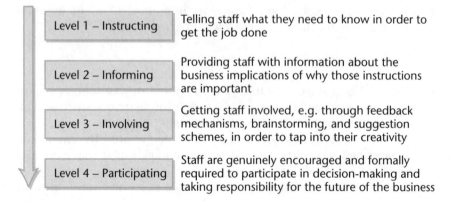

Figure 9.3   The evolution of internal communication

There are a number of tools and processes relevant to internal communication, all of which have a different part to play. They can be broken down according to their formality or informality and their regularity or irregularity (see Table 9.1). The extent to which each is appropriate to your firm and how important a role it assumes will depend on factors such as the size of your firm, whether or not the firm operates over several sites, the physical layout of your offices, the range of services you provide, and the culture of your firm and the predominating personality type within it.

Table 9.1 Internal communication tools

	Regular	**Periodic**
Formal	Meetings Reports/minutes External newsletter Management e-mails/memos	Staff surveys AGM Staff appraisals New protocols Training sessions Awaydays or weekends
Informal	Team social events Internal newsletters One-to-one staff meetings with managing partner	Brainstorming sessions Firm-wide social events Suggestion scheme

The advantage of developing an internal communication strategy which uses a number of these tools in different ways is that the strategy is likely to work because you have agreed:

- what information will be communicated;
- how often;
- by what means;
- in what tone;
- to whom.

All you have to do is to manage the process and make sure that you, and every one else involved, delivers on time. As a starting point, we suggest the following:

1. Be clear about what the firm as a whole is trying to achieve. Your values, vision, business and marketing strategies will underpin all that you're trying to communicate. However, remember that your communication objectives need to be as SMART as any others (see Chapter 1) if they are to be effective and help take the business forward to where you want it to be.
2. Take an inventory of all the information which is distributed around your firm at present – and the channels through which this takes place.

3. Make a list yourself of what information could possibly be communicated and divide the list into two columns:

    (a) That which currently is being communicated;
    (b) That which isn't.

    Consider list (a): Who is it going to? Who should it be going to? Are there any better ways (less time-consuming, more interesting, faster) of distributing it at present? Is it a one-way process? What channels are there for input and response?
        Now consider list (b). Assess each item individually: What would be the benefits and drawbacks of distributing that information? If there would be benefits, how would the information best be disseminated, bearing in mind the criteria given above?
4. Discuss with your partners the issue of information dissemination. Gauge their views on transparency of information. Persuade them to agree to an internal staff survey relating to communication, conduct it and see what it produces.
5. Revisit list 3(b) above, taking into account any additional information thrown up by the survey.

You should then plot your communication channels into a similar format as Table 9.1, but include detail (as an appendix) of exactly what information will be communicated. Remember to take into account the tone of each piece of communication – from highly formal and prescriptive to chatty and informal. And don't forget a touch of humour – used judiciously it can be very effective.

Next, plot a Gantt chart over the year showing times/dates of what will be communicated, and when, to ensure there is not overload in preparing information, that information is available at the right time (e.g. prior to meetings) and that people are not submerged by too much information arriving at one time.

Put your proposed plan to your partners for their discussion, input and agreement and set about introducing the scheme throughout the firm, one step at a time. The implications of what will happen for non-delivery of information, lack of contribution or refusal to cooperate must be taken on board. As always, the reasons behind the new programme must be carefully explained to all from the outset, the schedule of introduction outlined, and each person's role – if appropriate – built into their individual objectives.

After a period of time (a year or so at least), having implemented most of the strategy, it is worth conducting another survey on communication and people's attitudes to it, to measure improvement and highlight ongoing problems.

If yours is a fairly small firm, you may rightly feel that this approach is taking a sledgehammer to crack a nut. While it's true that you probably don't need quite as structured a communications programme as a larger firm, you should still take the same structured approach to assessing your communication needs. Even when there are only two of you, the ability to selectively impart information with damaging results – for whatever reason – is a common problem. Just think of the relationships between some husbands and wives . . .

Communication tools and processes

As Table 9.1 above illustrates, processes can be either formal or informal.

Formal

Meetings

> 'A meeting is an occasion when people get together, some to say what they do not think and others not to say what they really do.'
> Vladimir Voinovich (*The Listener*, 1988)

Meetings are potentially, and actually, one of the greatest time wasters within a firm so their usefulness must be regularly assessed. Most firms spend hours of valuable time a week on holding meetings from which little emerges. Worse, because of the way they are allowed to drift, people come away feeling frustrated, angry and resentful rather than motivated, empowered and clear about the way ahead.

For now, just remember the following points:

- Only hold a meeting if there's no better way you can achieve the same purpose.
- Circulate any material relevant to the meeting in good time so attendees have time to read it.
- Have an agenda and an allocated time for the meeting and stick to it.
- Ensure someone chairs the meeting and keeps matters strictly under control.
- Use the meeting for discussion and decision making, not information reporting.
- Record the outcome of meetings and circulate the minutes promptly after the meeting with action points clearly highlighted.
- If meetings are a problem in your organisation, ensure everyone receives training in holding effective meetings.

Reports/minutes

These should be the means of circulating regular information. As mentioned above, a meeting is not the place for simply reporting information

– so ensure any relevant reports are attached to agendas or minutes, or circulated independently.

Ideally, reports or minutes should be disseminated in some form to everyone in the firm, although there can be an argument for presenting information in summary form to those who are likely not to be interested in the full picture (with it made clear that they can have access to this information should they really require it). In the past, this would have led to accusations of paper mountains and wasted effort. These days it's a simple matter of computer storage and distribution, which is where the value of an intranet comes into its own.

Never assume that people will remember what took place at a meeting. Rather, ensure that someone attends specifically to take minutes and that these are written up, approved, and circulated as quickly as possible after the meeting. Minutes and reports should both focus on being concise, clear, accurate and readable. Any long or detailed information should either be attached as an appendix or a reference given to where it can be accessed.

Ensure that further action is highlighted (in graphical style if possible). For minutes, this may be a format which clearly shows task, name of person responsible, date to be achieved. In the case of reports, it may be better to condense further action into the format of a mini plan or Gantt chart.

A central archive of minutes and reports should be maintained – ideally on computer – so that no one is at the mercy of the filing system of the person generating the material.

Management e-mails/memos

Keep these brief, to the point and, if possible, consolidated. It's better to get one e-mailed message covering several points, once a week than random drips of information. If your information is still paper based, keep the paper mountain down as much as possible. A common complaint is that an e-mail isn't as formal as a memo and therefore some firms still waste time, money and energy on paper transmission of information. Stop! Just explain at the outset that from now, e-mail is how it will be done and that particular types of e-mails are to be taken seriously and are formal. This will grow on the dissenters over time.

If you are struggling, as many firms are, with those who still refuse to use e-mail as a valid form of communication, basing your entire communication strategy around it can be remarkably effective. What this means is that anyone who won't use the system is effectively excluded, and over time, invariably comes on board. Of course, they will need training, encouragement and often a degree of hand-holding but at the end of the day, you are guaranteed 100 per cent compliance.

New protocols

If a particular communication is outlining a new regulation, procedure, or system of conduct, it is essential that:

- it is clearly flagged up as such;
- the date of introduction is clearly given;
- penalties for non-compliance are clearly given;
- it is accompanied by details of any related training (should it be required);
- it is stored in a central knowledge bank (e.g. staff manual, intranet file, whatever) for easy reference and retrieval.

These protocols or policies are the systematic rules by which you run your business. Particularly in this increasingly litigious age, it is vital to have them if you intend to have enforceable standards throughout your firm and cohesiveness in respect of service delivery. They should form the foundation stone of the induction process for any new employees, and current employees should be reminded, as appropriate, of their existence on a regular basis.

Training sessions

As mentioned above, it is often not enough just to communicate information. Training in some form or another will need to be given in order to effect change and ensure action. Although you may picture training as a room full of people being formally lectured on a specific topic, there is a more pragmatic definition of 'practical education' or 'process of acquiring skill, qualifications, etc.'. So training can mean a team leader discussing an issue with their team; practical demonstrations of how something should be done; or one-to-one conversations with employees to confirm that they fully understand the new situation and its implications, and offering them the chance to raise any questions.

Staff appraisals

More information on staff appraisals and training is given in Chapter 10. However, the role of the appraisal in internal communication should not be underrated. It is the most essential of all internal communications tools in as much as its purpose is to deal one-to-one with the performance, feedback and objectives of the individual, couched in terms which are relevant to them, their aspirations and challenges. It is the most important tool you have for engendering change.

The key message to take on board is that the appraisal system is a communication tool, and as such is a two-way process. Many appraisal systems simply focus on the individual and what's required of them, without giving them the opportunity to feed in their comments both in respect of how the operational management of the firm impacts upon them, and also their reactions and suggestions concerning the 'bigger picture' – the firm as a whole, how it operates and where it is going.

Staff surveys

Once a firm has got to a certain size, periodic staff surveys can be a useful means of gauging satisfaction, issues of complaint, views and feelings. They can be anonymous, but as long as the respondents have to indicate their status, e.g. partner, secretary, they can be a useful means of comparing how various groups within the firm feel about different issues.

People like to be asked, and even though over time, the response rate to these surveys may drop away, they still have a benefit in being a means by which people can provide input and feedback. Of course, there will be cynics, but often they can be countered by taking the line that staff can best effect change by responding positively rather than simply complaining and belittling the process. When you present the exercise it should be with the expectation that everyone will respond, especially partners. If you undertake the exercise at all, in order for it to have any validity, it must be taken seriously.

Several points need to be borne in mind if the survey process is to be successful:

- The purpose of conducting a survey should be made very clear (with any sinister connotations or repercussions removed).
- The survey should come from the managing partner and individual responses should only be seen by him or her (anonymous aggregated responses can be widely circulated).
- There should be a balance of closed (multi-choice) and open (free-text) questions.
- Questions should deal with hard (e.g. provision of suitable equipment, salary levels) and soft (e.g. are respondents made to feel valued? Is bullying or intimidation an issue?) aspects of life within the firm.
- Aggregate results should be reported back to the firm.
- Action must be taken in respect of at least some of the main findings, or the exercise will be completely discredited.

It should also be made known that the managing partner is prepared to discuss the questionnaire with any staff – which can be a useful communications exercise in itself.

Like several other areas of specialist communication, it may be worthwhile calling in a specialist adviser (a marketing or market research professional) to conduct the survey and to analyse the results. The added benefit of doing so is the additional confidentiality in not having the raw data scrutinised by anyone in the firm.

AGM

Many large professional firms who model themselves more closely on commercial companies now hold Annual General Meetings – although they may refer to them by a variety of different names. Even for smaller firms, however, they are valuable and can be a great motivational tool. Most firms have held an assessment of annual performance at the year-end among the partners, but few have extended this to a formal presentation of results to the firm as a whole.

An effective AGM can have several purposes:

- It brings all the staff together, formally, once in the year.
- It reports on what the firm has achieved in the past year in respect of financial results, business development, staff, IT development, etc.
- It outlines plans for the coming year – and can include special (short) presentations on, for example, plans for upgrading the IT system, or a new client care programme.
- It provides an opportunity to acknowledge publicly and reward those who have contributed outstanding performance throughout the year.

An AGM should be short, punchy and informal. Ideally it should be held at a time and place where everyone can be gathered together – a room outside the office should be hired if necessary. If it can be combined with a social event – even just drinks – so much the better, though care should be taken that none of the seriousness of the atmosphere is lost in the event which follows. It's relatively cheap, easy to run but incredibly effective in boosting morale and levels of motivation.

Awaydays or weekends

These can be essential as a means of reviewing progress, planning for the future and achieving consensus on important issues. Commonly they are held by and for the partners and combine the benefits of team social events and brainstorming sessions. However, over time they can become boring, repetitive and non-productive – more a means of rubber-stamping the financial decisions and socialising than achieving anything meaningful.

If you suspect this is happening in your firm, try the following:

- Speak to each of your partners well in advance and ask them for their frank opinion of the current format and content.

- Ask them what they would like to see, and for their suggestions.
- Look at what the key issues are for the firm and see how these can be usefully considered at the get-together.
- Consider bringing in an outside facilitator to direct the meeting or external contributors (from within the firm, external advisers or clients) to present some sessions.
- If it becomes obvious that you could handle the business aspect of the meeting in one day, stick to that and don't drag it out all weekend, even though drinks and dinner in the evening are a good bonding opportunity.

External newsletter

Your external newsletter (see Chapter 2) also has important implications for internal communication. For one thing, it may be the only way that many staff know that you have particular expertise in a certain field – or that certain developments have taken place. It also underlines to them how the firm presents itself to the outside world. It is surprising how proud staff can be of an external newsletter – give them each their own copy and many will take it home to show their family or pass it on to interested friends.

The information conveyed through your newsletter can have far-reaching effects internally. This can be as simple as a secretary or switch-board operator saying 'a client rang and asked who dealt with such and such and I wouldn't have known except that I remembered they'd written something about it in the external newsletter'. (Of course, you should have other systems in place for dealing with this.) Or, better still, it may jog someone's memory and remind them that, yes, they had always meant to cross-sell another of the firm's services to a client – and now it's in the newsletter, there's a perfect excuse to bring it up in conversation.

Informal

Team social events

There's work and there's enjoyment. The two should go hand in hand, but, even in the best-run offices they don't all the time. For a team to be really effective, you need to get behind the veneer imposed by the operational structure and ensure that there's inter-personal bonding so that each individual really and truly feels part of the team.

An effective means of doing this is for the team to have periodic social outings, with no purpose other than to let their hair down, gossip, moan and probably end up with a collective hangover. What and when is organised depends on many factors – the age of the group, location of offices, travelling time from the office to home, etc. At the very least, each team should meet for a drink every couple of months, with the understanding that everyone in the team – from team leader to most junior support staff – is expected to attend unless they have some legitimate excuse. In some instances it may be more appropriate to go for a pizza at lunchtime, but whatever you choose, make sure it happens and happens regularly.

If the team members seriously don't want to spend any time with their colleagues outside the office then, quite frankly, you have a problem with that team – they are not bonding and never will and that could cause serious problems at some stage on the work front. Of course, not all team members will get on together as well as others, but such events provide a forum for finding other platforms on which to communicate and for members to see a different side to their colleagues. For example, many partners can reveal a much more likeable and approachable persona once out of the office environment. When floating the idea of team events you may come up against the response, 'junior staff won't enjoy themselves, they'll be overawed', however, it's up to the more senior members of the team to include them and ensure they don't feel overawed. Although respect is important between all parties it's impossible to have an effective team if one or more of its members feels intimidated by one or more of the rest. Also, don't forget inter-team bonding – getting together with another team every now and again can boost knowledge, camaraderie and cooperation.

You may wish to consider making some sort of contribution towards team events from the firm (but be aware of the tax implications), although it is not unreasonable for the partner(s) or team leader to dip into their own pocket and at least pay for a couple of rounds of drinks as a personal thank-you to their team.

Internal newsletter

An employee newsletter is a much underrated vehicle for internal communication, yet most firms tend to use it for the wrong purposes, or more commonly don't have one at all. 'Issue one and two came out on time, issue three was two months late, and then it folded completely!' is a common tale. Having a newsletter depends on allowing someone (with a degree of flair, literacy and editorial judgement) the time and resources to produce it. With desktop publishing, e-mail and photocopiers, an internal newsletter need not be terribly expensive or time consuming.

Such a newsletter can be a great leveller, containing information solicited from both the managing partner and the office junior. The key to a successful internal newsletter is informality and there should be plenty of room for humour as well as news (internal, client and any other external news of interest), human interest features, interviews, sport and even recipes. Here are some tried and tested tips for producing an internal newsletter:

- When first establishing (or reviving) your newsletter you need to work out precisely what you want to do based on what you perceive as the firm's particular communication needs and interests.
- Consider the practical details of how you're going to introduce the newsletter, including access to a computer, photocopier and physical distribution.
- Agree a publication schedule and produce something every publication day.
- It's important that your newsletter is not a management mouthpiece but does have management support. (It's a good idea for the managing partner or other senior manager to review the content before it's published to avoid major faux pas or communication disasters.)
- Communicate with everyone in the firm telling them what you are going to be doing, why you are doing it (information and amusement), the sort of thing you're looking for, and eliciting their help.
- Aim to establish a balance between the deathly dull (the need-to-know articles often concerning administration matters), the possible pontifications (management telling it how they'd like it to be) and the very specific human interest (weddings, exam results, birthdays, etc.).
- Always be positive and never enter into any sort of comment or criticism on matters directly to do with operations in the workplace (although if the newsletter highlights something that everyone complains about – for example, the coffee – in a humorous way, then you'll be on to a winner).
- Before each issue is published, start work on the next. Forward planning is crucial so that you have a good stock of 'timeless' material to provide the background if you need it for issues where more immediate news is short.

As an adjunct to staff newsletters, bulletins and noticeboards – physical or on the intranet – should not be overlooked as a valuable means of communication and dissemination of information. People will only look at noticeboards if they know there is regularly something new to see. However, if the boards become cluttered with rubbish of interest to very few, staff won't pay them attention (you should have a policy outlining who decides what is posted). And if you have an intranet-based, interactive bulletin board, it's once again important that procedures are outlined in respect of responses, adding comments, and so on, if the exercise isn't to be hijacked and discredited.

One-to-one staff meetings

One of the most effective forms of management is 'management by walking the floor'. This allows the managing partner or other senior managers informally to observe their troops at work and discuss any topical issues. Indeed, taken to extremes, one of the most radical and even more effective forms of management is actually going back to the floor and working alongside people for a period of time while they carry out their day-to-day duties.

Motivation and management are all to do with communication and aside from any formal or informal coaching or mentoring processes that may be taking place, it's a good idea for the managing partner to make time to meet informally and individually – even if just over a cup of coffee, or breakfast – with his managers, team leaders and other significant members of staff. This gives them an opportunity to report on how they feel things are going, any particular problems or issues they may be wrestling with and any recent successes, as well as providing the managing partner with a sounding board about how effectively and efficiently the firm is being managed and the current state of motivation and morale.

This is, if you like, the means of finding out the true picture of what's going on behind the information contained in the formal reports, and the conduct of formal meetings. The fact that a team leader knows that they'll have an opportunity for informal discussion will also help resolve many issues which may either have been presented as crises or been allowed to fester unresolved. The team leader or manager will tend to think, 'when we next meet, I'll make sure we discuss that' – by which time, the issue may have been resolved, or the person involved will have had time to take a more reasoned view.

Brainstorming sessions

Just because you're a manager doesn't mean you have to have all the answers, nor should you try to. Often when you're presented with a particular issue or challenge, the best approach is to start off with a brainstorming session in the hope of generating the widest possible range of workable options and solutions. Although by their very nature they should be freeform and wide-ranging, there are a few points to bear in mind about brainstorming sessions if they are to be effective:

- Be clear about what you want to achieve at the outset.
- Set a timetable and stick to it.
- Try to hold the session at a time and in a place with few other distractions.
- Involve a range of people – some of whom are close to the issue and some who have very little knowledge. The outsiders can often see more possibilities than those who are too close to the problem.

- Hold a warm-up session to get the ideas flowing (e.g. 'different uses for a matchstick').
- Record the outcomes as you go along.
- State at the outset that none of the outcomes may necessarily be implemented.
- Report back to the group following the meeting and indicate the next stage.

Firm-wide social events

What is it about Christmas? We're not knocking its religious or social significance, but in today's commercial world why is it that in many firms the only regular communication clients will receive from the firm is a Christmas card and the only regular social event for the staff is a Christmas party, or Christmas drinks. Yes, the staff Christmas bash certainly has its place and one could still argue that it's a good time to get together and for the management to show their appreciation. However, for many it is now an unwanted formality held at a time when they'd rather be doing something else, and felt to be hollow and meaningless.

If you suspect this is the situation in your firm, look at what you want to achieve by holding the event (a means of thanking the staff, an opportunity to bond, etc.) and then discuss the matter with your fellow partners and the rest of the staff. Working on their feedback, come up with a range of options and hold a referendum. You won't get 100 per cent support for any one option but at least you'll know why you are doing it and that there is majority support. Depending on your objectives, you may be better doing away with the one or two big, expensive firm-wide events and having a regular monthly 'drop-in' drinks session for those who want to attend.

Suggestion schemes

One tool which can have the lateral thinking advantages of brainstorming without the time and administrative encumbrance, is the suggestion scheme. We have included it here as an 'informal' communication channel simply because the regularity of input cannot be controlled as can more formal channels. However, the scheme itself, if it is to be effective, needs to be formalised, treated seriously, and suitable suggestions regularly considered, acted upon and rewarded.

Suggestion schemes have been discredited in many firms simply because they were introduced as 'a good idea' and a way of encouraging staff to be 'involved', placating their view that their ideas were neither sought nor considered. However, as with many other areas, the process was rarely tightly managed and staff were not motivated to participate, so the whole thing fell into disrepute.

Although we have listed suggestion schemes as an 'internal' communications process, client suggestion schemes can also be very effective in generating new ideas and new ways of doing things.

Problems/solutions

Effective internal communication is not without its problems and you may need actively to manage the following aspects.

Confidentiality

Underlying the concept of free speech and open communication is the concept of confidentiality in those situations where it is patently reasonable and desirable. For example, an employee who wants to discuss a personal matter with their manager in confidence, should not then find that information has been passed on unless the manager has sought their permission to discuss it with someone else and given the reason why.

Security

It goes without saying that computer-stored material can be password protected and, while not absolutely impervious, it is far safer than methods of physical distribution and storage. Practical problems occur with the dissemination of information by e-mail or other electronic means when partners or others are unable or unwilling to access or print off their own material. In this case they need to make clear to their secretaries the confidentiality of the information they are handling, and the dangers of leaving material on shared printers or photocopiers.

Resentment

Unfortunately, because communication is often concerned with change, no matter what you try and do, you will end up receiving complaints and generating resentment in some. People will say they are now bombarded with information, and many of those who previously complained that they were never told anything, now resent the number of e-mails they receive. You will hear complaints about tone of voice, speed of communication, imagined slights and inferences. It is important, however, to focus on the benefits and improvements brought about for the majority – undoubtedly they will recognise and appreciate this, although human nature being as it is, their views are more likely to remain unspoken.

POINTS TO REMEMBER

➤ Understand what communication really means – it is not a one-way process.

➤ Start by examining what you already do and where your communication gaps lie and aim to use a range of internal communication channels – one or two is rarely sufficient to cover all communication needs.

➤ Set SMART communications objectives and make sure everyone understands what they are aiming to achieve.

➤ Devise a communication strategy and get buy-in from your fellow partners.

➤ Don't try to improve everything at once – start with the worst areas and progress gradually.

➤ Make maximum use of IT – don't pay lip-service to it.

➤ Use the full range of communication tools – they all have a significant and slightly different role to play.

➤ Periodically re-examine how well communication is working – it is not a static process.

➤ Don't be discouraged by minority complaints or resentment. Investigate their cause and deal with them appropriately, but always focus on the benefits that effective internal communications can generate for the majority.

10

Individual performance

KEY ISSUES

- The importance of motivation
- Incentive and reward
- The role of induction
- Training
- Coaching and mentoring
- Appraisals

Think about your firm – do you recognise any of these problems?

	YES	NO
We pay our staff more than the going rate so I can't understand why they aren't more motivated.		
There isn't really any proper induction process – newcomers are usually shown around the office but that's about it.		
Sometimes the first we get to know that someone new has joined the firm is when their leaving card is sent round for signing!		
We must spend a fortune each year on training – I don't know that we ever see much benefit from it though.		
We don't actually have a formal training plan as such. The fee-earners are responsible for making sure they attend enough courses to get their CPD [continuous professional development] points for the year.		
Coaching and mentoring – that's just where you follow someone more senior around for a bit, isn't it?		

The partners here really struggle with appraisals – they never seem to be carried out in any truly objective manner and hardly ever recognise individual effort.		
Personal objectives are all very well in the big firms but we just don't have time for that sort of thing here.		

Assuming you didn't answer 'no' to all the above, then you should read on.

Individual performance is an area of crucial importance to the professional services firm simply because:

- by its very nature, the service can't be separated from the individual(s) supplying it;
- the firm's performance is made up of the aggregate performance of the individuals within it;
- the firm's brand is based on promises relating to consistency and quality, and delivery of these is dependent on individual attitudes and motivation.

An individual's performance is related to:

- their level of understanding of client needs and of what they are expected to do;
- their level of motivation and acceptance of shared values;
- their knowledge of how to perform the task in hand;
- their general well-being.

The first can be bettered through effective initial induction and by setting and reviewing clear personal objectives. The second two can be improved through coaching, training and mentoring. The whole process can be steered, monitored and measured through a proper system of appraisal.

Before we look in detail at each of these, let's look more closely at exactly what's meant by motivation.

The importance of motivation

Understanding what motivates individuals is essential if you are to bring about real change within the firm, as overall achievement of goals depends on the extent to which each individual is motivated to perform and deliver. It is an area with which managers often struggle; it's not that they don't care, more that they don't know what to do.

For example, there is a common misconception that if you put right the things that your employees complain about, they will be happy and motivated. In fact, studies show that this is not necessarily the case.

Satisfiers and dissatisfiers

The psychologist Herzberg discovered that things that satisfy people are very different from those that dissatisfy them, so that eliminating dissatisfaction does not automatically create satisfaction. For example, in his study, dissatisfiers (aspects relating to what he called 'hygiene' factors) included:

- company policy;
- supervision methods;
- working conditions;
- salary.

However, satisfiers (motivating factors) were:

- achievement;
- recognition;
- nature of the work itself;
- responsibility.

What this showed overall was that dissatisfiers can be corrected by attention to hygiene factors. However, doing that won't make other problems – that is, areas where there is a lack of real satisfaction – go away. In fact, every individual will be at some point along a sort of continuum ranging from actual dissatisfaction through to true satisfaction (motivation). See Figure 10.1.

Positive and negative reinforcement

Often, and especially in relation to business development issues, a firm will complain that its efforts are failing because it 'hasn't got the right people' for successful marketing. However, the firm probably doesn't really need to change its people – more likely, it needs to change the

Figure 10.1 The dissatisfaction–satisfaction continuum

behaviour of its people. Training, coaching and mentoring can all help to bring about change and much of that will be involved with addressing issues related to the individual's motivation. This is especially so in areas such as business development where there is plenty of uncertainty associated with what people are trying to do (for example, they generally feel awkward and inadequate trying to win new business) but there may be very little positive reinforcement for performance (many firms offer no bonuses or other recognition for business development successes).

What we need to look at here is the concept of positive and negative reinforcement. Positive reinforcement works on the premise that positive feedback on a successful outcome is a far more effective motivator than negative feedback as a response to failure or shortcoming. Motivators are in fact positive reinforcers – those things that encourage an individual to repeat their behaviour.

That's fine if the behaviour is 'good' and you want it to be repeated (and copied by others in the work group). But you need to take care here – in practice, positive reinforcement is often inadvertently given to negative behaviour. For example, someone in the team is set a task or objective and fails to perform. If the outcome is that the individual isn't tackled about the lack of performance but is simply not asked to perform the task again, this becomes positive reinforcement of the non-performance and will act as a powerful signal to the individual that it is okay to repeat the poor behaviour. Other team members will be affected – they may either think that the poor behaviour has been condoned by the powers that be and that it is acceptable for them to copy it, or they may see it as a case where someone in the team has been allowed to get away with lack of performance and feel resentment at what they perceive as unfair, unequal treatment.

At the other end of the spectrum, negative reinforcers – overt criticism, blame, removal of status or reward, ridicule – invariably carry side-effects such as apprehension, aggression and misinterpretation. It has been found that blaming or punishing approaches can produce hostility and resentment in the individual which can foster and linger, and can cause permanent damage to the culture and morale of the team as a whole on a scale completely disproportionate to the original poor behaviour.

It clearly makes sense therefore to try and positively reinforce good behaviour wherever possible and, in those situations where you do have to deal with negative behaviour, make sure you do so in a constructive fashion:

- Spell out the individual's current shortcomings in neutral but specific terms – for example, don't say 'you're letting your team down by not carrying out your marketing responsibilities'. Instead, try, 'did you know that your team is very upset because you haven't contributed to achieving their cross-selling targets?'.

- Ensure that the individual concerned has a clear understanding of exactly what you are talking about and where you feel the problem lies (they may not even have realised there was a problem).
- Discuss the individual's reason for their non-performance, listen to their response and provide constructive, practical guidance on how they might improve.

In all cases, be aware that, as a manager/leader, you will have a choice in how you deal with individual performance or lack of it but the choice you make will, in turn, determine the future development of the individual as well as impacting on the whole team. Figure 10.2 illustrates behavioural reinforcement.

Incentive and reward

Another thing you need to know about motivation is that different things motivate different people. For some, financial incentive is the be-all and end-all while for others, a timely word of praise or acknowledgement of a job well done is enough to put them on cloud nine and inspire even greater performance next time.

Let's look more closely at this. Money is (often erroneously) viewed by those in authority as being the prime motivator. However, it will only

		Reinforcement	
		Negative	Positive
Behaviour	Good	**De-motivated culture** • No incentive to repeat good behaviour • Individuals feel betrayed and undervalued • Low team morale	**Highly motivated culture** • Individuals likely to repeat 'good' outcomes • Improved self-esteem • High individual and team motivation
	Bad	**Blame culture** • Individuals feel hostility and lingering resentment • Low individual and team morale	**Confused culture** • Individuals likely to repeat 'poor' behaviour as message received that this is acceptable • Other team members may copy the 'poor' behaviour which they perceive as being condoned by management

Figure 10.2 Behavioural reinforcement

work in this way if there is a need within the individual to be met – for example, offering to pay overtime at double rate may be enough to entice a junior secretary into the office to work over the weekend. On the other hand, paying, say, a senior surveyor a salary which is above the norm will tend not to be a motivator (although it may have been a key incentive for him or her to join the firm). The surveyor will view it as salary – no more and no less than they deserve in return for taking on their normal work-load. A discretionary performance-based bonus, on the other hand, might inspire extra performance in the individual, and a monetary bonus awarded on a team basis, in return for team results, can also work very effectively, bringing about not just increased productivity but also improving team involvement and morale.

But money doesn't talk to everybody and some people will respond better to other forms of incentive. A number of firms have put on their thinking caps and come up with an impressive array of alternative incentives – private healthcare, company cars, contributions to personal pension plans, gym and leisure club membership, even on-site physiotherapy, yoga and stress counselling. Flexible working methods (discussed fully in the next chapter) are often viewed favourably – by employees at any rate – because they help to preserve quality of life and can engender a sensible work–life balance.

Some, however, might view perks such as free late-night taxis home, in-house restaurants, gyms and so on in a more cynical light – namely, as a means of the employer effectively exploiting the individual, finding ways of keeping them in the office as long as possible so they can do more and more work and therefore promulgating an unhealthy long-hours culture.

So it is not easy to come up with a scheme which is acceptable to all and which actually produces the desired result of providing motivation for improved individual performance. What firms must do is:

- decide exactly what level of performance they want to inspire;
- ascertain what will provide the necessary incentive for each individual;
- be clear about how certain benefits offered might be viewed (that is, be clear about your motives);
- work at introducing a reward system which can be tailored to individual needs.

The role of induction

With motivation, it pays to start at the very beginning . . .

Most businesses admit that staffing is one of their biggest challenges. The problem isn't just recruitment; holding on to staff and helping them realise their maximum potential once they have joined are equally important concerns. For the firm, a departing employee potentially means wasted recruitment costs and time, bad publicity for the company and a negative impact on the morale of remaining staff.

So what goes wrong and what is the solution? Analysis shows that if a new employee does not have a good understanding of an organisation, this may lead from the outset to poor integration into the team, low morale and loss of productivity. Therefore one of the key factors in not just retaining staff, but keeping them happy and productive, is having a formal induction programme which starts on day one.

What is induction?

The first step in implementing a really successful induction programme is understanding what it actually is. Far from the ten-minute tour of the building that many organisations regard as induction, it is, in fact, a structured programme of information giving and familiarisation with the aim of ensuring the effective integration of the new recruit into their surroundings.

The length and nature of each induction programme will vary according to the size and type of your company. Figure 10.3 describes typical areas that should be included.

Creating an induction programme

Before you can implement an effective induction programme, certain issues must be resolved:

- Who is to be responsible for the induction process? Normally this is the new recruit's team leader or line manager, but allocation of tasks may extend to several people including HR personnel, the training manager and IT manager, depending on who is best informed to contribute.
- What are the objectives of the induction programme? What specific outcomes do you wish to achieve and what information do you need to deliver and when in order to ensure the new employee achieves a particular level of knowledge within certain timescales?
- How do you intend to deliver induction information – verbal or video presentation, written or on-line material or a mixture of these?
- Is the programme sufficiently tailored towards the needs of the individual? Particular attention needs to be paid to certain categories of newcomers such as college leavers, the long-term unemployed and physically disabled employees.
- Is the programme compliant with the requirements of relevant external quality standards such as the Health and Safety at Work Act 1974

or the Investors In People standard? For example, the latter sets a standard that companies should adhere to in looking after employees, and outlines key principles such as *commitment* to developing people, *planning* through the establishment of aims and objectives for each member of staff, *action* to effectively improve staff performance, and *evaluation* of each employee's performance. (This and other quality standards relevant to professional services firms are discussed in detail at Chapter 12.)

Job specification	Give a clear outline of the requirements and standards expected
The organisation and department	Show how the employee will fit into the team and the rest of the company, including organisation charts and site map
Office facilities	Cover location, operating procedures and internal rules or protocols governing the use of telephones, copiers, fax machines, computers
Company culture and values	Provide an outline of the firm's background and mission statement and explain quality systems
Rules, procedures and policies	Provide information on security systems, dress codes, private use of telephone/e-mail, breaks, etc.
Grievance and disciplinary procedures	Explain communication methods, appeals procedures, employee representation
Employment conditions	Provide contract of employment and information on hours, holidays, probationary period, sickness, maternity/paternity leave
Financial matters	Cover details of salary and benefits, payment dates and method, expenses and expense claims
Health, safety and welfare	Identify emergency procedures, safety rules, first aid, accident reporting
Training	Explain firm's training policy and appraisal system and procedures relating to attendance at in-house and external courses

Figure 10.3   The induction plan

Showing you care

How well an employee fits in is all to do with people – so making an effort to make them feel valued and welcome is vital. For example,

- Prepare their workplace before they start. Remove the previous incumbent's possessions and ensure the area is clean, fully equipped and functional.
- Give them some practical work to do from day one. Not only will it assist their learning and lead to a sense of achievement, it will also help them feel part of the workforce from early on.
- Don't overload them with information. Ensure that you stage the induction process so they can absorb information gradually.

Some organisations operate, very successfully, a buddy system whereby someone (usually a member of the same team) is officially allocated to every newcomer so that they can use them as a on-going (say for their first six months) source of advice, an initial 'friend', confidant(e), etc. In most firms, this operates on an informal basis, but because it is informal, the new employee can often feel they mustn't bother the person next to them by asking too many questions, while on the other side, although well-intentioned, the new employee's busy colleagues feel it isn't part of their role to train and support and so quickly start to resent having to mother someone new.

Remember, however, that induction should be just one part of an on-going communication process throughout the employment cycle. Review induction with the new recruit to establish whether objectives have been met, then ensure they participate in a programme of on-going training and staff appraisal, thus allowing both employers and employees regularly to discuss objectives and exchange feedback.

Part of induction should be ensuring that over time (not during their first week!) all new employees are brought up to speed on all of the firm's marketing initiatives, client care standards, knowledge management procedures and so on. Although those who were on the staff when these initiatives were introduced were probably given intensive training, new joiners are generally just expected to pick up such important information by osmosis. It's not surprising therefore that, over time, initiatives start to slip and become diluted.

Training

Training means bringing a person up to a state or standard of efficiency by instruction and practice. But why do we have to bother about training at all? Don't people enter the professions already suitably qualified? What are we trying to get out of it? Increasing emphasis is placed these days by all the professions on the importance of lifetime learning, with a programme of continuing education being a matter of compulsory professional compliance for solicitors, accountants and surveyors – so there's one good reason for doing it!

Here are some others:

- Training leads to an increase in knowledge and – crucially – skills.
- It helps maximise the investment made by a firm in its employees.
- It can provide competitive advantage over other firms.
- A firm with a renowned training programme will have an advantage in the recruitment market.
- It can provide an opportunity for team building and bonding (in the case of group training).
- Rather than letting people loose on clients before they have been 'tried and tested', training sessions can be a safe opportunity in which to practise and to give and receive feedback, constructive criticism and corrective advice.
- Training can also be a partnership opportunity – both with clients and other professional contacts. Run training courses that will be of interest and benefit to both.

This is how a partner in one large firm put it: 'training is as important as fee-earning . . . firms need to get a proper balance between the two'.

Training topics

The Law Society is currently considering a training motif which is designed to provide a framework for all sizes of firm to follow and which identifies three training areas: knowledge, skills and ethics. A slightly simpler model, we would suggest, is capable of applying across all the professions, and addresses two basic elements of training need – technical knowledge and business skills, see Figure 10.4.

Evaluating training

Training is a way of increasing the experience of individuals without each of them having to go through their own learning curve. However, although seminars, workshops and similar training sessions give people a more detailed understanding of what their problems are, a greater sense of urgency in respect of doing something about them and usually, improved willingness to try and do the right thing, they are often inadequate in giving the individual sufficient information about exactly *what* to do.

Training within professional services firms must concentrate as much on soft topics – the business skills identified in Figure 10.4 – as it does on

Figure 10.4   The training plan

technical ability. Training a person in technical skills is comparatively easy but these other areas can be much harder for some people to grasp and tend to need continuous attention.

A lot of training involves telling people how things should be done without giving them the opportunity (preferably immediately) to practise doing it. Try to ensure that your training plan coordinates the two. For example, hold training in networking a few days before one of the firm's client hospitality events and get everyone to put what they've learned into practice and give them an opportunity to report back.

Similarly, on close examination, a lot of training doesn't actually involve any learning – people attend, listen (for at least some of the time), but don't modify their behaviour. Ensure mechanisms are in place for testing that there has been a behavioural change. An effective system of training involves employing standard planning procedures, as illustrated in Figure 10.5.

Coaching and mentoring

What's the difference?

Although they are often, erroneously, used as interchangeable terms, coaching and mentoring can and should be distinguished from each other although both involve methods of learning and personal development.

A comparison of the dictionary definitions is helpful when considering the distinction between the two:

- A mentor is 'an experienced, trusted adviser'.
- To coach means 'to tutor/train intensively and individually'.

Figure 10.5   The training process

Consequently, mentoring can be viewed as a long-term relationship in which the mentor provides on-going support; (possibly) counselling; the benefit of their wisdom and experience; the benefit of the mentor's influence and independent 'sounding board' facilities.

Coaching, by contrast, suggests a shorter-term process in which training, advice and guidance are given in response to an identified learning need. It is the process of bringing about improved work performance in a specific area through individual instruction and can be a way of bringing about real change in an individual's behaviour plus improved results for the organisation as a whole. It is, however, a process of helping to learn rather than teaching.

CASE STUDY   **Coaching and mentoring**

It is decided, in XY & Co, that a partner, who is about to be involved in making a pitch for a major work project, needs to sharpen up her presentation skills and a short series of one-to-one sessions with a specialist trainer is arranged. This is coaching.

Another of the partners, returning to work after a long career break, turns for advice to a colleague in a different firm who did much the same thing five years ago. During a series of conversations and meetings spread over a period of time, the colleague passes on the benefit of her own experience, providing useful guidance and pointers that had not been considered by the returner. In this scenario, the colleague is a mentor.

Selecting a coach/mentor

The big question is, should you select from inside or outside your organisation? Internally, the choice of potentially suitable candidates is likely to be as follows:

- the managing or senior partner of the firm;
- the head of the team to which the person being coached/mentored belongs;
- the head (or someone sufficiently senior) from another team in the firm;
- the head of an appropriate support department (marketing or personnel).

Externally, there are a number of commercial and business organisations which can offer specialist coaching and mentoring services on a consultancy basis. In addition, some professional bodies – for example, the Association of Women Solicitors – have set up free mentoring programmes available to their membership.

One area which is absolutely essential to consider is the extent to which the managing partner of the firm has some source of advice and support externally – be it a coach or a mentor. There are no truer maxims than 'you can't see the wood for the trees', and 'it's lonely at the top' and having some facility where problems can be discussed and examined, ideas sounded out, and new ways of thinking introduced, can be invaluable. Although the usefulness of going outside the profession should not be overlooked, it can also be the case that benchmarking partners within your own profession – depending on the nature and non-competitiveness of your relationship with them – can be a useful source of mentoring support. Someone who is impartial yet has a deep understanding and experience of the challenges and opportunities you face can be extremely helpful. Whichever source is chosen, it is clearly essential that the coach/mentor possesses the necessary skills to be able to perform their role meaningfully.

Coaching and mentoring are often applied to soft skill areas (on the basis that technical skills are usually easier to learn through other means). For example, take marketing skills where people (especially at a senior level) feel:

- they ought to know what to do;
- their personality possibly isn't up to the job;

- shy, inadequate or hesitant;
- overcome by fear of failure.

Remember, these symptoms may not be expressed overtly but may be disguised as lack of interest, aggression, cynicism, refusal to participate or take things seriously.

What skills are required?

A good coach or mentor needs to possess a healthy mix of the following skills and attributes:

> **C** *communicator – good at listening and questioning*
> **O** *open-minded observer – unbiased and non-judgemental*
> **A** *adaptable – to individual learning styles and abilities*
> **C** *confidence-builder – able to generate a relationship of trust*
> **H** *helpful – providing constructive feedback and encouragement*

It can (we hope) be presumed that external consultants will be both able and experienced. The same presumption may not apply when looking within an organisation, however, and for your internal coaches and mentors to be effective, it may be necessary to arrange for them to receive appropriate training (or should we say coaching).

Before moving on, it is worth pointing out one or two further considerations which apply when selecting a coach or mentor.

Conflicting roles

Conflicting roles could prove a problem for the managing/senior partner or for the team leader when they are embarking on a coaching or mentoring role. It can be difficult to reconcile a coaching role with that of a leader/appraiser/disciplinarian as the pre-existing, conflicting role can prevent the build-up of trust which is an essential feature of any coaching or mentoring relationship.

Too close

The idea behind both coaching and mentoring is that the individual is helped to find their own solution to the defined problem. If the coach/mentor is the person's team leader, however, they may find they are too close to the problem to be able to stand back from it. This is particularly the case where the problem involves technical issues – the coach/mentor can become sidetracked by them and end up imposing a solution which then means that the objective of the exercise – to enhance the personal learning and development of the individual – fails.

Not close enough

Sometimes the converse situation applies. Depending on what the learning need consists of, coaching and mentoring skills in themselves are sometimes not enough and some technical knowledge is required in order for the exercise to work. If this is the case, then an external consultant or the internal head of marketing/HR may prove an inappropriate choice.

Appraisals

In the dark ages, professional services firms had never heard of appraisal. The only way for an individual to measure their rate of career progression was to compare how long it took them to make partner as compared to the time it took their peers.

In the middle ages, many firms began to see the sense of introducing fee-earner evaluation (although it did not necessarily cross their minds to extend this to partners or support staff). This evaluation sometimes took the form of a 'headmaster's report' – a paper-based exercise in which the head of department filed a report to the managing partner giving an opinion on how they thought the fee-earner was matching up to (completely arbitrary) expectations. At the other end of the spectrum, it consisted of the occasional unscheduled coffee-and-chat much favoured by partners who (mistakenly as it often turned out) prided themselves on being in tune with their team – thanks, presumably, to some sort of telepathy.

CASE STUDY   **Getting the message**

We know of a firm which, some years ago, decided (for reasons only ever known to the partners) that one person out of a group of half a dozen newly qualified accountants did not 'fit in' and had no long-term future with the practice. This decision coincided with the launch of a brand new incentive scheme – the first the firm had ever had and quite sophisticated for its time – under which all qualified fee-earners were to be given a company car with the keys to be handed over at a special celebratory event.

All fee-earners, that is, except for the unfortunate, unwanted, newly qualified who instead received a terse memo from her head of department to the effect that she need not bother attending the celebration. Needless to say, the individual concerned quickly took the hint and moved within weeks to a different firm. She never did discover what she was supposed to have done to provoke such treatment.

Nowadays, it is probably fair to say that the passage of time has seen a large number of firms progress to some type of formal appraisal for the majority of their workforce. Sadly, many systems remain ineffective with the result that they are, by turns, abused, feared and regarded in some quarters as a comprehensive waste of time. The reason for this is that the true concept of appraisal continues to be misunderstood and so it takes place as a once-a-year, one-way process where outcomes, if any, tend to be fairly mechanical.

Properly and consistently run, however, appraisal is a key tool in the quest for enhanced individual performance and development.

Why bother with appraisals?

As we saw earlier, satisfiers – things that motivate people – include recognition of achievement, positive feedback and increased responsibility. However, even though the individual might merit this, the reality of business life is that, all too often, team leaders and managers are 'too busy' or too absorbed in their own client work either to notice or bother. The reverse usually isn't true – if the individual fails to perform or does something wrong, blame or criticism are often a rapid response. Appraisal addresses this imbalance and provides a regular opportunity for such issues to be met head on.

Appraisal is a method of formal communication in which individual performance can be evaluated and, if handled well, improved. This then results in increased motivation at both personal and team level and benefits the firm as a whole. Appraisals should not just be concerned with technical performance – there are arguably better ways to monitor this on an on-going basis. Rather, they provide the perfect forum for reviewing individual performance in respect of:

- client relationship building;
- new business development;
- team working;
- internal communication;
- client care standards.

After all, if these areas are not made the focus of objective analysis, measurement and appraisal, what is going to ensure that they happen?

Effective appraisal

A properly run appraisal system is a firm-wide interactive process in which the actual appraisal interview is merely a summary of what has taken place in the previous period and is a taste of what is to come.

It is important to be clear about what the objectives of the appraisal itself are. Appraisal objectives will differ from firm to firm but the list is likely to include all or some of the following:

- to give and receive feedback on past performance;
- to measure achievement of personal objectives against target;
- to refine previously set objectives where necessary;
- to agree new objectives for the future;
- to identify skills gaps and training needs;
- to identify individual potential;
- to assess whether rewards/incentives or sanctions should be recommended;
- to assess whether salary increases should be awarded;
- to discuss problems and difficulties;
- to review career development;
- to provide a channel for communication of management information.

Remember, although it is a review process, its main focus should be on looking forward. Also, to be effective, it is essential that the appraisal culminates in meaningful and measurable outcomes.

Finding time

It can easily be imagined that conducting a full and effective appraisal for even one individual is a time-consuming exercise. If the appraisor has to multiply the process several times over (for example, if they are head of a large team) then it quickly becomes a full-time job and usually means that most organisations only manage to go through the exercise once a year. This is probably adequate if other regular team and one-to-one meetings are taking place as they can provide sufficient opportunity to check individual progress – in relation to achievement of personal objectives, for example – and ensure that momentum is maintained.

Gaining commitment

What is crucial to appraisal is that it is fully supported from the top of the organisation. Paying lip-service to the idea or treating it as a mechanical, administrative exercise is not good enough. Senior management must ensure that appraisal is budgeted for – that it is built into the management calendar with sufficient time set aside by all those involved to carry it out properly. The requirement to conduct appraisals is something which should form an official part of a team leader's duties. To gain buy-in from reluctant or sceptical partners, try making their commitment to carrying out effective appraisals something on which they are evaluated each year. As management expert David Freemantle has said, managing people 'is a complicated task that cannot and should not be reduced to mere procedure'.

The role of personal objectives

Underpinning the process of effective appraisal is the principle of setting and monitoring clear personal objectives.

In reality, achievement of the firm's overall business aims and objectives is ultimately brought about by performance of personal objectives. This makes sense because a firm consists of individuals and its success or failure depends on what those individuals either do or don't do. It makes sense in turn, therefore, that, as we show in Figure 10.6, each layer of goals – from personal objectives outwards – must be reflective of the next layer in order to achieve consistency.

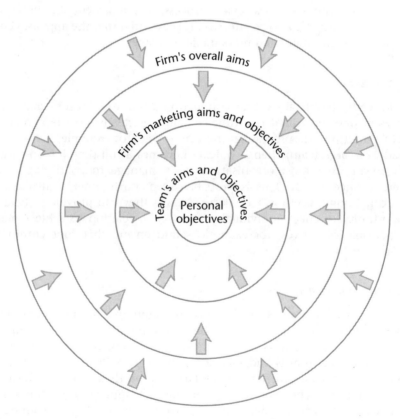

Figure 10.6 The hierarchy of objectives

In order for personal objectives to work, it is not enough for them simply to be communicated to the individual. Instead, they should be fixed only after a proper process of consultation, frank discussion and ultimately consensus, for only this degree of participation will lead to the goals and objectives being 'owned' by the individual and therefore stand a good chance of being performed.

The whole concept of personal objectives is, however, something with which professional service organisations (more, it would seem, than any other sector of industry) have wrestled.

The good news is, it needn't be so difficult. Go back to basics: when fixing personal objectives, the same rules apply as those seen earlier in relation to business, marketing or departmental goals – personal objectives must be SMART. They must, in addition, be relevant and it is by remembering this aspect that the exercise suddenly becomes easier. *Relevant* personal objectives can be defined as ones which either:

- help to perform or fulfil team objectives; and/or
- perform/achieve personal career development goals such as those identified in the course of personal appraisals; and/or
- fulfil private personal goals where these legitimately overlap into the work arena.

Even more difficult than defining personal objectives, it seems, is the awesome task of implementing them. If the SMART test has been followed, there should be no problem in knowing what is to be done and in what time frame, and the objective should, from the outset, be clearly capable of achievement. So what is wrong exactly?

Procrastination is one of the most common problems, and that is all to do with fear of failure: the individual is afraid of doing a less than perfect job – especially in unfamiliar territory such as marketing – so engages in what psychologists call 'displacement behaviour'. Basically, this means doing anything but the task in hand, and hence the common cry of 'too busy!' when the individual is called to account.

Ways of tackling this problem, and coaching others to tackle it, are:

- Break the specific task up into chunks – instead of tackling 'contact ten new clients', think 'today I'll do the first draft of what I might put in a letter to prospective new clients . . .'.
- Positively develop and encourage in your team a 'failure isn't important' mindset. Everyone fails now and again, and people tend to be sympathetic rather than scathing. After all, today's great entrepreneurs fail spectacularly every so often and no one thinks the worse of them for it. As for past inventors – as Thomas Edison said at one stage, 'Results! Why, man, I have gotten a lot of results. I know several thousand things that won't work.'

- Prioritise what you have to do in terms of its importance, urgency and difficulty and write next to each task the worst-case scenario of what could happen if you don't deliver, or don't give the task enough consideration. The idea of being unprepared for a new business pitch, or having your colleagues single you out for attention because you've let them down can often sharpen the mind wonderfully. Once you've done that, start at the top and work your way through the list.

Finally, in relation to personal objectives, it is worth bearing in mind the following key points.

Clarity

When setting objectives, the manager and employee each need to be clear (each should write down if necessary and compare lists) exactly what the employee is expected to *do*. What commonly happens is that the objective deals with responsibility rather than action so the person involved is unclear as to what is expected of them and the performance criteria against which they will be judged.

Performance criteria

When running through the individual's objectives, performance measures should be made clear at the outset and the consequence of non-performance spelt out. Regardless of what penalties are to be put in place, performance measures are fairly straightforward – acceptable behaviour is to carry out the behaviours outlined by the objective; unacceptable behaviour is not to carry them out. This is the baseline for motivation.

Feedback

Many so-called motivational problems are caused by lack of feedback, in as much as if people believe they are actually doing what they are supposed to be doing, why would it occur to them to do anything different? Similarly, failure to give praise and encouragement – for example, in recognition of a job well done or for the contribution of an innovative idea – can prove intensely demoralising for the individual who then sees little point in continuing to make the effort to perform well. Remember our earlier discussion regarding positive and negative reinforcement, and always aim to give constructive (as opposed to purely negative) feedback when things are not quite right and plenty of positive and timely encouragement where it is due.

Appraising the appraisor

It is generally accepted among professional services firms (and so we have assumed for the purposes of this chapter so far) that it falls to the head of team or department to conduct appraisals in respect of those individuals who work in their groups. Alternatively, appraisal might – if there is a sufficiently large and recognised department as is common in larger firms – be an HR responsibility. The main problem in this area concerns the thorny subject of partner appraisal.

Many firms (certainly the bigger ones) now include their partners in the appraisal process, some even operating 360° appraisals where not only the partner's fellow partners (peers) but also their subordinates participate in the review. A number of others, however, struggle with the idea. There are a variety of reasons for this:

- Natural psychological barriers come into play when it comes to assessing the performance of someone who is supposed to be an equal. Partners can feel extremely uncomfortable if they think they are being asked effectively to sit in judgement over another partner.
- Partners tend to co-exist in a very close relationship which can lead to unfairness in the appraisal situation. There might be too much personal knowledge, producing bias.
- Partnership tensions or politics can also generate bias. One party to the appraisal might feel, for example, that the other has a personal agenda of some description.

These are all valid issues and must be taken into account when structuring any partner appraisal scheme and deciding who is going to appraise whom.

One answer might be to look outside the firm and appoint external HR consultants to conduct partner appraisals. Provided they are conducted on a fully confidential basis, except for the 'grandfather' involvement of the managing/senior partner or management board, and provided, of course, the appraisor is fully acquainted with the individual's performance as well as with corporate goals and values, this can be a way of ensuring a completely even-handed process.

POINTS TO REMEMBER

➤ Correcting issues and problems that produce dissatisfaction does not automatically lead to motivation. The process you need to think through is

Dissatisfaction → Absence of Dissatisfaction → Satisfaction (Motivation)

➤   Think about how you deal with good and with poor performance: failing to reinforce 'good' behaviour and positively reinforcing (implicitly condoning) 'poor' behaviour are intensely demotivating.

➤   Induction is the first stage in an on-going process of internal communication.

➤   Effective training should focus on soft as well as technical skills and should be regularly evaluated to ensure that learning has taken place leading to a change in behaviour.

➤   Consider the use of coaching and mentoring programmes as a means of improving learning and individual development.

➤   When setting up an appraisal system, make sure it is structured, formal and two-way. Define appraisal objectives beforehand so you know what you want to get out of it and *give it time*! It usually takes a couple of years before a new scheme really starts to produce benefits.

➤   Clear personal objectives are a crucial feature of effective appraisal in that they underpin the whole process of motivation and individual performance.

11

Flexible working practices

KEY ISSUES

- Drivers for change
- A tool for differentiation
- The options and what's involved
- Implementing a flexible working system
- Inherent problems and some solutions

Think about your firm – do you recognise any of these comments?

	YES	NO
I don't think our clients would be impressed if we introduced flexible working – I'm sure they would rather know they can contact our fee-earners in the office just like they always have done.		
It would be great to be able to work from home but it would be viewed as a weakness by the partners here and would have a negative effect on my career.		
We have decided against a formal flexible working policy because of the danger that deadlines and calls would be missed and cases not progressed with proper continuity.		
Yes, our assistants work long hours but it's because they want to do well. If it's all too much for them, then perhaps they are in the wrong job.		
It's upsetting when good staff leave the firm but then no one is irreplaceable are they?		
I wish we knew how to get the extra mile out of our staff – we pay them the going rate but there's no real loyalty to the firm.		

If we let one work part time, they'll all want to.		
We have enough difficulty managing people when they're here, let alone trying to cope if they're working off-site.		
We're at complete overload in terms of office accommodation – but bigger premises will send our overheads sky high.		

Assuming you didn't answer 'no' to all the above, then you should read on.

'Flexible working' comes in a multitude of guises and is something which is talked about by many but actually adopted in any meaningful fashion by very few. There is little doubt, however, that the winds of change are beginning to blow within the professions. Technological advance is a key facilitator of that change and can be seen as a symptom of it, as can the various 'family friendly' legislative concepts which, to date, have introduced the prospect of extended maternity leave, paid paternity and (unpaid) parental leave as well as the possibility of post-maternity part-time working.

Drivers for change

Overall, we believe there is an irrefutable case for flexible working, and there are four main reasons why we think professional services firms should take it seriously and move it to the top of the agenda in terms of business development:

1. *Client needs* – for delivery and continuity of services at times convenient to them.
2. *Staff needs* – to cope with the hard, immutable facts of working parents, commuting times, and so on.
3. *Business needs* – to counter the increasing costs of business premises, recruitment and retention of skilled personnel, and the resource required to deal with physical business growth.
4. *Staff motivation* – the impetus which can be provided by offering and supporting another way of working.

Client needs

Many clients – both private sector and commercial – have needs which entail working outside normal hours, holding on-site meetings, or other service requirements which do not adhere to traditional working patterns. Matching such needs with more flexible working systems will result in distinct benefits in terms of achieving client satisfaction and producing competitive advantage and differentiation for the firm.

Many firms dismiss the idea of flexible working on the basis that 'organisational goals must take priority over employees' wishes. Those that do offer some form of flexibility, do so, mainly, in an informal manner and often with the attitude that it is only available as a somewhat reluctantly given personal concession to one or two key employees, as if rolling it out in any more widespread or formal fashion would be seen as pandering to the demands of capricious and spoilt staff.

The organisational goals and aspirations of the business must take priority but such goals and aims ought, primarily, to centre on clients – what are *their* needs and wants and how can they best be satisfied? Although a quantum leap in terms of cultural thinking might be required, the logic of matching staff who want for their own sakes to work flexibly with satisfying clients whose needs are for more flexible service delivery is both simple and undeniable.

CASE STUDY   **Open all hours?**

Consider the law firm based in a picturesque, albeit rather remote, part of the country, the mainstay of whose business consists of residential conveyancing work. An increasingly large element of their client base is made up of city business men and women who purchase second or weekend homes in the area. The reason why the firm in question successfully acquired virtually all the new instructions (and continues to do so) is that they took a deliberate decision to open their offices in the evenings and at weekends in order to coincide with the times when the prospective purchasers were most likely to be doing their house hunting. None of their competitors had thought to do the same thing, which meant there was an immediate marketing advantage simply by demonstrating a more flexible approach.

Staff needs

Much has been written about the effects of excessive stress in the workplace and the extent of employers' duties to take measures to mitigate it. Several high-profile cases illustrate the point that consideration must be given to accommodating vulnerable employees where possible if substantial damages cases are to be avoided. Human beings, pushed to mental and physical limits over a sustained period of time, will eventually burn out. While most employees will not consider litigation, employers must still question whether high-pressure working practices are really an effective way of maximising the working life and potential of their staff. A bit of lateral thinking on the subject of working patterns and staff bonuses and benefits can help preserve quality of life and provide an unprecedented boost to motivation.

A common reason given by many employees who participated in a recent survey about wanting to work from home is that significant time is wasted on commuting each day. And frequent interruptions when working in the office are often reported as being the most annoying part of their job.

At its simplest level, home workers have more time available each day:

More time = Increased productivity = More work billed = More fees

It doesn't stop there, however. Avoiding the hassles of commuting and having more quiet time throughout the day, leads to a less stressful working life for the employee who is likely to feel more motivated as a result. A happy, motivated employee will show a greater throughput of work, which translates into increased productivity and tangible financial benefits for the firm.

Recent surveys have underlined the fact that whilst the (not unreasonable) wish of the many is to enjoy an acceptable balance in the work–life equation, achieving this is easier said than done. Nowhere is this more apparent than in the case of those with primary care responsibilities. The surveys include a study on the work–life balance carried out by the Institute of Employment Studies on behalf of the DfES entitled *Family Friendly Employment: The Business Case Report* (DfES Research Report, September 1999) and research into flexible working practices conducted for the Institute of Chartered Accountants (stage 1 of the 'Flexible Futures' project carried out by the Work-Life Research Centre for the ICA, March 2001).

Business needs

At the risk of stating the obvious – given that it operates in a 'people' industry – the biggest asset any professional services firm can have is . . . its own people.

From the most senior members of the organisation to those in the junior ranks, few firms relish the prospect of losing valued staff. The old attitude of regarding nobody as irreplaceable is one which most managers will hesitate to articulate these days, knowing full well that a more realistic viewpoint would be 'everyone is of course replaceable . . . but at a cost'.

Specifically, that cost is represented by:

- *Lost investment cost*: some other firm or organisation gets to reap the benefit of your carefully trained, nurtured and developed employee. In addition, the professional services market is especially competitive and it is far from guaranteed that the right replacement candidate will materialise quickly if at all.

- *Lost opportunity cost*: the outgoing fee-earner is no longer there to bring in fees and potential new business for your firm.
- *Replacement cost*: you now have to incur the expense of management time and recruitment agency fees in securing a replacement to fill the gap.
- *Relationship cost*: both clients and colleagues will have to get to know and build relationships with the new recruit whilst weathering the downside of their learning curve in terms of initial inefficiency.

Although it would be nonsense to suggest that introducing flexible working will provide an instant panacea to all your recruitment problems, don't imagine that it isn't capable of making a difference. In some cases it can make the vital difference: research has found that two in every five employees would consider quitting their job if denied the chance to work flexibly. In some firms – as, for example, in one of the large national legal practices – lack of office space and spiralling overheads may prompt the decision to investigate and to try out flexible working. Benefits come not only in terms of lower rental costs but also in the form of reduced administrative/secretarial overhead. This particular firm also reported noticeably improved cross-selling caused by staff at different levels and from different practice areas regularly being mixed and brought together depending on who was sitting next to whom in their open plan hot desk area.

Introducing flexible working styles can also help firms boost their marketing efforts. One of the biggest reasons for ineffective marketing is that those who should be doing it say they have no time. Flexible working in the form of home working could free up, on average, an additional 2–3 hours a day for those who no longer have to commute. If that extra time each day were to be spent on developing the business, the pay-off could be enormous. Of course, the figures in this example are simplistic, but the logic is there.

Staff motivation

A key finding in the DTI survey was that, according to employers, the main advantage of facilitating a work–life balance is that it results in a happier workforce.

This is excellent news in terms of staff motivation. Consider the motivation equation illustrated in Figure 11.1.

The desire among many to bring about lifestyle and cultural changes has itself been the driver for many of the legislative developments outlined at the start of this chapter. Much of the impetus has come from employees who are increasingly prepared to be creative when it comes to settling

Figure 11.1   The motivation equation

salary and benefits packages, often more than happy to give up a portion of salary in return for extra holiday.

Perhaps the greatest benefit for employees allowed to work flexibly is their increased self-esteem and self-motivation brought about by being able, to some degree, to govern their own daily schedule. Empowering an employee to control their own destiny, even in a small way, can be an extremely effective motivator.

A tool for differentiation

Not known, as a rule, for being early adopters of communications technology and IT wizardry, some professional services firms have nevertheless taken flexible working to considerable lengths and, in doing so, have given themselves tremendous competitive advantage.

One or two brave pioneers have set up completely virtual offices, in which a number of fee-earners and secretaries work from home, linked on a day-to-day basis by computer and telephone and reliant on the Internet for document transmission, exchange of correspondence and internal communication. When they need to meet clients, the fee-earners visit them at the client's own premises; when they need to meet each other, a meeting or conference room in a central location is hired.

The advantages for such firms include the following:

- considerable client benefits, in the sense that a 24 hour 7 day a week service can, if called for, be provided;
- there is obvious differentiation from competitors;
- there is no confinement to a local market;
- overheads are cheaper.

Of course, not every firm will want to go to such radical lengths in their service delivery and nor should they. But equally, the days of offices opening from 9.00 to 5.00 and closing for an hour at lunchtime are gone – any firm still closer to this end of the flexibility spectrum must wake up and re-assess how services should be delivered in a way which is acceptable and sufficiently flexible to meet the changing needs of both clients and staff.

In the following sections, we consider various flexible working methods which can be adapted and employed to internal (motivational) and external (competitive) advantage by all firms.

The options and what's involved

Home working

Generally speaking, out-sourced office workers will aim to spend the majority of their working week in a home office and the remainder of their time at the firm's usual business premises, with communication on home-based days principally being by telephone, e-mail or fax. Best practice would see a home working charter or protocol drawn up (in addition to the usual contract of employment). This will typically specify how many and which days over what period are to be spent working from home and how many in the office, and what the preferred channels of communication are. It will also need to cover IT provision and reporting methods and frequency.

The home-based employee should be as accountable as any other member of staff for completing work records or timesheets, attending team or other staff meetings and attending to administrative tasks.

Hand in hand with all this goes a degree of flexibility on the part of the employee as to the days on which their attendance at the main office is required. Effective use of communications technology – for example, video or telephone conferencing – may circumvent the need for the homeworker's physical presence whilst still allowing them to participate fully in meetings and discussions.

It is becoming more widely accepted by those in the professional services sector that there are mutual benefits to be had in several areas from this type of working arrangement:

- The employee gets to avoid many of the stress 'triggers' which disturb the work–life balance (such as commuting difficulties, long-hours culture, difficulties in arranging child care etc.).
- The employer has not only found a way of retaining a valued member of staff but also is probably providing the motivation to inspire a better performance from the employee.
- Best of all, flexibility can translate into improved and differentiated service for the client. For example, the fee-earner is available for longer each day and is more likely to arrange face-to-face meetings at the client's own premises, saving the client travelling time, cost and inconvenience.

Part-time working

This might entail the employee working *short days* – that is, fewer hours but on each day of the working week or working *short weeks* – normal hours but only on certain days of the week. Whichever option is chosen, consideration must obviously be given to how the employee's job will be covered for the remainder of the time. In the case of fee-earners, presence in the office (which often, although not always correctly, translates as availability to clients and colleagues) might be the key factor and mean that the short days option is preferable. This might be less of a consideration in the case of secretarial and support staff, however, who generally interface less with clients. In both cases, the short week method of part-time working combines well with job sharing.

Successful part-time working requires good management: roles, responsibilities and workloads will need to be adjusted to take account of the fact that the part-timer will not be available for work for the same amount of time as before. This sounds simple – and it is – yet many a disillusioned employee has described how, after switching to part-time working and taking the corresponding reduction in salary and benefits that that entails, nothing has changed on the other side of the equation. The workload stays the same, with the result that either the employee ends up continuing to work a full week but in return for a part-time salary or team mates become disgruntled and resentful because they have to carry the burden of the additional workload not being handled by the part-timer.

Job sharing

In this scenario, two (or, theoretically, more) workers between them cover one full-time job. Managed correctly, this can be an extremely effective working method – particularly for the employer since the combined output of two part-timers usually exceeds that of one full-time worker doing the same job.

Essential elements of successful job sharing are:

- to draw up a precise job definition and ensure each co-worker knows exactly which part(s) of it will be their responsibility;
- to get the right combination of co-workers. They will need to be well matched on various levels: similar technical ability and competence; good personal rapport and strong communication skills. A lack of liaison and smooth handover can produce chaos and confusion which is unsettling for all and will send out a negative message to clients;
- to manage peer pressure. This will come into play and, if appropriately harnessed, can be a powerful motivator, driving each co-worker to perform well in order not to let the side down.

CASE STUDY   **Love match or mismatch?**

Problems can arise from mismatched job sharers. A firm of surveyors experienced teething problems with two secretaries who shared a job on the basis that each worked for half of the week. Although their technical abilities and speed of work were similar, the fee-earner they worked for reported a noticeably slower output of work during the latter half of the week. It transpired that the secretary covering the early part of the week happened to work in an untidy, haphazard fashion to the considerable annoyance of her co-worker who then spent her first day each week tidying up after her colleague.

Hot desking

Whilst job sharers will share not just the work itself but also the necessary office facilities, a flexible working system might involve having several employees who work part time or work partly from home and attend the office on an intermittent basis. If this is the case, setting up a hot desk area can help to solve problems of accommodation and management of internal office routines. A hot desk will need to be equipped with essential communications facilities – for example, a PC or network portal for connecting up a laptop computer – allowing a succession of different individuals to work partly from the office base.

Adaptability on the part of the flexible worker is required – those who need to have some office space to call their own or want a place to put their family photographs will probably not settle well to the concept of hot desking. For the rest of the office, however, a separate hot desk area will mean less disruption to their normal office routines and, for the employer, there may be economic and administrative benefits – for example, fewer desks and computers to provide. Sound operational management of the process is again required – for example, a system whereby desks can be reserved in advance and double-booking avoided.

Annualised hours

With this method of working, a certain number of hours per annum are identified as being necessary to complete the required work. The employee then has a measure of flexibility (subject to any interim deadlines or other particular stipulations) as to when to work. Salary is agreed at the outset and paid at the usual intervals, meaning that the employee has the benefit of regular, stable income and the employer has the advantage of fixed, predictable labour costs.

The annualised hours system lends itself to work which is seasonal or where the nature of it means it comes in peaks and troughs. While the team manager has the comfort of knowing that staff are bound to work during the busy times, meaning that client needs can be properly served, the employee gains the flexibility of quiet periods which might accommodate family commitments or personal leisure interests.

Variable hours

Flexibility in terms of when hours are actually worked emerges from almost every research survey as the most common flexible working practice. Usually this occurs on a strictly informal basis – for instance, the team leader who turns a blind eye to the secretary who routinely arrives in the office half an hour late because she has to drop her children off at school first, but on the (also tacit) understanding that she will work through part of her lunch break.

More rare, in professional services firms, is the scenario where flexi-time (the gradual building up of time off in lieu of additional hours worked) or compressed hours (regularly working longer but fewer days) are formally allowed. Research has shown that the majority of staff are significantly happier just to have occasional flexibility on an informal basis in the hours they work – proving that, often, it's the little things that make the biggest difference.

Using temporary staff

A major problem faced by law firms and other professional services organisations is how to persuade clients – particularly those with sudden or large-volume transactions on offer – that you have the necessary skills and resources to be able to handle their work effectively.

A common scenario is a small to medium-sized firm successfully dealing with a small number of matters each year or handling a particular aspect of the client's service requirement but failing to cross-sell other teams or departments because the firm as a whole is perceived as being too small or insufficiently specialised in the sought-after area of work. Or genuine lack of resource may be the reason why a firm reluctantly decides it is simply not in a position to pursue a potentially lucrative new source of work.

The problem is a thorny one: the seemingly obvious solution – go out and recruit – is often easier said than done. The right candidate can be elusive, taking considerable time, effort and money to find. There may be uncertainty about exactly how much work is on offer from the client which does not sit well with the fundamentally long-term implications of recruiting permanent staff. Resources may suddenly become stretched due to unforeseen circumstances – a key employee leaving the firm or needing long-term sick leave, for example. If this happens in the midst of a high-volume or complex matter, there is a very real danger of the client suffering a crisis of confidence and looking elsewhere or, at the very least, of remaining team members becoming disenchanted under the weight of extra responsibilities suddenly thrust upon them.

At times like this, what is needed is skilled resource at the right level and immediately available. The answer might be to recruit a temporary worker from the growing numbers of locum professionals or, in the legal world, for tasks of a more administrative nature, consider taking on paralegals.

Bringing in freelance workers as temporary reinforcements to assist with one-off transactions can make the difference between meeting and exceeding the expectations and timetable of important clients and seeing them reconsider their service providers because of a loss of confidence caused by a missed deadline or shoddy performance. For example, many law firms faced with suddenly urgent, voluminous transactions where more hands to the pump are required for seemingly menial but crucially important tasks (such as a court case involving meticulous preparation of large numbers of trial bundles) are turning to paralegals for occasional assistance. Many work on either a temporary or permanent basis, some as a way of gaining valuable experience of life as a lawyer before embarking on professional skills training, others as their chosen career.

Many freelance professionals operate in niche practice areas and might therefore be taken on as a means of avoiding a valued client being, effectively, forced to look elsewhere if a particular matter requires special-ist knowledge not otherwise available within the firm. Unless the special-ist knowledge is likely to be required on an on-going basis, it probably will not be financially worthwhile taking on a permanent niche practi-tioner and so, in this context, the freelance acts as an ad hoc consultant able to augment the team as and when the work demands it. Growing numbers of locums now work on a freelance basis and are experienced, commercially trained individuals who have made a choice to work more flexibly. The combination of long experience and excellent technical qualifications means that they are able to settle quickly into new environments and get on with the job without the need for detailed initial induction and training.

Freelance workers often go on to accept permanent positions with the firm they work for. For the employer, this can prove to be a low-risk method of recruitment, allowing the candidate to be vetted at close quarters with no strings attached – nothing is lost if, at the end of the day, the freelance is deemed unsuitable as a permanent employee. On the other side of the coin, some freelances will take the opportunity to size up a firm before deciding whether they wish to take up a permanent position, if one is on offer.

For the freelance, flexibility again emerges as the main attraction, producing the ability to work intensively for short bursts of time interspersed with work breaks (which might tie in with family commitments or personal interests) or to accept longer commitments with more conventional hours but leave options open by still having an end date in sight. There may be financial rewards – niche area practitioners can often command high fees to reflect the specialist skills they can bring to the arena.

A common criticism of the idea of using temporary staff is that there is a risk of them fragmenting the team they are attached to or that their personal style of working does not coincide with service levels agreed with or that the firm wishes to provide to its clients. It is important to bear in mind that, for however long they work with you, the freelance becomes a full (albeit temporary) member of the team they are placed with. So it is important to ensure the freelance is fully briefed on the team's objectives and on any applicable service delivery and quality standards.

Implementing a flexible working system

Having looked at what's involved with various flexible working options and considered what is causing other firms to adopt some of them, the big question is – do you want to? First, you need to examine, frankly, the culture of your firm with regard to the whole flexible working issue:

- Is there a genuine desire to adapt to the present-day requirements and desires of many employees and clients?
- Or will there be an underlying current of resentment and scepticism, promoting a feeling within the firm that flexible working is a soft option, a sop to those faint-hearted, family-challenged individuals, who are probably not tough enough to make it to the top anyway?

- How will it really be viewed by the powers-that-be in your firm? As an option that will genuinely benefit the firm as a whole and its clients as well as the individual, or as a personal concession made reluctantly to those who are brave enough to ask, demanding of the quid pro quo of promotion sacrifice?

Flexible working can either be the new nirvana or ... a complete shambles. If you decide it is for you, effective implementation will depend on properly managing the process and paying real attention to the (positive and negative) motivational implications, both for those directly participating and for those who are not.

Managing the process

Managing flexible working involves dealing with a number of different issues, most of which are recommended as a standard approach to managing:

- Set objectives: what are you trying to achieve by introducing flexible working?
- Research the needs of clients and staff, and evaluate the fit between the two.
- Evaluate what practices are potentially applicable and find out from others how they have made them work.
- Weigh up the benefits and the disadvantages in respect of your clients, your personnel and your firm in terms of both hard (financial) and soft (morale) factors (see Figure 11.2).
- Plan how you will introduce and run flexible working practices – ideally conducting a pilot project.
- Establish how you will monitor and evaluate success, both internally and externally.
- Communicate, communicate, communicate – with staff, clients and any other potentially affected parties – on an on-going basis.

Maximising the motivational aspect

Motivational aspects are not all positive. You may be surprised at some of the problems you will have to deal with from staff, who for one reason or another are having difficulty in coping with the amount of change involved when flexible working practices are introduced. For example:

- You will need to have mechanisms in place for countering the isolation, loneliness and uncertainty which will, to some degree, be experienced by all flexible workers.
- There may be arguments over benefits or lack of them (e.g. those who work at home don't need as many business clothes, don't have to pay

Conventional working

- Management and supervisory simplicity in having everyone under one roof
- IT provision is simpler and may be cheaper than providing for flexible workers
- Ease of communication
- Facilitates team working and parity amongst colleagues
- Avoids need to introduce and manage change as preserves the status quo
- (Perception of) greater availability to clients

Flexible working

- Potential for greater productivity and profitability
- Can provide competitive advantage
- Assists with recruitment and retention of good-quality employees
- Positive effect on organisation and management of resource (e.g. office space and administrative resource)
- Flexibility and control over management of own workload is motivating experience resulting in higher commitment and loyalty to firm on part of employee
- Results in noticeably reduced staff absenteeism
- Results in genuinely greater availability and more flexible service delivery to clients

Figure 11.2   Weighing up the benefits

travel expenses, but do have to fund the additional costs of home working such as heating and lighting, and so on).

- Conventionally working staff may feel that they are put upon in the sense that they believe they have to do more work to compensate for the times that the flexible worker is absent from the office.
- Flexible workers may feel aggrieved if there is a perception that their contribution is less valued and if this is believed (or seen) to hamper career prospects.

Inherent problems and some solutions

Introducing flexible working practices such as those described in this chapter into a professional services organisation is more likely than not to produce real benefits in terms of increased staff motivation, improved management efficiency and – as a result of this combination – marketing gains. Sadly, however, the vast majority of firms either steer away from such practices altogether or put a toe tentatively into the water only to deeply regret the experience. In both cases this is usually due to their inability to overcome fundamental cultural change which is vital if the project is not to be doomed to failure from the outset.

For those brave enough to make the required quantum leap and give innovative working styles a chance, it is important to recognise that there are still a number of possible problem areas each of which, if not dealt with properly and in time, is a potential barrier to success.

Here are some common concerns which have been expressed regarding implementation of flexible working practices together with some thoughts on how to tackle them:

'If we let one, then they'll all want to do it!'

The assumptions

Flexible working is somehow 'easier' than conventional working methods with the flexible worker able to escape the usual tedium of office disciplines such as time-recording, administrative tasks, achieving elusive fee targets, making contributions to the day-to-day running of the team or department. This misplaced train of thought leads to a fear on the part of the employer that, if the practice is advertised, then before long the whole of the workforce will demand a similar soft option and the firm will be transformed overnight into little more than a virtual office consisting of a typing pool and a couple of hot desks! Sometimes, the employer knows full well that this is not the reality but fears that the rest of the workforce will misconstrue the situation and so wants to keep things quiet – the ostrich approach.

To avoid this, what happens in many firms is that flexible working is permitted only in very isolated cases with the whole concept given a low profile and little or no information disseminated about what it entails, what is expected of the flexible worker or how it is likely to impact on the rest of the staff.

Ironically, this lack of information and general air of secrecy surrounding the terms upon which certain individuals are permitted to work flexibly is precisely what generates and sustains the myth that the flexible worker is somehow favoured, which leads to resentment and, occasionally, threatened mutiny among colleagues – terribly destructive in

CASE STUDY   **Unpleasant side-effects**

A home-based surveyor spoke of her frustration and anger at what she saw as an unjust – and unjustified – side-effect of her flexible working status. She said: 'I am actually 50 per cent more productive than I used to be and, because I also always travel to them instead of having them come to see me, have massively improved my client relationships. It has been made very clear to me, however, (unofficially, of course) that I will never make partner because none of the partners believe that I can possibly be working as hard as the others who work conventionally. Although the figures speak for themselves, I am made to feel that I don't really pull my weight or as if I have somehow voluntarily opted out of career development.'

terms of team relationships. The flexible worker is also, understandably, likely to react badly in this situation.

The ICA research mentioned earlier echoes this with a finding that 'the potential gains of flexible working are undermined ... in many organisations by workplace cultures in which non-flexible workers are the most highly valued'.

The solution

First, make sure that the flexible worker knows the score: there is no particular reason why home workers, part-time workers or employees retained on any other flexible terms should be any less accountable for how their time is spent or for meeting time/profitability/marketing targets.

Next, take steps to communicate this to the rest of the workforce (or, at least, the part likely to be affected). Up-front communication in this way is healthy – it levels the playing field and reassures the workforce that everyone is being treated equally and fairly.

Consider what criteria will apply to all flexible working requests. Increasing sophistication in communications technology and changing social–cultural views will without doubt mean that the incidence of flexible working requests will tend to increase not go away. The progressive firm will accept this and will already be giving thought as to how the firm's policy on working practices can be developed.

'How can we ensure that staff who are not there all the time are properly managed and supervised?'

The problem

Emanating no doubt from the 'jackets on chairs' culture of the past two decades, the popular misconception here is that if someone cannot physically be seen to be working, then they must not be working at all. This can be a problem, particularly for home workers whose lack of physical presence in the office can lead to them becoming almost invisible.

A common barrier to effective implementation of flexible working practice arises from poor management ability leading to a fear, on the part of the manager, of loss of control and supervision of the out-based or part-time fee-earner. On a more practical note, many managers express concerns about how to keep track of files, documents and correspondence especially in the case of out-based working. This can be an important consideration where the firm has gained or is applying for a quality mark (e.g. the Lexcel mark for lawyers) where effective case management is a quality requirement.

The solution

Introduce structured lines of communication, making sure the flexible worker knows what is expected of them, when feedback and progress reports are to be given and when they are expected to appear in the office. Because of the 'out of sight out of mind' syndrome, it can be easy for drift and lack of discipline to set in. To avoid this, the team manager must be rigorous in ensuring that feedback sessions are put in the diary and actually take place.

Measure, regularly, the tangible output of the flexible workers and compare it against that of conventional employees.

Consider appointing a single coordinator – for example, someone with HR responsibility – to act as a central reference point to help tackle any logistical problems or lapses in communication that occur either from the point of view of the flexible worker or anyone affected by the working system.

Set up a paper trail system to record files and correspondence leaving and coming back into the office. The spectre of missed calls can easily be dealt with by having office telephone numbers diverted to the out-based worker's home or (for instance if hot desking is used) equipping staff with portable digital telephones – such solutions actually benefit the client who only ever has to remember a single contact number and need not be aware of whether the person they are speaking to is working from their kitchen table or is in the office.

'How can we manage the feelings and motivation of the non-flexible workforce?'

The problem

Resentment, envy, team fragmentation. Those who are left behind in the office may well feel sidelined or overlooked unless their understandable feelings can be correctly anticipated and dealt with.

In the case of all flexible workers, the permanent, conventional workers are the ones who will inevitably have to provide cover in certain situations and, in some cases, continual back-up and support. This will usually be in addition to their own daily responsibilities and can represent a considerable extra workload.

The solution

First, draw up a precise description of what the flexible worker is responsible for and what lines of support they are entitled to call upon. If flexible working is a new venture for the firm, the flexible fee-earner will often not know exactly what their requirements in terms of support and assistance are until they have the benefit of some hindsight, so constant review and refinement of the processes involved will be required.

Communicate loudly and clearly to colleagues and peers that the flexible worker is subject to the same demands and rules as anyone else.

Thirdly, recognise – demonstrably – the contribution that those in supporting roles are making to the smooth running of the flexible working system. Individual motivation and team morale can be substantially enhanced simply by making sure that those concerned know you are aware of the extra effort they have put in.

Consider rewarding additional contribution with some form of incentive – for example, a monetary or other bonus.

Dealing with client perceptions and misconceptions

Common myths

These include the myths that clients will be naturally averse to the introduction of flexible working schemes; that clients believe their work will be mismanaged and cases will go wrong because the fee-earner is not always in the office; that – in the case of job-sharing fee-earners – their matter will fall between two stools because there will be handover problems; and that everything will grind to a halt for the part of the week that the part-time fee-earner is not there.

The reality and some solutions

Actual client views often differ from a firm's perception of what they will be. The trick is to communicate with and involve clients in the planning process.

- This will enable clients to tell or warn you of their actual fears (if any) in advance, allowing you, in turn, to take appropriate preventative action.
- It will make clients feel valued and important by virtue of being consulted at all.
- It may generate some new ideas and thinking on the subject as clients share their own experiences of flexible working practices.
- And it may even pleasantly surprise you. Numerous clients will say they prefer a more flexible delivery of service as it fits better with their own working practices and their business needs.

The reality is that clients are often a lot less conventional than we fear they might be and, in the main, they don't have a problem with the way in which work is organised and performed. Their principal concerns are usually that they can get hold of you when they need to and that the job gets done.

CASE STUDY   **Consult your clients**

One firm of solicitors, faced with the prospect of losing two experienced fee-earners unless they were allowed to work from home, was nervous about what their clients would think. They were advised to consult clients before-hand to put them in the picture and, to their surprise, found that the reaction was universally favourable, with one firm praising the firm's flexible approach.

Crisis cover

The problem

No matter how smoothly a flexible working system normally runs, occasionally a problem will suddenly occur on a matter, or there may be a crisis within the organisation. The knee-jerk reaction to such emergencies is that nothing short of presence in the office will do if the problem is to be sorted out. This is because the office is seen as the command centre – the centre of operations.

The solution

The answer to this understandable worry is that every organisation, large or small, should have a workable plan to cover any emergency or contingency situation. The problems that can occur in the context of flexible working are just one example of a number of potential crises that a firm might conceivably have to face. For example, what happens if a key member of staff is suddenly absent due to sickness or is away on holiday?

As ever, the importance of good communication cannot be stressed enough. This, together with sensible advance and contingency planning, will ensure that even a sudden crisis can be not simply weathered but managed head on and controlled.

POINTS TO REMEMBER

> Modern working practices must respond to changes in client needs and wants as well as evolving business needs.

> Flexible working can provide not only competitive edge and differentiation but can also respond to staff desires to achieve a comfortable work–life balance.

> Remember the motivation equation – happy and fulfilled staff results in clients being better served which is ultimately reflected in improved profitability.

> There are various forms of flexible working which, facilitated by advances in communications technology, can feasibly and effectively be used by professional services firms.

> The fundamental obstacle to successful implementation of a flexible working policy often lies in the firm's culture.

> Implementation requires clear and effective management of the process – continually plan, monitor and *communicate*.

> Be aware of the positive *and negative* motivational consequences that flexible working might entail.

The question of quality

Think about your firm – do you recognise any of these problems?

	YES	NO
Well, we operate a complaints system and give information on costs, so you could say we have a quality assurance programme.		
We don't have a formal quality programme here, we just tell everyone to do as good a job as they can in the time available.		
Two of our departments have a legal aid franchise but we don't think it's necessary for the whole firm to gain a quality mark.		
We did look into it but seeking quality accreditation looks so time consuming we decided not to bother.		
The trouble is, no one here really understands the true nature of quality – they think it's just about getting the right result at the end of the day no matter what happens in between.		
We're supposed to provide good service to all our clients aren't we – and so is every other firm. I don't see how introducing quality assurance can provide differentiation.		

When we applied for IIP last year, there was a flurry of activity from everyone leading up to the assessment and the partner in charge of it nearly had a nervous breakdown – frankly, I don't think it was worth all the hassle.		
Since our Lexcel assessment, everyone has been slipping back into bad habits – how can we keep up the momentum?		

Assuming you didn't answer 'no' to all the above, then you should read on.

We have deliberately made this the last chapter of our book. This is because, although in many respects quality lies at the very centre of the most important considerations for professional services firms (and so you may be forgiven for expecting to see a discussion of it earlier on in the text), an examination of its nature and impact here acts as a natural and rather neat summary of all the issues considered so far.

What is quality?

Introducing and maintaining a quality culture in your firm will involve constantly looking at:

- The marketing of your organisation – how services are delivered, how clients are dealt with and what their experience of the firm is like; what sort of image and brand values are presented to the outside world.
- The way in which it is managed – whether there is an appropriate structure and proper lines of authority and supervision; what the firm's vision and values are; whether it has appropriate operating systems and procedures.
- The willingness of every individual in the firm – whether the potential of each and every one of them is being recognised and developed to the full, whether they fully understand what is expected of them and whether they have the necessary incentives and motivation to do it.

In other words, quality assurance entails achieving the right balance – for your firm – of what we have identified as the three interrelating essential ingredients for business success: marketing, management and motivation.

One of the biggest lies in the English language, they say, is: 'I'm from the Government and I'm here to help you'. Second, or maybe equal to this is the promise emanating from the marketing and promotional material of most professional services firms which proclaims: 'We make it our priority to offer the highest quality service'.

Perhaps many firms could justify this by saying that yes, they do in terms of the technical service they provide – but evidence abounds, as we have demonstrated in earlier chapters, that the quality of the entire service experience is generally mediocre.

Professional firms are currently in danger of being left behind in the market place for specific reasons:

- Consumers these days know what they are entitled to; very few people are prepared to put up with a shoddy service.
- The majority of other industries – particularly service industries – have long recognised the importance of quality in providing a differentiated service, and have developed sophisticated techniques for providing added value.

What does quality really mean?

'Quality is about attitudes, culture and commitment within an organisation.'
Ron Collard, *Total Quality, Success through People*
(Institute of Personnel Management, 1989)

In the realm of professional services, quality is not a tangible thing. It is not even an objective concept. It is any number of subjective perceptions that will chop and change according to the eyes of the beholder.

This, in essence, is the reason why so many professional services firms fail to understand the concept of quality and find it difficult in the extreme to introduce any meaningful and lasting quality assurance programme in their organisation.

What they are doing wrong is to consider quality through their own eyes. Simplistic though it may sound, the only eyes that matter when it comes to delivering quality are those of the client – or, rather, clients, because quality will mean different things to different clients.

Of course, reality and common sense dictate that you will not be able to please and delight all of your clients all of the time. What you need to do is to work out:

1. What are the needs and perceptions of your clients in general (so that you start to see things from their point of view, not yours).
2. Which quality issues concern clients across the board (this will help determine your minimum service levels).
3. Who your key clients are (remember the relationship ladder in Chapter 5) and what their particular needs, wants and perceptions are. Work at meeting those extra quality requirements since this is where your investment in high-level quality assurance will pay the greatest dividends.

The starting point, when considering whether and how you deliver a quality service, however, must always be what does the client see as being important?

There are many practitioners in professional services firms who retain the view that what is important in delivering good service is to:

- be technically competent or even expert in the relevant field of practice;
- achieve a successful outcome to the transaction.

To most practitioners, the bits in between are less important, and not necessarily anything the client needs to know about anyway. 'You're only as good as your last job' is a common cry.

While it is true that the client would also generally hope for a satisfactory conclusion to their matter, aspects such as technical competence are pretty much taken for granted. The client would no doubt notice if competence was absent, but it does not of itself add to the quality of the client's experience. Many people find technical excellence impossible to judge – in their eyes, being good enough to do the job in hand is usually sufficient.

What does make a difference – and what adds up to quality – for most clients of professional services firms are the intangible 'soft' elements such as frequency and tone of communication, attitude of staff with whom they deal, receiving timely advice on progress and costs, proactivity on the part of their adviser rather than reactivity, whether the offices are pleasant and tidy, and so on. Figure 12.1 illustrates the internal and external elements of quality.

Quality and client care are not the same thing. Client care is part of the whole package of quality – but only a part. Quality cannot just be good in parts – it must be consistent, all pervading, and all embracing.

Quality is an ephemeral notion which resides in the eye of the beholder, and as such can easily be damaged. However, any organisation which truly operates quality standards throughout can withstand such damage – quality, in this sense, becomes the firm's protective and defensive shield. For example, a quality firm will have mechanisms in place for dealing with complaints such that the complainant will feel even better about the firm after the complaint has been dealt with than before. They will say things like: 'Of course they're not perfect, nobody is – but this was one slip-up, it was put right and, considering the benefits of the way they operate, I'm happy to take it.' Without the quality shield, that one slip-up could be fatal for most firms.

Beware, however, believing that anything goes as long as you apologise afterwards, because sometimes, saying sorry is not enough. Think how infuriating and empty the mechanical apologies of train managers of late running services sound on the second or third hearing, week in week out. Quality means saying sorry, and meaning it, and then going on to do

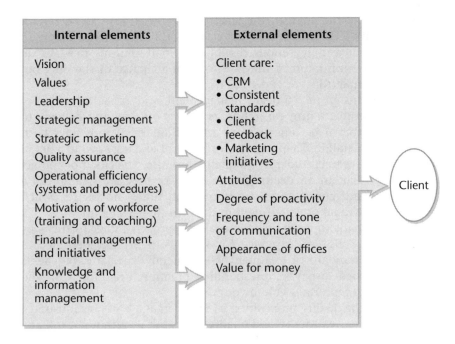

Figure 12.1   Elements of quality

something about it. It means making sure you get it right next time and, the time after that, making it even better. Quality is about continuous improvement.

Achieving differentiation through quality

Because lay clients find it difficult to assess whether service has been technically excellent or not or, indeed, whether it has been merely competent, they will be unable to differentiate the service offering of one firm above another on the ground of competence/excellence alone.

Rather, technical skills will be taken for granted and clients will choose their lawyer/surveyor/accountant and so on, on the basis of the aspects about which they are able to form a judgement.

Increasingly, professional regulatory bodies (particularly the Law Society in the case of the solicitors profession) are making adherence to a basic level of client care obligatory as a matter of professional conduct. Nowadays, therefore, anyone needing to purchase legal advice and services cannot only assume their lawyer is technically able to accomplish the task in hand but also (in theory at least) that the lawyer will give basic costs information at the outset, will regularly update them on progress and will even tell them who to complain to if things don't run according to plan.

Bearing in mind that, in the legal profession at any rate, a certain level of quality assurance is now obligatory for all firms (with failure to comply an increasingly serious disciplinary matter) firms need to do better than the minimum if they are to have a chance of standing out from their competitors.

Through insightful strategic management and proactive development of its people, a firm can refine its service offering and delivery to such a point that it becomes part of a brand image. Brands have been considered in detail in Chapter 3, but one way of looking at what a brand actually means is to consider it as a quality promise. The client or contact then knows that, in all dealings with X & Co, they are guaranteed a certain level and consistency of service at all times, no matter which particular individual or department in the firm they deal with.

Effective marketing can take the quality approach a stage further – by developing a Rolls Royce service for key clients. Those identified as meriting this standard of treatment will, generally speaking, be clients who are prepared to pay a corresponding premium price for it or who generate work of a certain volume or prestige.

In effect, the quality proposition can be seen as a tower, as illustrated in Figure 12.2 – the firm can add quality layers but it cannot remove any of the basic elements otherwise the foundation will be laid bare and the whole thing starts to topple.

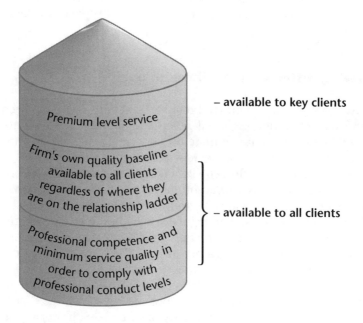

Figure 12.2   The quality tower

Implementing a total quality approach

Step 1: Client audit

The starting point, as we have said, is to find out what clients really want – how do they actually want services to be delivered; how much are they prepared to pay for it (a sense of realism must be maintained); what sort of issues are they bothered about? This will involve communicating meaningfully and regularly with clients, for example, through feedback questionnaires and partner visits.

Step 2: Internal audit

Next, put yourself in the client's shoes and cast a critical eye over the internal functioning of your firm:

* How are things really being done at the moment?
* Are systems working effectively?
* Are all departments (including internal support teams) working to a similar standard or are some better – more efficient, more friendly, more productive or proactive, more innovative – than others?
* What are things like at the sharp end? Are your employees enthusiastic and motivated in their work or do they mechanically go through the motions, doing things in a certain way because that's the way it has always been?

CASE STUDY   **Back to the floor**

Try emulating the tactic of the managing partner of a firm of solicitors who, from time to time, employs two simple but effective management techniques as a means of keeping a watchful eye on quality of service.

The first is mystery shopping in which you arrange for a 'plant' to contact the office as if they were a potential new client asking for information and initial guidance. A lot can be learnt from this, ranging from how quickly the telephone is answered in the first place to how efficiently the enquiry is dealt with through to the response of the fee-earner who might ultimately be responsible for the new matter.

The second technique is that of going back to the factory floor (which we mentioned in Chapter 9). Spend a couple of days working in the post room or on the reception desk and make as objective an assessment as you can of how truly well-oiled, efficient and client-oriented your firm is (or, maybe, isn't).

You will be amazed by how much you can discover.

Step 3: Set standards

Remind yourself of the firm's vision and core values. What does it need to be doing – how should it act – in order to live the vision and breathe its values? Once you have defined to yourself the standards that the firm as a whole must strive to achieve, you must communicate them to all.

Quality standards will inevitably cover a wide variety and number of different matters, from the very big, important issues down to seemingly quite trivial ones. It will be impossible for everyone to remember everything so a quality manual – in computer or printed format – will be essential.

It is helpful, at this stage, to mention the various official quality standards that exist. Those most often used in the professional services sector are ISO 9001 (the European successor to the old British Standard 5750); Investors in People (IIP); and, for law firms, the Lexcel Practice Management Standards. We discuss these in more detail below but suffice to say for the moment that any one of these can provide a useful framework to follow when devising and implementing a quality system for the first time.

Although there are obvious cost and time implications to be taken on board, there are also benefits to be had in terms of competitive advantage and promotional value in achieving the award of an official kite mark. Even for those firms who elect not to gain a quality mark, the concept and processes of quality assurance must be understood and embraced if the firm is to survive and succeed in the long term.

Step 4: Lead from the top

Although some individuals – even some whole departments – may already be doing all the things you want them to do, for many in the firm adopting a total quality approach will represent a major departure from the habits of a lifetime. If commitment to change is not seen to be supported and led from the top, then be warned that it will never be embraced by the rest of the workforce and, really, how could you expect it to be?

The results of your internal audit, when compared with the service standards you have just defined in Step 3 will undoubtedly reveal degrees of variance in all areas of the firm. Plug these gaps – in skills, abilities, attitudes – with appropriate training and coaching and in leading by example.

Step 5: Review and revision

Like marketing and management planning, a quality assurance programme is cyclical and never static. Clients' needs and expectations change; the people working for you change in terms of their abilities, motivation and ambition. Consequently, there is a need constantly to review the whole process, to seek on-going feedback and to adjust the system where necessary.

Figure 12.3 shows the sequential steps involved in implementing a quality programme.

Here are some further points to consider when implementing a quality system in your firm:

- Work outside the box and don't be hidebound by the standards of your particular profession. Look at best practice in other service industries.
- Get in touch with business advisers (e.g. Business Link) or independent quality advisers. Ask to speak to organisations which have gone through the process and come out the other side. Find out from them the real pain and the benefits.
- Work with your key clients to devise formal, measurable service standards in respect of your service delivery to them.
- Look at the approach to quality being taken by your clients' other advisers. Get together with them where appropriate and devise some common standards which you can all adopt.
- Assess the expectations and requirements of client groups in respect of quality. Many public sector organisations now expect all their suppliers to have relevant quality accreditation. Many SMEs who have themselves gained IIP accreditation seek to do business with other organisations who they can trust to operate to similar standards.
- In motivational terms there's a lot of mileage in being able to say 'We're the best' – it's incremental, and people will devote more and

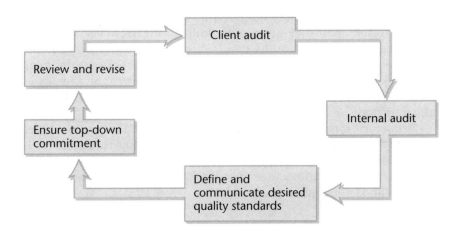

Figure 12.3   Implementing quality assurance

more effort to maintaining that position. But one external award or a kite mark on the notepaper won't be enough. Think about having your own internal awards and recognition, for example 'employee of the month' or a dynamic suggestion scheme – they can be enormously motivating.

- Quality should be driven from the bottom, managed and supported from the top – it's one area where ownership is the key to success. Whether you have regular quality circles or committees or working parties, ensure that those at the sharp end regularly meet to review and progress quality issues – possibly inviting external speakers to come and provide input periodically. Also, ask people to report regularly on their experiences of quality in the outside world – good or bad – and learn from these examples.

Official quality standards

ISO 9001

This was one of the first recognised quality marks to appeal to professional services firms (formerly, in pre-European Community days, it was BS 5750). Intended to be used as a model for a quality system rather than the system itself, ISO 9001 concentrates very much on process elements including:

- design and development;
- servicing;
- production;
- installation.

Clearly, these headings apply more readily to organisations operating in industry sectors than they do to professional firms. However, firms that have successfully applied for the standard report that the rigorous procedural and system control that it entails has brought about greater management knowledge, reassuring levels of risk management and increased levels of consistency across the firm as a whole in respect of the way things are done.

Detractors from ISO 9001 say they have found it too process-driven and industry-oriented – great for manufacturers of widgets but not really appropriate in the world of professional services. Indeed, one law firm senior partner has commented: 'ISO standards are incomprehensible to anyone who is not a quality consultant'.

Investors in People (IIP)

> 'You can take my factories and burn up my buildings but give me my people and I'll build the business right back up again.'
>
> Henry Ford

The Investors in People standard operates on the premise that the firm's achievement of business success derives from the strategic development of its main asset, its people. It says that if people are properly nurtured, developed and motivated, they will want to do well and that, through this, the business will by definition also succeed.

IIP concentrates on four areas which, on the one hand, are aimed at setting out a clear approach to defining and communicating business aims and objectives, and, on the other hand, at developing people to meet these aims and objectives.

The four areas are:

- business planning;
- communication;
- training and development;
- performance review.

A widely adopted standard, IIP clearly works well in the professional services sector precisely because of its people-oriented philosophy.

Lexcel

Lexcel was developed by the Law Society as a means of providing external assessment of adherence by law firms and in-house legal departments to the Practice Management Standards. Lexcel sets out to specify standards but not actual procedures – in other words, it indicates what to do but not how to do it.

The Practice Management Standards cover six headings as follows:

- management structure;
- services and forward planning (this includes marketing planning);
- financial planning;
- people management;
- office administration;
- case or file management.

Its emphasis on developing people through on-going training and appraisal, coupled with attention to systems and procedures such as the way in which files are managed on a day-to-day basis, means that Lexcel sits neatly somewhere between ISO 9001 and Investors in People.

Since Lexcel has been specifically designed for those in the legal profession, only they are eligible to seek formal assessment against the Practice Management Standards leading to the award of the Lexcel quality mark. However, it could also serve as a useful benchmarking model for other professional services disciplines whose objective is not so much to acquire a mark on the notepaper as to set about introducing an appropriate and effective quality approach.

More than any other, the Lexcel standard draws together the three critical areas identified as being necessary to achieve business success:

1. The need for strategic and systems management.
2. The value of effective marketing planning.
3. The benefits to be gained from developing and motivating the workforce.

Dealing with problem areas

Most of those responsible for introducing quality systems in their firms would report that the process proved fraught to say the least. Difficulties generally arise from people's natural resistance to change which, often necessarily, occurs on so many fronts.

Particular problem areas tend to concern the following:

- The level of investment required – the partnership must invest time, money and effort and be prepared to embrace change and signal to everyone else in the firm that this is the behaviour required of them too.
- Gaining commitment – often, during implementation of quality assurance, people will become weighed down by what they see as a pointless, and seemingly endless, procedural maze. To counteract this, the quality manager must consistently restate the aims and objectives of the exercise, point out the benefits and explain what is required of each individual. Wherever possible, involving others in the firm in the drive to implement the defined standards will help to secure buy-in and commitment.
- Maintaining discipline – a firm which has been newly successful in achieving a recognised quality mark can find that momentum and enthusiasm are suddenly lost, seemingly as soon as the assessors have left the building and the award ceremony is over. People slip back into bad habits and it is easy for the hard-earned investments and gains in quality to recede quietly and ebb away. On-going measurement and review is vital to ensure that everyone continues to follow

the rules and that service quality really and truly becomes part of the new culture of the firm – the new way of doing things – rather than a flash-in-the-pan effort to impress the assessment body.

- Raising expectations – this is a tricky one. There is an argument that the more you do, the better you perform and deliver services, the more you have to keep on doing in order to meet raised expectations. All we can say is, keep your eye on the game – constantly measure and evaluate your performance to ensure it meets your own defined standards; regularly benchmark your efforts against your competitors and, for the really innovative, look at what those in commercial or industry sectors are doing in terms of service delivery.

The benefits of achieving total quality

Introducing a true ethos of quality – paying rapt attention to the crucial areas of marketing, management and motivation – affects the very heart and soul of professional services firms. We are talking about improving the culture of the firm, from the way it does business to the way in which it looks after and develops its staff and the nature and quality of the relationships it can then aspire to with clients.

Improved quality assurance will give your firm a variety of advantages in the market place, including:

- greater and more informed management control;
- more developed people, which translates into increased motivation and a better service to clients;
- increased client satisfaction. Quality influences clients' purchasing decisions and is critical to the battle for differentiation. Consumers are more preoccupied than ever before with quality and many are prepared to pay more for it, provided there is corresponding value for money;
- improved risk management;
- improved marketing awareness and initiatives;
- better operating efficiency, leading to greater productivity and profitability – quality basically means doing things right first time. Although the initial investment in quality may seem high, it is a front-loaded cost – over time, it costs less than regularly doing things wrong which then have to be put right.

Moreover, it can provide a holistic framework allowing you to move logically and effectively on the three critical fronts leading to business success – marketing, management and motivation.

POINTS TO REMEMBER

➤   Quality – an intangible concept in professional firms – concerns the subjective perceptions of clients and other stakeholders of the whole service experience.

➤   Clients are entitled to take technical competence for granted – quality consists of the soft elements of service delivery, client care and the firm's attitude and culture.

➤   Maintaining an effective quality programme relies on bottom-up implementation coupled with top-down commitment and support.

➤   A quality programme is never static – like planning, it requires continual audit, review and refinement.

➤   Consider using quality circles or quality teams to maintain momentum.

➤   Official quality standards commonly used in professional firms are ISO 9001 (largely process-driven), Investors in People (focuses on developing people) and Lexcel (designed for the legal profession but could be a quality blueprint for other professional firms).

➤   Work outside the box when considering quality. Benchmark against and seek advice and ideas from those in other service industries.

➤   Achieving quality in your firm means finding the right balance between the three crucial areas for success – marketing, management and motivation.

Index